P9-DHQ-504

Foreclosure
Self-Defense
FOR
DUMMIES®

Foreclosure Self-Defense For Dummies®

Cheat Sheet

Foreclosure Self-Defense Strategies and Tactics

When you're facing foreclosure, you may think you have only two options — pay up or move out. As we reveal, however, you have a host of options to explore, and the faster you take action, the more options remain open:

- **Reinstate your mortgage** by borrowing money to catch up on missed payments.

- **Negotiate a forbearance** or payment plan with your lender.

- **Negotiate a mortgage modification** with your lender to make the monthly payments more affordable.

- **Borrow from friends or relatives** to catch up on missed payments.

- **Refinance your mortgage** to pay it off completely with a new loan.

- **Sell your home** (with the assistance of a qualified real estate agent) to cash out the equity and buy a more affordable abode.

- **Sell your home to an investor and buy it back** on contract or via a lease-option agreement.

- **Sell your home to an investor and rent it back** for several months or years. This is a great option if you want to remain in your home until your kids are out of school.

- **File for bankruptcy** to liquidate assets, pay off as much debt as possible, and free yourself from unpayable debts (under Chapter 7 bankruptcy) or to restructure your debt to pay it off over a three- to five-year period (under Chapter 13 bankruptcy).

- **Offer the lender a deed in lieu of foreclosure** to shed yourself of the property without having the foreclosure show up on your credit report.

- **Live in the house for free** and move out just before eviction day, so you can save up a bunch of money in anticipation of moving. This approach can be a great option if you have little equity in your home and don't really care about saving it.

Got a Foreclosure Notice? Here's What to Do

You just received a foreclosure notice. Now what? Don't make the common mistake of ignoring it. Take action right away:

1. **If you have a significant other who's out of the loop, inform him or her.**

   Your partner is going to find out eventually, and you need all the help you can get.

2. **Contact your lender to describe your situation and discuss options.**

3. **Contact a housing counseling agency approved by the U.S. Department of Housing and Urban Development (HUD) by calling 800-569-4287 (TTY**

   800-877-8339) or by going to www.hud.gov/ offices/hsg/sfh/hcc/hccprof14.cfm.

4. **If you financed the purchase of your home with a guaranteed loan from the Veterans Administration (VA), contact the VA for assistance; call 800-827-1000 and ask for the number to reach a loan service representative who can assist you.**

5. **Start exploring your options and deciding which of those options you want to pursue.**

Rounding Up the Troops

Although your first impulse when you receive a foreclosure notice may be to hide somewhere, that's often the worst move you can make. Isolating yourself makes you more vulnerable to foreclosure and a bigger target for con artists. Seek assistance from the following people:

- Your spouse or partner
- Your lender
- Your lender's attorney
- Your county's register of deeds
- A foreclosure attorney

- A reputable bankruptcy attorney
- Friends and relatives who can offer guidance or assistance
- An honest, reliable mortgage broker or loan officer

- A highly qualified real estate agent who has experience with foreclosure
- A real estate investor who has a platinum reputation

For Dummies: Bestselling Book Series for Beginners

Getting Up to Speed on the Foreclosure Process

Understanding the foreclosure process often improves your chances of navigating foreclosure. When you know exactly what's about to happen, you experience fewer surprises and can deal with the situation more rationally. Depending on the foreclosure rules and regulations in your area and your particular situation, the foreclosure process can take anywhere from several weeks to over a year. However, it generally proceeds along the following course:

Pre-foreclosure: You receive missed or late payment notices in the mail and perhaps phone calls if you fail to respond to the written notices.

Foreclosure notice: The lender delivers an official foreclosure notice, publishes a notice in the local newspaper or county news publication, and posts the notice on or near your home.

Reinstatement period: For some time prior to the sale, which varies depending on your jurisdiction, you may be able to stop the foreclosure by catching up on missed payments and any penalties and fees that accrued due to the missed payments.

Auction or sale: Assuming you do not reinstate the mortgage or take other actions to stop the foreclosure, your property goes for sale. An investor purchases the property or, if nobody bids, your lender ends up with the property.

Redemption period: In many jurisdictions, you have one last chance to save your property by redeeming it — buying it back from your lender or the investor who purchased it at the auction. To redeem the property, you must pay the buyer whatever the person paid at auction plus interest and any other qualifying expenses the person paid and filed an affidavit for paying.

Eviction: After the redemption period (if applicable in your jurisdiction), you must move out. If you don't move out, the court sends someone over to remove you and your belongings from the property.

Foreclosure Do's and Don'ts

Foreclosure can be a mind-blowing, emotionally-draining experience. The pressure can drive you to make mistakes — either doing the wrong thing or failing to do the right thing. To deal with the situation rationally, keep the following foreclosure do's and don'ts in mind:

- **Do tell your spouse or partner, if you're in a relationship.**
- **Do contact your lender immediately.**
- **Don't move out prematurely.** As soon as you vacate the premises, you lose control of the situation.
- **Do take copious notes and document everything for future reference.**
- **Don't believe everything you hear.** Verify everything with a reliable source.
- **Do tell the truth.** Any solution founded on a lie is sure to unravel later.
- **Don't borrow trouble.** A loan that addresses your current crisis could put you in even worse shape down the road, so do the math.
- **Don't sign a quit-claim deed.** Fraudsters may try to con you into signing over your home to them so they can "fix your problem." When you sign a quit-claim deed or any other kind of deed, you essentially give your home to the fraudster and may still have the obligation of repaying your mortgage debt. *Remember:* Check with your attorney before you sign any kind of deed.

For Dummies: Bestselling Book Series for Beginners

Foreclosure Self-Defense

FOR DUMMIES®

by Ralph R. Roberts, Lois Maljak,
and Paul Doroh, with Joe Kraynak

WILEY

Wiley Publishing, Inc.

Foreclosure Self-Defense For Dummies®

Published by
Wiley Publishing, Inc.
111 River St.
Hoboken, NJ 07030-5774
www.wiley.com

Copyright © 2008 by Wiley Publishing, Inc., Indianapolis, Indiana

Published simultaneously in Canada

For general information on our other products and services, please contact our Customer Care Department within the U.S. at 800-762-2974, outside the U.S. at 317-572-3993, or fax 317-572-4002.

For technical support, please visit www.wiley.com/techsupport.

Wiley also publishes its books in a variety of electronic formats. Some content that appears in print may not be available in electronic books.

Library of Congress Control Number:

ISBN: 978-0-470-25153-9

Manufactured in the United States of America

10 9 8 7 6 5 4 3 2 1

WILEY

About the Authors

Ralph R. Roberts is a master of transforming crises into opportunities. After losing one of his own homes to foreclosure early in his career, Ralph added a foreclosure division to his real estate business. Its goal was to assist distressed homeowners facing foreclosure and earn a profit in the process. Since then, Ralph and his team have led thousands of families through the foreclosure maze, informing them of their options, steering them clear of the most common pitfalls, and empowering them with the information required to get on with their lives. Ralph is the official spokesperson for Guthy-Renker Home (HurryHome.com), is on the board of directors for the Macomb County Chapter of Habitat for Humanity, and has a host of Web sites and blogs, including FlippingFrenzy.com and GetFlipping.com.

Ralph is also an experienced mentor, coach, consultant, and author who has penned several successful books, including *Flipping Houses For Dummies* (Wiley), *Foreclosure Investing For Dummies* (Wiley), *Advanced Selling For Dummies* (Wiley), and *Protect Yourself from Real Estate and Mortgage Fraud: Preserving the American Dream of Homeownership* (Kaplan). To find out more about Ralph Roberts, visit www.aboutralph.com.

Lois "Lane" Maljak is Ralph's second in command and a foreclosure specialist in her own right. Lois formerly ran Ralph's foreclosure department, HomeSavers, during which time she met with hundreds of distressed homeowners every year, assisting people in foreclosure and pre-foreclosure, counseling them on their available options, and helping them leave a difficult situation in their past. Lois has a combination of compassion and expertise that makes her uniquely qualified to counsel hapless homeowners.

Paul Doroh is also a foreclosure expert working directly with clients and prospective clients at Ralph Roberts Realty. In addition to meeting with homeowners who are facing foreclosure, Paul represents the company at fore-closure auctions. He has been thoroughly trained in the Ralph Roberts approach to foreclosure investing — assisting people through the foreclosure process so they can gain more control of the situation and improve their outcome.

Joe Kraynak is a freelance author who has written and coauthored numerous books on topics ranging from slam poetry to computer basics. Joe teamed up with Dr. Candida Fink to write his first book in the *For Dummies* series, *Bipolar Disorder For Dummies*. He has since teamed up with Ralph Roberts to coauthor *Flipping Houses For Dummies, Foreclosure Investing For Dummies,* and *Advanced Selling For Dummies,* and with Dr. Robert Wood to coauthor *Food Allergies For Dummies.*

Dedication

From Ralph: To all homeowners and their families who have found themselves staring foreclosure in the eye and praying for hope. May your prayers be answered in the information, resources, and guidance we offer in this book.

From Lois: To my husband Michael, for understanding my need to spend hours with other families sharing what I learned the hard way. Without his support, I never would have gained the insights and experiences revealed in this book. Thank you!

From Paul: To my beautiful wife Stacy, who more than ten years ago bravely said "yes"; and to my children: Emma, Anna, Clara, and Otto. Collectively, they help make me who I am.

Authors' Acknowledgments

Special thanks go to acquisitions editor Lindsay Lefevere, who chose us to author this book and guided us through the tough part of getting started. Elizabeth Kuball, our project editor and copy editor, deserves a loud cheer for acting as a very patient collaborator and gifted editor — shuffling chapters back and forth, shepherding the text and graphics through production, making sure any technical issues were properly resolved, and serving as unofficial quality control manager. We also tip our hats to the Composition Services crew for doing such an outstanding job of transforming a loose collection of text and illustrations into such an attractive bound book.

Throughout the writing of this book, we relied heavily on a knowledgeable and dedicated support staff, who provided expert advice, tips, and research, so we could deliver the most comprehensive and useful information.

We owe special thanks to our technical editor, James P. Caher, for ferreting out technical errors in the manuscript, helping guide its content, and offering his own tips, tricks, and insights from his perspective as a bankruptcy specialist. For additional information about playing the bankruptcy card, we encourage you to check out his book, *Personal Bankruptcy Laws For Dummies*.

Publisher's Acknowledgments

We're proud of this book; please send us your comments through our Dummies online registration form located at www.dummies.com/register/.

Some of the people who helped bring this book to market include the following:

Acquisitions, Editorial, and Media Development

Project Editor: Elizabeth Kuball

Acquisitions Editor: Lindsay Sandman Lefevere

Copy Editor: Elizabeth Kuball

Technical Editor: James P. Caher

Senior Editorial Manager: Jennifer Ehrlich

Consumer Editorial Supervisor and Reprint Editor: Carmen Krikorian

Editorial Assistants: Leeann Harney, David Lutton, Erin Calligan Mooney, Joe Niesen

Cover Photos: © Comstock/Corbis

Cartoons: Rich Tennant (www.the5thwave.com)

Composition Services

Project Coordinator: Katie Key

Layout and Graphics: Claudia Bell, Stacie Brooks, Alissa Ellet, Melissa K. Jester, Barbara Moore, Christine Williams

Proofreaders: John Greenough, Todd Lothery, Sean Medlock

Indexer: Potomac Indexing, LLC

Publishing and Editorial for Consumer Dummies

Diane Graves Steele, Vice President and Publisher, Consumer Dummies

Joyce Pepple, Acquisitions Director, Consumer Dummies

Kristin A. Cocks, Product Development Director, Consumer Dummies

Michael Spring, Vice President and Publisher, Travel

Kelly Regan, Editorial Director, Travel

Publishing for Technology Dummies

Andy Cummings, Vice President and Publisher, Dummies Technology/General User

Composition Services

Gerry Fahey, Vice President of Production Services

Debbie Stailey, Director of Composition Services

Contents at a Glance

Table of Contents

Foreword

Owning a home is a lot more complicated than it used to be. As market fluctuations and mortgage industry woes continue to wreak havoc on the real estate boom of the early 2000s, many homeowners are left scrambling to protect their investment, keep a roof over their heads, and continue living the so-called American Dream. That's why this book couldn't come at a better time.

Make no mistake — foreclosure is happening everywhere: the inner city, rural areas, ritzy suburbs, towns, and villages alike. Foreclosure doesn't discriminate, either — it afflicts the affluent, the poor, and all those in between. At last count, consumers owed nearly $8 trillion in debt, according to the Federal Reserve. Shockingly, this is double the amount consumers carried into the last recession. Homeowners need to be armed and ready to fight foreclosure. The time has come to prepare yourself and protect your assets, the largest and most significant of which is more than likely your home.

Foreclosure Self-Defense For Dummies shows you how to identify and evaluate all the options available to you before, during, and after foreclosure strikes. What's more, author Ralph R. Roberts and his team of foreclosure specialists present this information in a positive, take-charge manner. Their goal is to move homeowners away from the intensely negative feelings surrounding foreclosure, in order to focus instead on proven strategies for emerging from foreclosure stronger than ever. Together, they masterfully reduce a highly emotional subject to a proactive game plan for building a brighter tomorrow.

This book leaves no stone unturned and provides hundreds of helpful tips, tricks, strategies, and warning signs for avoiding or recovering from foreclosure. It also guides you through the process of choosing and working with a real estate professional on the purchase of a new home. I firmly believe that *Foreclosure Self-Defense For Dummies* will become the quintessential guide to navigating the foreclosure process, helping homeowners cope, make the right decisions, and move confidently forward toward a secure and stable future.

John E. Featherston
President and CEO
RISMedia, publisher of *Real Estate* magazine

Introduction

Foreclosure is not biased. It afflicts homeowners all over the country, from the inner city to the suburbs to rural areas, and from all socioeconomic backgrounds. While skimming the most recent foreclosure listings in our area, we saw houses in foreclosure owned by well-known real estate agents and other professionals — people considered by their friends and neighbors to be highly successful.

Homeowners end up in foreclosure for all sorts of reasons, many of which are beyond their control. Perhaps you've been the victim of predatory lending practices, an unexpected job loss, reduction in overtime opportunities, the illness or death of a loved one, or a series of unexpected bills. Or maybe you or a loved one made some bad choices — excessive gambling, overspending, or alcohol or substance abuse. Perhaps a recent divorce led to a loss of household income.

As we explain to the homeowners we assist, the series of circumstances that led you into foreclosure matters very little — and it certainly doesn't matter much to the bank who holds your mortgage. You can leave all that in the past, as long as you recognize what happened and take action to prevent it from happening again. What matters most is how you deal with the situation that's staring you in the face — foreclosure.

To deal effectively with foreclosure, you need guidance and assistance. We have led thousands of homeowners through the foreclosure minefields — homeowners who listened to our advice, planned well, and took appropriate action. In this book, we offer you the same advice and point you toward the people in your circle who can provide you with the assistance you need. With the advice we provide, some assistance from those around you, and your own *sticktoitism* (a word we use to mean "dogged determination"), you can take control of what may seem to be an overwhelming situation and significantly improve the outcome for yourself and your family.

About This Book

Most homeowners facing foreclosure think they have two options — pay up or move out. Because they don't have the money to pay up, they resign themselves to the mistaken belief that, no matter what they do, they're going to lose their home, so why bother? They end up doing nothing and losing their home and any equity they have in it.

Equity is the amount of cash that's left over when you sell something and pay off what you owe on it. Lose your home in foreclosure, and you may lose not only your home, but a nice little nest egg — perhaps tens of thousands of dollars!

We hate to see people lose their homes just because they were unaware of their rights and their options. We wrote this book for people like you who are facing foreclosure and don't know what to do, what not to do, and where to go for assistance. In these pages, we reveal more than a dozen options — including borrowing money from friends and relatives to catch up on your payments, negotiating a deal with your lender, selling your home to cash out the equity, and simply heading out of town and leaving the keys behind. We also show you how to spot a con artist or opportunist from a mile away, and how to recover your financial footing after foreclosure.

Following the advice we provide in this book, you can increase your chances of saving your home (if that's what you want to do), delay foreclosure to give yourself more time, and negotiate deals so you have more money in your pocket if you decide to move out and move on. You may not be able to save your home, but you can significantly improve your outcome. All you need is the right information and the determination to take action.

Conventions Used in This Book

Foreclosure Self-Defense For Dummies is anything but conventional. In fact, we've seen very few books on the subject. We do use some conventions, however, to call your attention to certain items. For example:

- *Italics* highlight new, somewhat technical terms (such as *equity,* in the preceding section) and emphasize words when we're driving home a point.

- **Boldface** text indicates key words in bulleted lists or steps to take in numbered lists.

- Monofont highlights Web and e-mail addresses.

In addition, even though four of us stand as the official authors of this book, only three of us — Ralph, Lois, and Paul — have experience advising home-owners in foreclosure. When you see *we,* Ralph, Lois, and Paul are talking. Joe's the wordsmith — the guy responsible for keeping you engaged and entertained and making sure that *we've* explained everything as clearly and thoroughly as possible. Joe is admittedly not much of a foreclosure expert, although he claims that, as a writer, he's always one paying project away from foreclosure.

What You're Not to Read

Although reading this book from cover to cover will certainly maximize the return on your investment, *Foreclosure Self-Defense For Dummies* facilitates a skip-and-dip approach. It presents the information in bite-size bits, so you can skip to the chapter or section that grabs your attention or meets your current needs, and then skip to another section — or simply set the book aside for later reference.

Feel free to skip any sections you feel as though you've already mastered. If, for example, you want to explore the option of refinancing your mortgage, skip to Chapter 12. If you have little equity in your home, can't possibly make the payments, and just want to dump the house, check out Chapter 13. Chapter 10 shows you how to play the bankruptcy card.

You can also safely skip anything you see in a gray-shaded box. We stuck it in a box for the same reason that most people stick stuff in boxes — to get it out of the way, so you won't trip over it. However, most of the sidebars contain real-life stories of people just like you (or perhaps nothing like you) that may shed some light on your current situation.

Foolish Assumptions

The premise of this book is based on several foolish assumptions, and at least one that is not so foolish. We assume that you

- Received some sort of notice from the bank or your county stating that your mortgage payments are late or that your home is going to be placed on the auction block at a foreclosure sale, or you're afraid that you won't be able to make your house payments
- Are unaware of all the options available in foreclosure
- Are committed to reducing the fallout from foreclosure and improving your outcome for yourself or your family

We can provide the information you need to defend yourself and your home from foreclosure, but we can't force you to contact your lender, document everything, seek the assistance of an attorney, or put into action any of the strategies we recommend. That's where you come in. Fighting foreclosure isn't easy, but the sooner you take positive steps to improving your situation, the more options you have and the more time you have to pursue those options.

How This Book Is Organized

We wrote this book so you could approach it in either of two ways. You can pick up the book and flip to any chapter for a quick, stand-alone mini-course on a specific foreclosure self-defense topic, or you can read the book from cover to cover. To help you navigate, we took the 18 chapters that make up the book and divvied them into 4 parts. Here, we provide a quick overview of what we cover in each part.

Part I: Warming Up for Your Foreclosure Fight

Although you want to act as quickly as possible when foreclosure strikes, you need to act rationally and with composure. In this part, we introduce you to the basics of foreclosure; step you through the process, so you know what to expect; assist you in dealing with the emotional aspects of foreclosure; introduce you to people who can be of the greatest assistance; and lead you through the basics of reading and understanding your mortgage and other legal documents.

Part II: Confronting Foreclosure Head On

When EMTs arrive at the scene of the accident, their first order of business is to stabilize the patient. The same is true when foreclosure strikes. You need to figure out where you stand and avoid doing anything that could make the situation worse.

In this part, we lead you through the process of getting a handle on your financial situation, sizing up your options, stopping the financial bleeding, and avoiding the con artists and other opportunists who are going to try to rip you off. As soon as you've established a foothold, you can begin taking positive action to turn things around.

Part III: Digging Your Way out of the Foreclosure Pit

Knowing what to do is only the first step in putting foreclosure behind you. You have to know how to do it. In this part, we show you how to execute several plans of attack. Here you discover how to negotiate any of several solutions with your lender, borrow money to refinance your current mortgage or catch up on missed payments, unload your home by selling it or giving it away, shut down the foreclosure process temporarily with bankruptcy, execute the stay-save-and-leave approach, and then restore your financial health post-foreclosure.

Part IV: The Part of Tens

Every *For Dummies* title comes complete with a Part of Tens — two or more chapters that each contain ten strategies, tips, tricks, or other important items to keep in mind. In *Foreclosure Self-Defense For Dummies,* the Part of Tens offers ten foreclosure delay tactics, ten foreclosure scams and schemes designed to rip you off, and ten ways to rebuild your life (and your credit) after foreclosure.

Glossary

At the back of the book, we provide a glossary of common terms you're likely to hear bandied about by lenders, lawyers, judges, and real estate professionals. If you come across an alien phrase in this book or in some correspondence from the bank, check out the glossary for a plain-English definition.

Icons Used in This Book

Throughout this book, we've sprinkled icons in the margins to clue you in on different types of information that call out for your attention. Here are the icons you'll see and a brief description of each:

We want you to remember everything you read in this book, but if you can't quite do that, then remember the most important points, which we flag with this icon.

Tips provide insider insight from behind the scenes. When you're looking for a better, faster, cheaper way to do something, check out these turbo tips.

"Whoa!" This icon appears when you need to be extra vigilant or seek professional assistance before moving forward.

Where to Go from Here

Foreclosure Self-Defense For Dummies lays out your options, so you can determine which ones are viable for you and which ones you want to pursue. In most cases, we recommend that you pursue several options and then choose the best option when the choice becomes more obvious. It's sort of like applying for a job or for admittance to college — keep as many options open as possible, for as long as possible.

If you're looking for a quick guide to foreclosure self-defense, check out Chapter 1. To get a bird's-eye view of the foreclosure process, visit Chapter 2. Chapter 4 points you in the direction of friends, relatives, and professionals who can support your efforts. If you want to skip the preliminaries, check out Chapter 7. After you've identified a few options you'd like to pursue, turn to the chapters in Part III, where we provide the how-to information and strategies you need to put in place.

As terrible as your situation may seem right now, keep in mind that very successful people have survived foreclosure and much worse situations. In fact, our team leader, Ralph, lost one of his first homes in foreclosure. You can fall backward or forward — and which way you fall is often your choice. Our hope is that you'll follow the advice we offer in this book and fall *forward* — toward a more prosperous future for you and your family.

Part I

Warming Up for Your Foreclosure Fight

The 5th Wave   By Rich Tennant

"Can you explain your loan program again, this time without using the phrase 'yada, yada, yada'?"

In this part . . .

When foreclosure rears its ugly head, you may feel as though you're fighting a mythological seven-headed dragon. Every time you cut off one of the beast's heads, it grows two more that are even more vicious. You can get so overwhelmed at times that you feel like giving up the fight.

In this part, our purpose is to calm you down, so you can deal with the situation more rationally. We lead you through the foreclosure process, so you know what's going on and what's about to happen; assist you in dealing with the emotional side of foreclosure; point you in the direction of people who can help; and lead you through the process of understanding your mortgage and other documents.

Chapter 1

Digging Into and Out of the Foreclosure Hole

Foreclosure has a distinct beginning and an end. A series of events usually triggers foreclosure, and in a matter of months or maybe a year in some cases, the foreclosure is usually behind you — whether you save your home or lose it. In a way, that's good news. Within a year, your foreclosure is likely to be no more than a bad memory — a passing blip on your radar screen.

In this chapter, we cover foreclosure from start to finish, beginning with common causes that trigger the foreclosure process. This gives you some comfort in knowing that you're not alone — foreclosure happens to more people than you can imagine, people from all different socioeconomic backgrounds. We then bring you up to speed on the stages of the foreclosure process and reveal the options you have to delay or terminate the process. We end the chapter by showing you that life goes on after foreclosure and, with the right approach, you can look forward to better times.

Stumbling into the Foreclosure Hole

Homeowners end up in foreclosure for any number of reasons, ranging from being the victims of predatory lending practices to abusing alcohol and drugs to having a family member with an expensive medical condition. Foreclosure happens in the inner city, in rural areas, and in ritzy suburbs, towns, and villages, and it afflicts the rich, the poor, and the middle class.

In the following sections, we reveal the most common foreclosure triggers, in the hopes that you may relate to at least one of them and realize that bad things can and do happen to good people. This may seem like little comfort, but by realizing how common foreclosure really is, you may begin to see it more as a problem that needs to be solved than an overwhelming crisis that will ruin your life. With the right attitude and understanding, you can overcome your current challenges and emerge a stronger person as a result.

The first thing we do when we sit down with homeowners facing foreclosure is let them know that they are not alone. We service a tri-county area in Michigan, where an average of 400 properties per week are scheduled for the foreclosure auction. Although some of these are properties owned by chronic deadbeats, foreclosure strikes diligent, hardworking Americans, too. Don't let foreclosure get you down. You have plenty of reasons to remain hopeful and leverage that hope into taking positive action.

Irresponsible lending practices

Major contributors to the foreclosure epidemic that started to heat up in 2007 included mortgage fraud and irresponsible lending practices. Mortgage lenders were offering risky loan packages to consumers, including adjustable rate mortgages (ARMs) with attractive teaser interest rates, interest-only loans, and mortgages that exceeded the value of the homes used to secure them. In addition, many loan originators actually encouraged borrowers to lie on their loan applications in order to get approved.

We were involved in one case in which a mortgage broker tricked a single mother with two children into borrowing so much money at such a high interest rate that over 90 percent of her monthly pay was required to cover her mortgage payment. After making her mortgage payment, she couldn't even afford to pay her utility bills or buy groceries.

Many people who purchased properties during this time were also involved in cash-back-at-closing schemes in which they agreed to take out a mortgage in excess of what the home they were buying was worth, so they could receive the excess cash back when they closed on the deal. In most cases they were misled; an inflated appraisal may have been used to trick the buyers into believing that the home was worth more than it really was. They spent the money, had huge mortgage payments, and, when they couldn't afford the payments, ended up in foreclosure.

Divorce

The mother of all foreclosure triggers is divorce, which is painful in itself but even more devastating when the couple owns a home together. Three major factors contribute to the connection between divorce and foreclosure:

- ✔ **Loss of income:** The household requires two incomes to support it. As a result of the divorce, only one or one and a half incomes are available, depending on the settlement.

- ✔ **Settlement woes:** The one spouse who is supposed to be making the house payment as part of the settlement can't afford payments on two houses (the ex's house and the new house he just purchased) and defaults on one or both mortgages.

- ✔ **Spite:** One spouse, out of sheer spite, allows the house to go into foreclosure, because "If I can't have it, neither can you" or "My husband (or wife) loved this house, and it will kill him (or her) to see it lost in foreclosure."

Overspending

We live in a consumer-based society based on deficit spending. Most people in the United States are living on the edge of foreclosure. A few months without income or one or two unexpected bills, and they're likely to end up in the same place as you. Overspending is commonly caused by one of the following three factors:

- ✔ Inability to budget or stick to a budget

- ✔ Unexpected expenses or loss of income

- ✔ Easy credit, including credit cards, leading to accumulated debt

For tips on how to slash expenses, check out Chapter 8.

Job loss

When income dries up after a job loss or layoff, foreclosure follows close behind. When times are great and everyone is working, families often upgrade into a bigger, better house, only to have the bottom drop out when the perfect job or overtime opportunities disappear. A job loss is less of a problem in a family in which both partners work, but it can still be a problem if both incomes are required to make ends meet.

If the cloud of a job loss has any silver lining, it has to do with the fact that most people understand it. Winding up in foreclosure due to a job loss is less embarrassing than losing your home because you blew a hundred grand in Vegas.

Illness

Illness often strikes with a one-two punch. It hits you in the pocketbook with increased medical expenses and may compromise your ability to generate income through work. You may not be able to generate income if the illness prevents you from working, or if the illness of a family member requires you to take off work to care for them.

Unfortunately, foreclosure has no emotions. It doesn't stop when you or a loved one becomes ill. The creditors move forward to collect the debt regardless of why you're experiencing financial setbacks.

Death

A death in the family can also function as a one-two-three punch, particularly if you experience the loss of a major breadwinner. The emotional blow can be so devastating that you may lose your ability to perform normal activities, such as working. The cost of the funeral arrangements can push your spending over the limit. And finally, the loss of income may add to your financial burden.

From grieving to foreclosure

You never quite know how the death of a loved one will affect a person. We had the good fortune of meeting a very nice gentleman who found himself in a very unfortunate situation. He was a successful, well-educated businessman in a managerial position at a well-known corporation. We met him on the day he was being evicted from his home.

We had been trying to contact him for months, but we couldn't track down his work number until the court officer showed up at his home to evict him. When we found the number, we called him at work, explained the situation, and asked him to meet us at his home, which he did.

He was calm the entire time the court officer arranged to have his belongings set out on the curb. We waited with his possessions while he went and rented a moving truck. A couple workers on the eviction crew loaded all his items into the truck.

While we waited, he explained to us that he had lost his mother some six to seven months before. She had been living with him for years, and they were very close. He took her passing especially hard — so hard, in fact, that he just stopped paying attention to things. He still went to work, but he ignored just about everything else. He had stopped paying his bills, including his mortgage, and was pretty much going through life in a haze.

What was odd was that he had over $100,000 in his bank account. It wasn't that he *couldn't* pay, he just *wasn't* paying. Never underestimate the power of grief.

Gambling

Gambling has become a huge problem in the United States, primarily because it's so convenient. You can go down to the local gas station or convenience store and load up on lottery tickets. In many areas, the casinos are a short drive away. And online gambling is huge — you don't even have to leave your home.

Gambling can start out innocently enough, as a form of entertainment, and quickly escalate as the gambler tries to win back her losses, which is always a recipe for major trouble. The losses pile up as quickly as the guilt and embarrassment, and it usually remains a secret until it's far too late and the damage is done. People are devastated when they discover that their homes are in foreclosure because, instead of making the house payments, their spouses have been gambling them away.

Alcohol and substance abuse

Alcoholism and substance abuse can be even more devastating than other illnesses due to the emotional fallout that typically follows. A breadwinner who is more committed to the bottle or a certain drug than to fulfilling his responsibilities to his family is eventually consumed by the substance. This often results in a host of problems, including increased medical bills, job loss, and divorce, any one of which can trigger foreclosure on its own.

Like gambling, alcoholism and substance abuse are often kept a secret. Many families are in denial about the problem until it's too late.

Whatever challenges your family faces, don't try to sweep them under the carpet. Confront those challenges head on, and work as a team to develop solutions before your problems get the upper hand. Thinking a problem is just going to go away often leads to foreclosure.

Digging Deeper Through Denial and Avoidance

One sure way to make matters worse in foreclosure is to deny you have a problem or avoid it entirely; yet, that is exactly what many people choose to do. Overwhelmed by their financial setbacks or the accompanying embarrassment, they spend all their time and energy trying to keep a secret. Unless they take a different approach, they're sure to lose their homes and all the equity they have in them.

The longer you put off taking action, the fewer your options and the less time you have to explore existing options.

In the following sections, we reveal three of the most common mistakes people make in an attempt to deny or avoid dealing with their situations. Our hope is that you won't repeat these same mistakes.

Say what?! Our house was auctioned off?!

We follow foreclosures in our area. We read the foreclosure notices, attend the sales, and network throughout the area to contact people as early in the foreclosure process as possible. When we discover homeowners who are facing foreclosure, we attempt to contact them and explain their options and rights. You see, plenty of people knock on the doors of distressed homeowners to capitalize on their misfortunes, but very few are willing to openly and honestly discuss the process and lay out possible solutions. We believe that informed homeowners are in a position to make educated decisions and are less likely to be conned into something that's going to make matters worse.

One day, after attending a foreclosure auction, we were out knocking on doors. We knocked on one door, and when the gentleman answered, we introduced ourselves and handed him one of our cards. We told him that we had just come from the sheriff's sale where his home was auctioned off. He looked at us as if we were standing there in Girl Scout uniforms trying to sell him a box of Thin Mints.

Finally he said, "You must be mistaken." We then asked whether his name was Mr. X and the address was 123 Main Street. He said, "Yes." We then informed him that there was no mistake. His home had, indeed, been auctioned off at the sheriff's sale.

He was pretty shaken. He looked like a dazed boxer who had just gone down after an eighth-round beating. He had enough composure left, however, to invite us in to have a seat. He explained that he didn't pay the bills — his wife did and she would be home from work any minute to clear things up. It was already clear to us from our past experience. His wife hadn't been making the mortgage payments and had kept him completely in the dark.

As we were walking into the house, the man looked over our shoulders out to the driveway and said, "Great, here's my wife now." We stepped out of the doorway to let her through. As she came up the sidewalk toward the front door, he said, "Honey, these folks say we're in foreclosure and our house was sold this morning at a sheriff's sale." If looks could kill, we would have dropped dead in the bushes.

Again he invited us in to sit at the kitchen table and explain what was going on, but his wife pushed past us and began to close the solid door. As she did we heard the husband say, "He's mistaken, isn't he? I mean, you pay the bills — please tell me our house didn't just sell at a sheriff's sale!" Before we could reach the end of the sidewalk leading from the front door to the street, it was all-out war.

Fortunately, the couple lived in a state with a redemption period and they had the opportunity to redeem their house. If they had lived in a jurisdiction that offered no redemption period, they would have lost their home.

Remember: As bad as you think it may be to let your spouse in on your little secret, it's a hundred times worse for your spouse to find out from a complete stranger. Let your loved one know early on, when you have options and time to explore them.

Failing to act quickly

The longer you wait to take action, the fewer your options and the less time you have to pursue whatever options remain. Keep in mind that foreclosure proceeds in stages. Your options and the prognosis vary according to which stage you're at in the process:

- ✓ **Stage 1:** You missed a payment, but the bank hasn't accelerated the mortgage yet (see Chapter 5). You probably still have the option to pay the missed payment plus a late fee and get off scot-free.

- ✓ **Stage 2:** You missed more than one payment, but the bank hasn't auctioned off your property just yet. At this stage, you can still negotiate payment options with your bank (see Chapter 11).

- ✓ **Stage 3:** Someone purchased your home at auction, but your jurisdiction has a redemption period, during which time (in some cases) you can still buy back your home, typically for more money than you owed at Stage 2.

- ✓ **Stage 4:** The redemption period (if any) expires, and you're now a trespasser in your former home.

- ✓ **Stage 5:** If you don't move yourself and your stuff out of the home by a specific date, the court sends an officer to evict you and your belongings.

- ✓ **Stage 6:** You feel the aftershocks. If you haven't planned ahead, you now have no place to live and damaged credit. If you did plan ahead, you may be able to start anew and leave this crisis behind you.

As you can see, your options dry up pretty quickly. By Stage 4, your fate is sealed and you're wondering what the heck just happened. Foreclosure runs a fairly fast course, particularly if you live in an area with no redemption period. Contact your lender as soon as you suspect that you're going to miss a payment — the sooner the better.

Paying unsecured debts first

When you start missing credit card payments, your phone starts ringing off the hook. Your credit card company wants its money immediately, if not sooner, and its representatives will badger you until they get it. Your first impulse is to shut them up by making a payment, but this is usually not the best move. The money you owe the credit card company is *unsecured debt* — you didn't put up your house, car, or other belongings as collateral for the loan, so the credit card company can't take that stuff unless it files and wins a suit against you.

Your mortgage and the loan you used to buy your car are secured debts — when you took out the loan, you put your home or your car up as collateral to secure payment. If you fail to make your mortgage payments, the mortgage company can take your home. Fail to make your car payments, and the bank that loaned you the money can repossess your car.

When you're facing foreclosure, pay your property taxes first, your secured debts second, utility and grocery bills third, and your unsecured debts last. Working out a payment plan with your credit card company or a hospital is easier than working out a payment plan with your mortgage company. If you miss one or two mortgage payments, the mortgage company may declare you in default, stop accepting payments, and file for foreclosure.

Your creditors can't throw you and your family into a debtor's prison, because such prisons no longer exist in the United States. The government has placed certain restrictions on what creditors can do to collect on debts. If you feel that creditors are harassing you, send them a "bug-off" letter, citing your rights under the Fair Debt Collection Practices Act (www.ftc.gov/bcp/conline/pubs/credit/fdc.shtm) and mentioning any state consumer protection statutes. If the collectors still won't bug off, file a complaint with the Federal Trade Commission (FTC) at www.ftc.gov.

Don't buy trouble

We recently met a woman who had just lost her home in foreclosure. She took the right first step and called her lender. Unfortunately, the person she got a hold of was clueless and transferred her to another department, where a representative told her that he couldn't do anything and didn't even know how she was able to secure the loan.

Next, she called the local Chamber of Commerce. The person she talked to there referred her to someone who came out to her home and charged her $500 for the initial consultation — to call and talk with the lender and assess options.

After trying to work with them for several weeks and seeing no progress, she filed a police report. When the scammers found out about the police report, they returned her $500, but not before they used up all the time she had to save

her home. She called back to the Chamber of Commerce and learned that this particular "foreclosure rescue" company wasn't even a member; the person answering the phone at the time referred the homeowner to one of her friends.

The ex-homeowner was now living in an apartment. She was doing okay, but she would have been doing much better had she not trusted her situation and her money to con artists.

No matter where you get a referral, if someone tries charging you money upfront to save your home from foreclosure, tread carefully. Ask what the fee covers and what the service provider is going to do for you, and make sure the company has an address (not just a post office box) and a phone number. Ask for references and check them out.

Seeking a quick fix

Foreclosure information is publicly accessible, so as soon as that foreclosure notice is published, everyone who follows foreclosures is going to know about it, and some of these people are shady characters. Foreclosure rescue crews may show up at your door offering to bail you out. All you have to do is sign on the dotted line. Don't trust them.

Far more people are going to show up at your door to take advantage of you than to offer real assistance. We strongly recommend that you work out solutions directly with your lender. If someone does show up to offer assistance and you want to pursue whatever solutions he offers, consult with a qualified attorney who's well-versed in foreclosure and bankruptcy before signing anything or handing over any money.

Boning Up on the Foreclosure Process

Most people think that as soon as you receive a foreclosure notice, you've pretty much lost your home. This is simply not true. The posting of the foreclosure notice is the first step in a process that may take several weeks or months to unfold. By understanding the process, you can often gain more control over the outcome.

In the following sections, we describe the various stages of the foreclosure process to give you a better understanding of how it works.

Receiving missed-payment notices

Although your bank expects to receive your monthly mortgage payment on or before the due date, it's probably set up to cut you some slack. Most banks offer a ten-day grace period. As long as the bank receives payment within ten days of the due date, you're okay. If the bank still hasn't received payment, then it sends you a missed-payment notice, typically stating that you need to send in your payment ASAP to avoid further action. That usually means you have some additional time, but not much.

As long as you send in your payment, you may not suffer much at this point. You may be required to pay a late fee, and the late payment could negatively affect your credit rating, but the bank is probably not going to initiate foreclosure proceedings.

Receiving a notice of default

If your payment is 30 days late or more, the bank may send you a notice of default (NOD), essentially telling you to "pay up, or else." This NOD includes the property information, your name, the amount you're delinquent, the number of days that you're behind, and a statement indicating that you're in default under the terms of the note and the mortgage you signed when you purchased your home. (See Chapter 5 for more information about your note and mortgage.)

The notice may also briefly explain that if the default is not cured immediately, the bank will be forced to take further measures, including foreclosure. Some notices are not that friendly and are, in fact, just a very coarse statement that you're in default, the bank has elected to accelerate the mortgage and note, and you have *x* days to cure the default.

You may receive the notice via certified mail, or your lender may have it published in a local newspaper or legal news publication. Sometimes, the court sends out an officer to post the notice on the home, usually on or near the front entrance. However the bad news is delivered, it still means the same thing — pay up, or end up in foreclosure.

Getting the dreaded foreclosure notice

If you don't respond to your bank in a way that satisfies the bank, it eventually sends you a foreclosure notice, like the one shown in Figure 1-1. The foreclosure notice informs you that the bank has initiated foreclosure proceedings and scheduled the sale of your home at auction. It also includes the amount you currently owe, the percentage interest, the name of your bank, and contact information for the bank's attorney.

Losing your home at a foreclosure sale

In some jurisdictions, the foreclosure sale is the end of the line — as soon as someone submits the winning bid (or nobody bids and the bank gets the property by default), you lose all rights to your home and either have to move out or be evicted. In states that have a redemption period following the sale (see the next section), you have one more chance to buy back your property.

At the foreclosure auction, the bank sets an opening bid at an amount that covers the balance you owe on your mortgage plus any interest and penalties that have accrued prior to the sale. If nobody enters a bid in excess of that amount, the bank obtains the property by default. Otherwise, the property goes to the high bidder.

THIS FIRM IS A DEBT COLLECTOR ATTEMPTING TO COLLECT A DEBT. ANY INFORMATION WE OBTAIN WILL BE USED FOR THAT PURPOSE. PLEASE CONTACT OUR OFFICE AT THE NUMBER BELOW IF YOU ARE IN ACTIVE MILITARY DUTY.

MORTGAGE SALE — Default has been made in the conditions of a mortgage made by **JOHN DOE** and **JANE DOE**, husband and wife, original mortgagor(s), to BIG BAD MORTGAGE COMPANY, INC., as nominee for lender and lender's successors and/or assigns, Mortgagee, dated September 1, 20__, and recorded on September 7, 20__, in Liber 123 on Page 456, in Wayne County records, Michigan, on which mortgage there is claimed to be due at the date hereof the sum of Two Hundred Thirty-Five Thousand Eleven and 01/100 Dollars ($235,011.01), including interest at 5.375 percent per annum.

Under the power of sale contained in said mortgage and the statute in such case made and provided, notice is hereby given that said mortgage will be foreclosed by a sale of the mortgaged premises, or some part of them, at public venue, at the place of holding the circuit court within Wayne County, at 10:00 a.m., on **SEPTEMBER 14, 20__**.

Said premises are situated in Township of Grosse Pointe, Wayne County, Michigan, and are described as:

The North 1/32 of Lots 400895, Supervisor's Plat of Mountain Cove View Lake Bluff Orchard Farms, according to the recorded Plat thereof, as recorded in Liber 1 of Plats, Page 2.

The redemption period shall be 6 months from the date of such sale, unless determined abandoned in accordance with statute, in which case the redemption period shall be 30 days from the date of such sale.

Dated: August 17, 20__

File # 12-10-123-456

For more information, please call:

ABC, P.C.
Attorneys and Counselors
123 Any Street
Detroit, Michigan 48201
313-555-1212
Attorneys For Servicer

Figure 1-1:
The foreclosure notice lets you know that the bank has initiated foreclosure proceedings.

We recommend that you attend a sale in your area to experience the process for yourself. You may even meet someone at the auction who can answer some of your questions. If your home ends up on the auction block, attend the sale, so you can be sure that your house has been sold and you know who purchased it. This information can come in handy later if you have the resources to buy back your home or if something happened to delay the sale.

The location, date, and time of the sale may be published in the local newspaper or legal news publication, or may be included in correspondence you receive from the bank's attorney or the court. If in doubt, contact your county's register of deeds and ask where the sales are held and the dates and times. Sales are typically held on the same day and time each week — for example, Wednesdays at noon.

Finding a glimmer of hope in the redemption period

Redemption is like a do-over. You lose your home at the foreclosure sale, but then you have an additional period of time to buy back your home from whoever purchased it at the sale. The only hitch is that you have to come up with the cash to cover what the buyer paid for the property at auction, plus interest and expenses that the person paid and filed an affidavit for having paid.

Not all states have a redemption period. Redemption periods range from a few days to up to a year, depending on the state and on your particular situation. In Michigan, for example, the redemption period is six months for most

---

Know your redemption rights

Some crooked real estate investors don't play by the rules, so you need to know your rights. In Michigan, one investor who didn't like the six-month redemption period decided to take matters into his own hands. As soon as he purchased a property at auction, he would visit the homeowners to inform them that he had purchased their home and they had to move out. He failed to mention that they had six months to move out.

We're not sure how successful he was, but we suspect that some homeowners who were unaware of their rights would have gotten scared and moved out as soon as physically possible. After they vacated the premises, the investor could have had the home declared abandoned — and abandoned homes have a redemption period of only 30 days.

Know your rights and don't be afraid to stand up for them. If you're not sure about your rights, visit your county's register of deeds or a community center and ask for the names of foreclosure attorneys who may be able to provide you with some free information.

residential properties, 30 days if the property is abandoned, and a year for any parcels of property 3 acres or larger or any original mortgage that has been more than 50 percent paid off.

In some jurisdictions, the method of foreclosure determines whether you have a redemption period. For example, if the foreclosure is nonjudicial, you may have no redemption period and the bank may not be able to pursue a deficiency judgment, whereas in judicial foreclosure, you may have a right of redemption but the bank has the right to pursue a deficiency judgment. (A *deficiency judgment* is a court order that the borrower must pay the balance that remains on the mortgage if the proceeds from the sale of the home did not fully pay off the mortgage.)

Spotting the Early Warning Signs of Financial Trouble

The early warning signs of financial trouble can be as obvious as a lost job, a layoff, or a huge medical bill, or as secretive as an addiction. In either case, you and your partner (if you have a partner) should remain on the lookout for these warning signs and work together to build a strong financial foundation that can protect you from foreclosure:

- **Budget.** Make sure you have at least as much money coming in as is flowing out each month. If you have a partner, you and your loved one should agree, upfront, on how much to spend and what to spend it on. When partners are off spending money on their own pet luxuries, problems often arise.

- **Pay your bills.** When the bills arrive, prioritize them and pay them as soon as possible, so they don't stack up. If you have a partner, pay your bills together. Blaming your spouse for overspending is easy when you don't know how much it costs to heat your house or feed your family. You both need to be aware of where the money's going, so you can hold yourselves, and one another, accountable.

- **Audit your books.** Add up all the money you spend each week on nonessentials and try to trim the fat. If you're teaming up with a partner, determine how much you're responsible for and how much your partner is responsible for. This shouldn't be a blame game, but it can open your eyes to any potential spending problems that could leave the checkbook short when it comes time to make the mortgage payment.

- **Watch for addictive behavior.** Any addiction can be a problem, including alcohol, drugs, or the Internet. Anything that takes time, energy, and resources away from a paying job and your family (if you're supporting a family) could cause financial problems. Identify addictions early and nip them in the bud.

If you and your partner can't have an honest discussion about household finances and troublesome behaviors, then your entire relationship is in jeopardy. Communication is key to avoiding the problem in the first place and recovering from it if avoidance isn't possible.

Brushing Up on Your Rights as a Homeowner

As a homeowner, you have rights, but those can vary a great deal depending on the jurisdiction in which you live and your situation. Redemption rights can vary depending on the state in which you live, whether you stay in the home or abandon it, and even the size of the parcel of land on which your home sits (see "Finding a glimmer of hope in the redemption period," earlier in this chapter).

We can't possibly cover all the variations for all jurisdictions, so you need to ask someone in your area who can answer your questions, preferably an attorney who has experience in foreclosure law. Here are some of the questions you may need to have answered:

- ✔ **Does my area have a redemption period? If so, how long is it?** Ask your attorney to explain any specifics.

- ✔ **How long after the sale do I have to move?** If you live in an area with no redemption, can the buyer kick you out the next day, or do you have some time to move your belongings?

- ✔ **How does the bank have to notify me of the pending foreclosure?** If the bank fails to notify you in the proper way, you may be able to file a suit to buy yourself some more time.

- ✔ **How long do I have prior to the sale to reinstate my mortgage?** If you want to catch up on payments prior to the sale, make sure you do it before the deadline.

- ✔ **If something happens to the property prior to the expiration of the redemption period, who gets the insurance money?** Do you get the money, or does it go to the bank or the investor who purchased your home?

Many of your rights and responsibilities are spelled out in your mortgage and promissory note. For instructions on how to decipher these legal documents, check out Chapter 5. You also have rights under the Fair Debt Collection Practices Act (as explained earlier in this chapter in the "Paying unsecured debts first" section) and under the Truth In Lending Act (see Chapter 4).

Drafting Your Plan of Attack

Before you even start missing payments, your bank has a plan in place to deal with the situation and collect on the debt. You need your own plan to counter that attack. Are you going to try to save your home? Do you want to sell it to get out from under the burden? Would it make sense to simply live in the home as long as possible and then bail out before the sheriff comes to evict you?

In the following sections, we provide a brief overview of your options and highlight the resources you may have at your disposal. When you know your options, you can begin drafting your own plan of attack.

 Purchase or create a large calendar on which to mark important dates, events, and conversations relating to your foreclosure. Mark the last day you have to reinstate, the date of the sale, the last day you can redeem the property, dates on which you discussed options with your lender, court dates, and so on. Make notations on dates when you had important conversations. You can then keep more detailed notes of the conversations in a separate notebook. Use the calendar to give you a big-picture view of what's happened and is about to happen.

Contacting helpful folks

Your most valuable assets in foreclosure are people who can assist you, so before you begin drawing up a plan, draw up a list of people you can lean on. Your list is likely to include the following:

- **Friends and relatives with money:** Your mom, dad, grandma, grandpa, or your rich aunt or uncle may be in a position to assist you financially, by loaning you the money you need to catch up on payments or redeem your property. Don't hesitate to ask for assistance. After all, if you were in a position to help a friend or relative in the same situation, wouldn't you want him to ask you for help?

- **Friends and relatives without money:** Even if your friends and relatives are not well off financially, they can assist in other ways, such as watching your kids so you can work overtime, cooking meals for you and your family, or offering moral support.

- **Bank representative:** Although you may see the foreclosing bank as your bitter enemy, the bank's representative or attorney may be your biggest ally or at least the person who can offer the most assistance. She may give you a few extra weeks to get your money together or work out a payment plan with you (see Chapter 11).

- ✔ **Real estate agent:** A real estate agent may be able to sell your house for you before you lose it and all the equity you have in it, through foreclosure. Even if you don't plan on selling your home, contact a real estate agent (see Chapter 13) to explore this option.

  We estimate that selling the home is the best option in about 90 percent of all foreclosure cases.

- ✔ **Register of deeds:** Your county's register of deeds is likely to be reluctant in offering any advice, but the person may be able to refer you to others who can assist you.

- ✔ **Sheriff:** If the county sheriff is in charge of handling the foreclosure sale, he may be willing to explain to you how the system works and provide you with some valuable information.

- ✔ **Bankruptcy attorney:** As we explain in Chapter 10, filing for bankruptcy may be your best option. Depending on your situation, you can either liquidate assets under Chapter 7 bankruptcy and have all debts erased, or reorganize under Chapter 13 bankruptcy to pay off as much debt as reasonable and possibly even save your home.

- ✔ **Foreclosure attorney:** A qualified attorney who has experience in foreclosures in your area is the ultimate go-to guy or gal, assuming you can afford the services. The attorney can review your mortgage, note, and other legal documents; inform you of your rights; let you know when the lender has failed to adhere to the rules and regulations in your jurisdiction; and represent you in court.

For additional information on obtaining assistance from people who can help you through the foreclosure process, check out Chapter 4.

Gathering important documents

Before you get too far into the foreclosure fight, gather important documents and other materials you're going to be called upon to deliver at some point in the process. In Chapter 5, we show you how to decipher the most important of these legal documents:

- ✔ **Mortgage, deed of trust, or contract for deed:** If you financed the purchase of your home through a bank, you have a mortgage or deed of trust. If the seller provided financing, you may have a contract for deed. All three documents stipulate the agreement between you and the lender, name the home as collateral for the loan, explain what the lender can do in the event of a default, and perhaps even explain what the bank must do before foreclosing.

- ✔ **Note:** The note or promissory note or contract is your promise to pay the loan in full. The mortgage or deed of trust backs up your promise by offering the home has collateral. The note explains what you agreed to when you took out the loan and what the bank can do if a deficiency arises; that is, if the proceeds from the sale of your home are not enough to cover what you owe on it.

✔ **Modifications to the mortgage or note:** If your bank agreed to modify the mortgage or note in the past, you should have the documents showing those modifications, including any forbearance agreements.

✔ **Deed:** Your deed shows you as the legal owner of the property, but it may also contain warranties from the seller. You need to know the type of deed you have and what that deed warrants (see Chapter 5).

✔ **Correspondence:** Save a copy of anything the bank and/or its attorney sends you and anything you send the bank. For additional instructions on the types of correspondence you should record, check out Chapter 3.

✔ **Notice of default:** Keep a copy of the notice of default (NOD). If your jurisdiction requires the lender to publish the NOD once a week for so many weeks in the local paper or legal news, then cut it out each week along with the cover section of the newspaper to show the date of publication. If you're going to challenge that the notice wasn't properly published, you need to have this information to prove your case. Read the notice to make sure the information is accurate and complies with what the bank agreed to in the mortgage or note.

✔ **Sheriff's or trustee's deed:** If your house has already been sold, obtain a copy of the sheriff's or trustee's deed, which should also include information about your redemption period (if any) and where you can go to redeem your property. Check the deed for any errors; you may be able to challenge the sale if the deed contains errors.

✔ **Canceled checks:** If you sent payments to the bank or the bank cashed your checks and failed to credit your account, you should have a record of the checks you sent. These can be invaluable in proving that you paid on time when the bank claims you didn't.

✔ **Bank statements:** Bank statements can come in handy to show checks that have been cashed. If you decide to refinance your way out of foreclosure or take out a loan to reinstate the mortgage, lenders are going to want to see your most recent bank statements, as well.

✔ **Listing agreement:** If you decide to place your home on the market, obtain a listing agreement from your real estate agent proving that you're trying to sell your home. You should also keep copies of any offers you receive. In addition, ask your agent to supply you with copies of all marketing fliers and ads and a history of how many times she showed your home to prospective buyers. If you're having trouble selling the home for enough money to pay off the loan, all this information can help you convince the bank to accept a *short sale* (less than full payment of the loan balance — see Chapter 11).

✔ **Current appraisal:** Although you may not want to pay for a new appraisal, if you already have a recent appraisal of your home's market value, keep it handy. This information can be valuable in convincing the lender to accept a short sale and can assist you in understanding the current market conditions so you can decide whether selling your home is a viable option.

✔ **Phone logs:** Keep a written journal of all your phone conversations, and include a copy of these in you files. These records can be useful down the line if and when you need to recall a conversation.

✔ **Other stuff:** Keep anything else you think may be relevant. Having more than you need is better than needing something later and not having it.

The best way to keep all this information accessible and organized is to use a three-ring binder. If you can't find a copy of your deed or mortgage or anything else that's part of the public record, schedule a trip down to your local county building; you can usually obtain copies of most documents by paying a small per-page copy fee.

Getting your financial house in order

When foreclosure strikes, the first order of business is to get a handle on your finances. Do whatever possible to keep more cash flowing in than flowing out — boost income with overtime or a second job, slash unnecessary expenses, and sock away as much money as possible.

What you do with the added income and savings depends entirely on your strategy. If you're committed to saving your home, set aside the extra cash for reinstating the mortgage (see the following section) or working out a payment plan with the bank. If saving your home is a lost cause, you may decide to squirrel away as much money during the redemption period as possible, so you have a sufficient nest egg to take with you when you move. (For additional details on getting your financial house in order, check out Chapter 8.)

Playing the bankruptcy card

Tucked in the sleeves of all homeowners facing foreclosure is the bankruptcy card — a powerful card that can stop foreclosure in its tracks. As soon as you file for bankruptcy, you receive an *automatic stay* telling all your creditors to back off.

Unfortunately, the automatic stay is only temporary until the court approves your bankruptcy filing or one of your creditors has the stay lifted. If your bankruptcy is approved, you can liquidate assets to pay off as much debt as possible and have the rest forgiven (under Chapter 7 bankruptcy) or reorganize your finances to pay off your debt over time (under Chapter 13 bankruptcy).

The court is highly unlikely to give the bank relief from the automatic stay if you have equity in the property, or if you and your attorney propose a feasible plan for catching up on back mortgage payments.

Reinstating your mortgage: Getting a second chance

When foreclosure is caused by a temporary financial setback, you may be able to reinstate your mortgage prior to the foreclosure sale and pick up where you left off, as though nothing ever happened. Reinstating consists of paying a lump sum to the bank that covers the total of your missed payments, plus any interest, penalties, and fees that the bank charges you for being late. Your bank may voluntarily accept reinstatement, or you may have the right by law — your mortgage may even include language describing your right to reinstate.

Where do you get the money to reinstate? If you come into some money prior to the sale (from an insurance payment, a client who owed you some money, borrowing against your retirement savings, or some other source), you can always use that money, but most people borrow it from friends, relatives, or a private investor. Just be careful not to borrow even more trouble. If you think you'll be unable to pay off the loan in addition to making your mortgage payments, reinstatement may not be the ideal solution for you.

Reinstating is less costly and painful than redemption. With reinstatement, you're catching up on back payments and penalties, whereas in redemption, you have to come up with a chunk of money to pay off the entire loan, plus any qualifying interest, expenses, and attorney fees that have stacked up as a result of the foreclosure.

Haggling your way to a forbearance

A forbearance agreement is similar to reinstating, except for the fact that you don't have to pay a lump sum all at once. Your bank may agree to let you make payments every month, in addition to your mortgage payments, until you pay the amount past due plus any interest, penalties, and fees. If you owe $2,000 in back payments, for example, your bank may allow you to pay $250 extra for eight months to pay it off. You can then pick up where you left off.

Negotiating a mortgage modification

With a mortgage modification, your bank tweaks your mortgage. It basically says, "Okay, you can't afford these payments, so let's make a few adjustments." The adjustments can include anything stated in the mortgage, including the interest rate and *term* (how long you have to pay off the loan). By dropping the interest rate and adding several months (or years) to the end of the mortgage, your bank may be able to bring your monthly mortgage payments down to an affordable range.

Refinancing: Borrowing your way out of foreclosure

If your current lender refuses to work out a solution with you, perhaps another lender will agree to pick up the slack. Contact a reputable mortgage broker in your area to check out your options. You may be able to consolidate all your debt (what you owe on your house, car, credit cards, student loans, and other loans) into a single loan that has a lower monthly payment than the total you're paying now. (For more about refinancing your way out of trouble, check out Chapter 12.)

Don't refinance to turn unsecured debts (such as credit card debt) into debt that's secured by your home, unless you have a very, very good reason to do so and have considered other options, including bankruptcy. Consult a bankruptcy attorney first, as discussed in Chapter 10.

Don't borrow trouble. Some shady loan originators may try to take advantage of you by selling you a loan that'll put you in worse shape months or years down the road. They may offer you a loan at 14 percent interest when you're currently paying 7.5 percent, or they may try to convince you to take out an adjustable rate mortgage (ARM) with a low teaser rate that's likely to rise suddenly, making your payments less affordable. Know what you're getting into before you sign on the dotted line.

Living off your home with a reverse mortgage

If you have plenty of equity built up in your home (it's worth a lot more than you owe on it) and you'd like to live off that equity for several years while planning to sell your home, consider a *reverse mortgage*. With a reverse mortgage, you receive monthly payments (tax free) from the mortgage holder instead of having to make monthly payments. Reverse mortgages are typically designed for older homeowners who have plenty of equity in their homes and need to draw on that equity to cover living expenses.

For more information on reverse mortgages, check out *Reverse Mortgages For Dummies,* by Sarah Glendon Lyons and John E. Lucas (Wiley).

Cashing out your chips: Selling the house

Almost everyone we meet in foreclosure wants to save the family home, because, well, it's the family home. Few people want to uproot their kids, leave their neighbors and possibly their family behind, and go through the hassle of moving. Yet, for a huge majority of people facing foreclosure, selling the home and moving to more affordable accommodations is the absolute best option. Here are some general guidelines that can help you determine which option is best for you:

- ✔ Filing for bankruptcy is always an option, but it could be a costly one. In any event, you should always consult with a reputable bankruptcy attorney in your area before making any final decisions.

- ✔ If you've experienced a temporary financial setback, you can get back on your feet to start making payments, and you really want to save your home, then reinstatement, forbearance, or a mortgage modification may be your best options.

- ✔ If you really can't afford the monthly mortgage payments and you have a moderate to large amount of equity in your home (you can profit by selling it), then selling your home and finding more affordable accommodations is best.

- ✔ If you can't afford the monthly mortgage payments and you have little, no, or negative equity in the home, then your best option may be to stay in the home as long as possible (for free), save your money, and move out just before you're evicted. Keep in mind, however, that if you live in a jurisdiction that allows for deficiency judgments, and your home does not sell for enough money to pay off the liens against it, lenders may sue you for the difference. (See Chapter 13 for more about this option.)

If you plan to sell your home, hire an experienced, top-producing real estate agent (see Chapter 13). If you had all the time in the world, you could possibly sell the home yourself, but when you're in foreclosure, you need someone who can sell it in a hurry for the highest price possible.

If you can't sell the house for a profit, you may be able to sell it to break even and pay off your mortgage, so you won't have the foreclosure on your record. Your bank may agree to a short sale, so you can sell the house without losing more money. (For more about short sales, turn to Chapter 11.)

Unloading your money pit

If you can't save your home or sell it for a profit or to break even, then bailing out may be your best option — cut your losses, load up your family and your belongings, and hit the road, Jack. In Chapter 13, we discuss several methods for ditching your home:

- ✓ **Deeding the house to your bank in lieu of foreclosure:** Your bank may agree to forgive your debt in exchange for the deed to your home and the keys. You move on without the drama, time, money, and hassle of foreclosure, and the bank gets the property without costly attorney fees and having to wait several weeks or months to place the home on the market.

  When offering a deed in lieu of foreclosure, make sure the bank provides you with a formal release of all obligations for repaying the debt. Otherwise, the bank may be able to file for a deficiency judgment if the house sells for less than what you owe on it; you're then responsible for paying the difference. Read the agreement and have your attorney review it and explain it to you before you sign anything.

- ✓ **Selling the house to an investor:** If you can't possibly afford to rehab your home to bring it up to market standards and then sell it for a profit, an investor may be able to. Investors can often negotiate short sales with your creditors that creditors are unwilling to offer you. An investor may even be able to give you a little money to cover your moving expenses. Before pursuing this option, consult a real estate agent or an attorney with experience in foreclosure; you don't want to sell your home for pennies on the dollar if you can sell it for a profit and keep the cash yourself.

- ✓ **Moving out and leaving the keys:** You can't sell your home even to an investor, the bank won't accept a deed in lieu of foreclosure, and you have no other options. What do you do? Your best option may be to live in your home for as long as the law allows and save your money for the eventual move. In areas that have a lengthy redemption period, you can squirrel away a lot of cash over the course of several months.

You can often score some additional cash by negotiating a cash-for-keys deal with your bank or the investor who purchases your property. You agree to vacate the premises on a certain date without trashing the place, and the bank or investor agrees to pay you for moving out early. You usually get a percentage now and the rest when you move out. (For more on cash-for-keys deals, check out Chapters 10, 12, and 14.)

Getting Your Life Back After Foreclosure

Whatever plan you have in place for dealing with foreclosure, or even if you have no plan, one thing's for certain: The foreclosure is eventually going to be over, and you'll need to get on with your life.

Having a plan in place to deal with the fallout from foreclosure can give you more control over the outcome and more opportunities moving forward. In the following sections, we show you what you can expect post-foreclosure and the steps you can take to improve your situation.

Starting from scratch

Chances are pretty good that, when you first set out to seek your fortune, you had very few possessions, no home of your own, and little to no money in savings. You had your youth and enthusiasm, and that was enough to get you through each day.

After foreclosure, you may find yourself in the same position, possibly complicated by the fact that you now have a family to support. However, you also have some additional skills and experience to offset the added burden, so you're pretty much starting from scratch.

Fortunately, you live in the United States, where starting from scratch is tradition. You may have to move to where the jobs are, take on some overtime or another job, and dramatically scale back your lifestyle, but relatively few people in the United States are destitute. As long as the foreclosure didn't crush your will to live, you can survive and thrive.

Getting a clean bill of (credit) health

Most people give little thought to their credit until they lose it, and when you suffer through a foreclosure, you usually end up grieving the loss of your high credit score. You may lose your ability to charge purchases on your credit card, borrow money from the bank, or even set up a cellphone account.

The good news is that all these inconveniences are only temporary. As soon as the foreclosure is a thing of the past, you can begin rebuilding your credit. You may have to start out slowly, by obtaining a secured credit card through your bank (see Chapter 15), but by paying your bills on time, you can raise your credit score and become a much more attractive borrower.

Bad or no credit history?

Couples who are first starting out often have trouble getting a mortgage loan, not because they have a *bruised* credit history but because they have *no* credit history. This pretty much puts them in the same boat you can expect to find yourself in after foreclosure; they can't qualify for a loan.

Some time ago, we were showing homes to a young couple who had no credit history. (We didn't know it at the time.) As any good real estate agent would do, we sent the couple to a mortgage loan officer to have them obtain preapproval for a loan. Later, when we called the couple to find out how the meeting went, they told us that they were unable to qualify for a loan at this time and that they needed to work on their credit first.

We asked whether they had any blemishes on their credit history. They said, "No," that the problem wasn't that they had bad credit but that they had no credit. They never used credit cards. They bought used cars for cash. They didn't really have a lot of utilities or other monthly bills in their names. They didn't even have a bank account, because they paid for everything with cash.

The couple had to do some work to build their credit history, and you'll have similar work to do to reestablish your credit.

Chapter 2

Wrapping Your Brain Around the Foreclosure Process

In This Chapter

▶ Getting up to speed on the foreclosure process

▶ Identifying the stages of the foreclosure process

▶ Understanding how a breakdown in communication can hurt you

*W*hen you first find out that your bank or some other party has started foreclosure proceedings against you, you're likely to be concerned about exactly what this means and how it will affect you and your family. What options do you have? How much time do you have to do something about it?

This chapter answers these questions by providing an overview of the foreclosure process and pointing out some of the variations in the process that may affect you, depending on where you live. If you know what to expect, you can calmly address what often feels like an overwhelming situation.

Identifying the Mechanics of Foreclosure in Your Area

The procedure that the bank follows to take possession of property in the event of a default on a loan varies, depending on the state and area where you live and on any special circumstances that apply. The three types of foreclosure are

- ✔ **Non-judicial:** This type of foreclosure is done by advertisement.
- ✔ **Judicial:** This type of foreclosure involves a court order.
- ✔ **Forfeiture:** This type of foreclosure is used if you purchased the home using a *contract for deed* or *land contract*, instead of with a mortgage.

In some states, a deed of trust may be used instead of a mortgage and may be treated as a mortgage for most purposes. With a deed of trust, three parties are involved: the trustor (borrower), the beneficiary (lender), and the trustee (an unbiased third party). If you default on the loan, the trustee can foreclose on the home without having to go through the courts.

If you have something called a *contract for deed, lease option,* or something other than a mortgage to prove ownership of your home, the foreclosure process in your area is actually a *forfeiture* process. If your area uses contract for deeds, pay close attention to the "Forfeiture" section of this chapter.

In the following sections, we describe each type of foreclosure in greater detail. For simplicity, we refer to the party foreclosing on your home as "the bank," even though it may be a creditor, lender, mortgage company, bank, or *assignee* (someone the loan has been signed over to). When exploring various solutions with your lender (see Chapter 11), make sure you're speaking with someone who has the power to make a decision — this is usually the party who owns the loan, not the servicer who merely collects payments.

Non-judicial foreclosure (foreclosure by advertisement)

When you purchased your home, you signed a mortgage and a note. The *note* is your personal promise to pay back the money you borrowed. The *mortgage* is the security used to guarantee the promise. Your mortgage may contain a clause that gives the bank the right to foreclose if you don't make your payments as specified in the mortgage. This grants the bank *power of sale.* If you live in a state that allows power of sale and your mortgage contains a

---

Can't I just send the missed payments now?

Bottom line: No. As soon as the bank begins to advertise, you can no longer simply send in a missed payment or two to "catch up." The bank is likely to refuse the payment. Why? Because if the bank were to accept the payment from you at this point, that acceptance could create the impression that your payment has cured the default, and the bank could be forced to start the process all over again if you stopped making payments again. Not surprisingly, the bank doesn't want to have to start all over again.

You may have other options for delaying or stopping the foreclosure after the bank begins to advertise (see the "Aborting or delaying foreclosure" section, later in this chapter, as well as Chapter 16), but simply sending in the missed payments is usually not a good idea. Contact your lender to learn more, or consult with an attorney to learn about your legal options.

power-of-sale clause, your bank can foreclose without having to file suit against you. The same may be true if you have a deed of trust instead of a mortgage. Some deeds of trust include in them the right to foreclose non-judicially.

The note and the mortgage can be enforced separately — the note is personal, and the mortgage is backed by collateral (your home). If the bank can get the money from you personally, it doesn't have to foreclose; it can collect the money and leave your collateral alone. People who aren't making their mortgage payments, however, rarely have much money lying around, so the bank usually goes after the collateral by foreclosing on the mortgage.

Read your mortgage and note carefully to determine your rights and the rights your bank has in collecting the debt. The mortgage typically contains one or more of the following:

- ✔ **Due on sale (due on transfer) clause:** The due on sale clause just says that if you sell the house, the proceeds of the sale must pay off the mortgage balance in full before you get any remaining proceeds.

- ✔ **Power of sale provision:** If your mortgage contains power of sale language, all the bank needs to do to foreclose is publicly advertise the intent to foreclose and notify you (or at least try to notify you) prior to the sale (which happens at an auction). The number of days or weeks the advertisement must be posted prior to sale varies by state. Without a power of sale provision or a deed of trust, a judicial foreclosure is typically required, assuming your jurisdiction allows for it. With a judicial foreclosure, the bank must work through the courts to foreclose, which may provide you with additional legal options to at least delay the foreclosure proceedings.

    Review your mortgage carefully to determine whether it grants the bank power of sale. A short phrase like "This mortgage is granted a power of sale by advertisement" may be all that's there — but that's all the bank needs.

- ✔ **Acceleration clause:** An acceleration clause allows the bank to call in the whole balance due in the event of missed payments. Without an acceleration clause, the bank would have to declare a separate default for each missed payment as each payment is missed. An acceleration clause allows a missed payment to be considered a default of the whole and allows the bank to call the full balance due.

In foreclosure by advertisement, the bank generally advertises by:

- ✔ **Sending a notice of default to you.** A notice of default is required in some states, but most banks do this even if they aren't required to do so by law.

- ✔ **Posting a notice on or near your property.**

✔ **Publishing a notice in a local newspaper (in the county where the property is located) and/or in a legal newspaper.** The advertisement will include your name, the bank's name, the property's legal description, the sale date, the name of the foreclosing attorney, the amount claimed due, the interest rate, the redemption period (if any), and other relevant information.

The advertisement may also be called an *insertion,* and depending on where the property is located, the bank may be required to publish the insertion for several consecutive weeks before it can sell the property.

If the foreclosure notice contains errors, you may be able to challenge the foreclosure for *failure of process,* which means failing to adhere to the statutes in your area.

In some states, homeowners can *redeem* a property they've lost in foreclosure even after someone has bought the property at auction (see the "Seeking redemption: Buying back your home" section, later in this chapter). Ask your county's register of deeds whether your area has a redemption period and, if it does, how many days or months you have to redeem.

After the advertising, notices, and postings are completed, the bank will try to sell your property at auction as soon as possible. (Auctions are commonly referred to as *sheriff's sales,* because the county sheriff usually conducts the auction.) If your property is going up for auction, here are a few key points to keep in mind:

✔ The person conducting the auction varies by state. In Oregon, for example, the lender's representative conducts the auction in nonjudicial foreclosures, while the sheriff conducts sales in judicial foreclosures.

✔ A sale may be *adjourned* (delayed) and possibly canceled if you can work out something with the bank prior to the sale, or if something goes wrong.

✔ If you're told that the sale will be adjourned, go to the sale and make sure it actually *is* adjourned.

✔ Keep in mind that if your state has a redemption period, the clock begins ticking from the date of sale.

Just like that, the house is sold. This is why banks prefer to foreclose via advertisement — it's quick, easy, relatively hassle-free, and inexpensive. The fact that foreclosure can happen so quickly is the very reason that we encourage you, throughout this book, to act quickly. Doing nothing always results in the loss of the home and any equity that you have in it. (*Equity* is the amount of cash you have in the house — the amount you can sell the house for minus what you owe on it.)

Foreclosure by judicial sale

In foreclosure by judicial sale, your bank must actually file a claim against you in court and proceed through the courts to foreclose on the property. Banks don't like the process because it takes longer, costs more, and gives

---

Know your redemption rights!

We were contacted by a loan officer who had a friend facing foreclosure. The loan officer knew we were foreclosure specialists who helped many distressed homeowners through the fore-closure process, so she contacted Lois for advice. She told Lois, "I know there's nothing that can be done to help save my friend's home, but I wonder if you could take some time with his wife to help get her through this final stage?"

The couple was actually in the process of pack-ing and needed to be out in a couple of days. Initially, we were convinced that the couple had waited too long to act and had severely limited their options, but we agreed to meet with them anyway. The couple came in that same evening with the paperwork that Lois had requested — the notice of foreclosure, the mortgage, the deed, and anything else they thought would help.

In preparing for the meeting, we did our own research and discovered that this was a nice, older farmhouse that sat on about 3.3 acres of land, a seemingly minor detail that would become critical in this particular case. As Lois reviewed the documents, she immediately dis-covered a pleasant surprise for these worried homeowners. The foreclosure notice claimed that the redemption period was six months. In Michigan, however, the redemption period for any property on a parcel of land that is more than 3 acres is actually 12 months!

As soon as Lois discovered this key piece of information, she stepped out of the room to verify with an attorney that these homeowners had a valid point for contesting the foreclosure. (You should always double-check your hunches and the information you have on hand.) Sure enough, the attorney agreed that the lender was at fault.

When we broke the good news to the home-owners, they couldn't believe it. We advised the couple to hire an attorney who was familiar with the foreclosure process. He took up the charge to inform the lender and the lender's attorney of their mistake. The lender had to begin the process all over again from scratch. That meant that this couple would have a total of 18 months to live in the house free — the 6 months they had already lived there, plus the 12 months they would have from the time that the bank initiated the process anew.

We now had some bargaining power. Ultimately, we were able to pay off the homeowners' mort-gage for less than what they originally owed (through a *short sale* — see Chapters 5 and 8), and the bank seemed pretty happy to get the money.

Remember: Knowledge is power. Don't just assume that everything the lender and the lender's attorney tell you is correct. If the bank makes a legal error in your favor, don't hesitate to take advantage of it. You may just be able to save your home!

the homeowner an opportunity to put forth a case and object. In some states, however, the lender may need to proceed with a judicial foreclosure in order to obtain a deficiency judgment. (With a deficiency judgment, if your home doesn't sell for enough to pay the total amount due, the bank can continue to try to collect the shortfall.)

Depending on your state, someone seeking to foreclose on a contract for deed (see the next section) may be *forced* to foreclose judicially.

In judicial foreclosure, the bank must follow some fairly strict rules when filing a claim, including the following:

- ✔ The claim must be filed in the circuit court for the county where the property is located.

- ✔ The judicial action cannot be taken if the homeowners make the payments current before the bank enforces the acceleration clause (see the preceding section) by notifying the homeowners.

- ✔ If the mortgage or contract for deed doesn't have an acceleration clause, the bank can foreclose only for the amount of delinquent payments, not for the full amount of the loan.

If the bank properly accelerated its mortgage, then it can file an action for foreclosure, which begins with the complaint. The complaint should include the following:

- ✔ **The bank's right and interest:** The bank's claim to the property and how much money it is seeking to collect.

- ✔ **The homeowner's interest:** That the homeowner has the right to redeem, what period in which to do so, or any information about possessory interest or right to cure the default.

- ✔ **The rights and interests of any other parties who have a legal claim to the property:** If any other parties have a claim to the property, the complaint needs to acknowledge their claims.

- ✔ **The legal description of the property:** The location of the property as recorded with the register of deeds.

After the complaint is filed, the court notifies the homeowners. If the homeowners do not respond or put forth a valid challenge to the foreclosure, then the court issues a default judgment in favor of the bank and sets a sale date, which varies depending on the jurisdiction. In Michigan, for example, the minimum time is three months on a land contract and six months on mortgages.

If you've been notified that your lender has filed suit against you and you disagree with the claims in that suit, be sure to file your answer within the specified period (usually 30 days). If you fail to do so, the court is likely to enter a default judgment in favor of the lender and grant the lender the right to foreclose. If you own a large tract of property, for example, you may file a claim that only a portion of the property needs to be sold to satisfy the debt.

After the judgment is issued allowing the sale of the property, the property must be published for sale, just as with sale by advertisement. Every state specifies that the sale must be published for a certain number of days prior to the sale, but the number of days varies from state to state. The property is then sent to sheriff's sale just like mortgages foreclosed by advertisement (see the preceding section).

Although it rarely happens, the court may order only part of the property sold if, by doing so, the sale can satisfy the full amount owed. This usually happens only if you own a large parcel of land and the loan balance can be satisfied by selling a portion of it. If you own 40 acres, for example, the judge can order that 10 acres be sold to satisfy the debt. This can also occur in situations in which ownership consists of *tenants in common* (two distinct owners reside in the same property) and the mortgage applies to only one of the owner's interests. The judge may then order half the property sold. This is rare, but it can happen.

After the property is sold, a sheriff's deed is issued on the property and must be recorded within a certain number of days from the date of sale. (If nobody bids on the property, the bank "bids in" for the amount owed and obtains the sheriff's deed.) The redemption period on the sheriff's deed begins running from the date of sale. To redeem the property, you have to pay the sale amount plus interest on the mortgage. You may also have to reimburse the buyer for any property taxes and insurance the person paid, legal fees, and other qualifying expenses, assuming that the buyer filed an affidavit proving that he paid those expenses.

When the redemption period expires, the buyer takes possession by seeking an *order of eviction* or *writ of restitution* (essentially the same thing). When a bank forecloses judicially, you can challenge the method of sale but not the fact that you simply lost the judgment. This characteristic makes judicial foreclosures more secure (for the bank), although that security comes with a cost (in time and money).

As someone who's facing foreclosure, you may not see a big difference between foreclosure by advertisement and foreclosure by judicial sale. After all, you're still losing the house, right? But the differences are significant. With judicial foreclosure, you have more rights and power to stall the proceedings:

✔ **In judicial foreclosure, the bank is suing you on the collateral, which means that the bank has to serve you with the complaint, and the court needs to review the filing.** If the courts are backed up, you may have more time to act.

- ✔ **The bank always hires an attorney, but in judicial foreclosure, the bank needs one to prosecute the foreclosure in court, not just publish a notice and oversee the process.** The attorney will have to show up in court, make the motion before the judge, and, if challenged, present the bank's case as to why and how you're in default. This gives you a better chance of taking advantage of mistakes and loopholes.

- ✔ **You or your attorney may show up in court and object to the judgment to at least buy yourself some additional time to work out a solution.** The key is to raise a successful challenge or present a reasonable argument to make the judge want to hear more arguments and see more evidence. Your goal is to get another day in court. The case will take time to prepare, and the court is usually never in a rush, so you may have a couple weeks or more before your court day arrives. Judges are likely to side (or at least err on the side) of the homeowner, so if you're able to present reasonable arguments why you're not in default (for example, you have proof of all payments and canceled checks to prove it), the judge is likely to award you a day in court. If you have a clever attorney who can make good "doubt raising" arguments (even if those arguments aren't substantiated on that particular day on the spot), the judge will be likely to order another hearing on the issue with proof to be presented at that time.

  The most common challenge results when the bank has a history of accepting late payments from you. If the bank accepted late payments in the past and is now refusing to accept late payments without having notified you of its change in policy, then you have a good chance of proving that the lender has waived its right to foreclose. Consult an attorney who specializes in foreclosure to file your challenge.

- ✔ **Even if the bank prevails, it still has to sell the property.**

- ✔ **If your area has a redemption period, the bank must wait even longer before it can sell the property and recover its losses.**

Why does any of this matter? Because all these delays are costly for the bank in terms of both time and money. As a result, the bank is likely to be more motivated to work out a deal with you that enables it to cut its losses and get this bad loan off its books. We're not saying that your job is going to be any easier, but potential hassles for the bank give you a stronger position from which to negotiate. For specifics on negotiating with your lender, refer to Chapter 11.

Forfeiture actions on contracts for deed

If you financed the purchase of your home with a mortgage, you can safely skip this section. However, if you purchased your home by signing a *contract for deed* (or *land contract*), pay particular attention.

Contracts for deed are typically used when the seller is financing the purchase. The buyer takes possession of the property but does not receive the title until he has paid the seller in full. Although a bank has only one way to regain possession of a property when the borrower defaults on the loan, the seller in a contract for deed has two options:

- Foreclosure, as discussed earlier
- *Forfeiture* (automatically relinquishing rights to a property by not fulfilling the requirements stipulated in the contract)

A contract for deed can only be forfeited if the contract expressly allows for forfeiture. If the contract is silent on forfeiture, foreclosure may be the only option. Check the contract for a forfeiture remedy clause and consult your attorney to find out about state statutes that govern land sale contracts and forfeiture in your area — just because the contract contains a forfeiture clause doesn't mean your state allows it.

If someone is filing a complaint against you in a county other than the one in which your home is located, you may file a motion for a change of venue in order to bring the case into your district court. In some cases, you may even be awarded court costs and attorney fees if the other party contests the change of venue.

Before the other party can file a complaint, he must serve you with a *notice of forfeiture*. The notice should state the names of the parties, the legal description of the property, the past-due amount, when payments were due, the date the contract was signed, and any other information deemed a material breach of the contract. You may be able to challenge the claim if any one of these points is inaccurate.

Ignoring the notice of forfeiture

If you're thinking, as plenty of people facing foreclosure do, of just saying that you never got the notice, you can certainly try that approach, but don't expect too much. When a notice of forfeiture is served, a copy of it is filed along with a record of how you were served. This can include postal mail, personal delivery, or (in some cases) advertisement. A copy of the contract for deed may, and probably will, accompany the complaint.

Instead of ignoring the notice, start taking positive steps to resolve the problem, as discussed throughout this book, including contacting your lender and perhaps even your attorney. Simply ignoring the notice and falsely claiming that you never received it can backfire on you and waste valuable time.

The bad news (for you) about contract for deed forfeitures is that if you remain in possession of the property after forfeiting it, you may have to pay additional damages, including rent. Some courts may even allow the addition of payments that become due during the redemption period. So if you're thinking of staying put as long as possible, that may not save you a whole lot of money.

In most cases, you have a set number of days to cure the default, typically 15 days, but check your contract to see if it gives you more time. If you don't cure the default in the specified number of days, you can expect to be summoned to court to stand trial. The summons will require you to bring proof of why the eviction should not proceed. Your best options at this point are as follows:

- ✔ **Present a great reason why you shouldn't be evicted.** If you can prove on paper that you did honor the contract or that the seller breached the contract, you may have a chance. If you fail to raise a defense, the plaintiff's attorney will request a summary judgment, and then you're pretty much at the mercy of the courts.

- ✔ **Consider claiming "lack of time to file an answer," and request an extension to do so.**

- ✔ **Demand a jury trial.** This is often the best tactic, if you're looking to buy yourself some time. If the courts are backed up and you won't be able to have a jury trial for some time, the plaintiff may be more willing to settle the issue with you and avoid all the hassle and cost of a jury trial.

Make sure you show up to court. Failure to file an answer or to show up for the initial hearing may result in a default judgment against you. That essentially means you no longer have a case unless you can successfully appeal, which is unlikely.

After the plaintiff wins a judgment and that judgment has been sent to the parties, the plaintiff may file the judgment and seek eviction if you fail to initiate a post-judgment motion or challenge, usually within ten days.

If your state has a redemption period, the clock starts ticking from the time the judgment is issued granting eviction. The redemption period is usually tied to how much of the purchase price you've paid; for example, if you've paid less than 50 percent, you get 90 days, and if you paid over 50 percent, you get 6 months. If you're able to *redeem the property* (pay the full amount due on the judgment), you get to stay and you've solved this forfeiture problem. If you don't redeem, the plaintiff will apply for, and the court will grant, an order of eviction or a writ of restitution, and the court officer will execute the eviction and restore possession to the plaintiff.

Stepping Through the Foreclosure Process

Although mistakes, delays, and other unexpected occurrences are common, the steps leading up to the loss of a property in foreclosure are fairly predictable. Knowing the sequence of events is important, so you can anticipate key events and have a better understanding of your options at each point in the process.

The following sections describe each stage in the process and highlight important information that applies to each stage.

Receiving nasty letters in pre-foreclosure

When you miss a mortgage payment by more than a few days, the bank begins sending you notices that request immediate payment. The later the payments, the nastier the notices become. These notices are no different from notices you may receive for missing a credit card payment, except, in this case, the bank has the power to foreclose if you don't catch up on your payments.

Typically, the bank sends you a few missed payment notices before it declares an all-out default, but this grace period depends on your bank. Some banks are more aggressive and won't let you get several months behind on payments before declaring default, while others may be more willing to work with you.

The earlier you contact the bank, the more options you have. Don't simply ignore missed payment notices. When your bank is calling you, you're playing defense. When you're calling your bank, you're playing offense. And playing good offense is often the best defense. Do the hardest thing first — call your lender.

Receiving a foreclosure notice — Ouch!

As soon as the bank determines that you're not going to make good on the back payments, it declares you in default and exercises the acceleration clause in the mortgage to declare the full amount due. When this happens, you'll receive the notice of default (or foreclosure notice). In a foreclosure by advertisement state, the notice is also published in a local newspaper; in a judicial foreclosure state, a court officer may serve you with a complaint.

At this point, your bank may or may not be willing to work out a solution with you, but regardless of how cooperative it is, you need to contact the bank and find out about your options. (We offer more about how to talk to your bank in Chapter 11.)

The notice of foreclosure puts you one step closer to losing your home, and if it hasn't set in yet, realize now that this problem is serious. Don't despair, but if you were daydreaming before, thinking this would work itself out, this is your wakeup call.

Aborting or delaying foreclosure

During the missed payment stage, you can completely avoid foreclosure by catching up on missed payments. After the bank officially starts foreclosure proceedings, however, stopping foreclosure becomes more challenging.

In the following sections, we explain the three primary methods for stopping foreclosure between the time you receive the notice of default and the time of sale.

Reinstating your mortgage with a promise of payment

Your bank doesn't really want your house; it wants you to make your monthly mortgage payments, so it can collect interest on your loan for 30 years or however many years you still owe on your home. Foreclosure costs the bank time and money — and banks aren't in the real estate business, they're in the money-lending business.

For this reason, banks are often willing to forgive and forget by allowing you to *reinstate your mortgage.* Reinstatement consists of paying the total amount of missed payments plus interest. If you missed two payments of $1,200 each, you can expect to need roughly $2,500 to reinstate (to cover missed payments, penalties, late fees, and possibly even legal fees); plus, you'll still have to make that next monthly payment on time.

Reinstatement is almost always the best and cheapest way to solve the problem and prevent the foreclosure. In Chapters 4 and 11 of this book, we suggest that if you get behind but can borrow the money from family or friends to reinstate, and can then keep up with your payments, you should do so.

If you had a great interest rate and the rates have gone up dramatically, the bank may not be so willing to allow you to reinstate. It may want to raise your interest rate and modify the mortgage. Read your mortgage agreement carefully. It may give you the right to cure the delinquency, regardless of whether your bank is willing to allow you to reinstate.

Playing catch-up with a forbearance agreement

A *forbearance agreement* is essentially a new payment plan that enables you to catch up on missed payments over time, in addition to making your regularly scheduled payments. If you experienced a temporary financial setback but now have a sufficient amount of money coming in, forbearance may be a realistic option.

Your bank is likely to require more in-depth information to enter into a forbearance agreement than it requires to reinstate the mortgage. The bank wants to make sure you can pay, so it'll require bank statements, pay stubs, and a host of other information from you to prove it. In a way, this is a good thing for you — you don't want to enter into a forbearance agreement that places you in a terrible financial situation in the future.

If the bank offers forbearance as a solution, you may have little say in how the payments are structured. Simply provide the bank with the information it requests and be honest about how much you can afford to pay each month. Try to negotiate for a realistic payment plan. Keep in mind that your monthly payments are going to increase, perhaps dramatically. If you can afford it and saving the house is worth the sacrifice to you, this may be a good option. If, however, forbearance is just going to put you in the same situation a couple months down the road, other options may be better. (To find out more about your options, check out Chapter 5.)

If you know that you probably won't be able to catch up on missed payments in forbearance, don't dismiss the option entirely. Forbearance may buy you some extra time to explore other options. Just the time spent negotiating the forbearance gives you extra time. Keep in mind, however, that the bank is most likely going to keep the wheels of foreclosure moving forward and probably won't stop them until all its conditions are met, some money is sent to the bank, and a forbearance agreement is firmly in place. (For more about negotiating a forbearance agreement with your lender in pre-foreclosure, check out Chapter 8.)

Stalling foreclosure in court

If you can't stop the foreclosure in time to come up with a reasonable solution, you may be able to slow the process in court. Your best option is to hire a good attorney. You may be thinking, "But if I had the money for an attorney, I wouldn't be *in* this mess." Remember, however, that an attorney may end up costing you less money than you stand to lose if your home ends up on the auction block. Do the math before dismissing the notion of hiring an attorney.

Not all attorneys have the same training and expertise. You don't want a divorce lawyer representing you in a foreclosure case. Hire an attorney who is trained and has plenty of experience representing homeowners who are facing foreclosure. State and federal consumer protection laws allow for some very technical defenses, but only a handful of lawyers in your area may be well-versed on these complicated statutes. Make sure you hire a specialist.

If you can't afford an attorney, you may be able to handle some court actions yourself, but keep in mind that you'll be going up against the bank's attorney, who probably knows a little more about foreclosure laws than you do. Turn over some rocks — you may have legal services available to you through your workplace or union, or you may have access to legal aid through state, county, or community organizations.

If you decide to take on the case yourself, read up on your state's foreclosure statutes and read materials that explain those statutes. Pay close attention to the details of actions that the bank must take to foreclose properly. If the law requires that the bank publish the notice for five weeks, but you can prove that it only published for two weeks, you may be able to challenge the foreclosure. For additional tips, visit the National Consumer Law Center's Web site at www.consumerlaw.org.

If you find yourself in court, here are some actions you can take to buy yourself some extra time and perhaps give yourself more bargaining power:

- **Attend all hearing dates.** If you're required to bring proof of payments or other information, bring it with you. Don't miss the hearing and allow a default judgment to be entered against you.

- **Demand the right for a jury trial or more time to file an answer (in judicial foreclosures).** This may buy you another day in court; if the court docket is severely backed up, it may buy you weeks. If nothing else, it may give you some negotiating power with the bank to help you settle. (A jury trial may not be an option in all jurisdictions.)

- **File a judicial action to a foreclosure by advertisement before the sale.** This may suspend the sale and force an adjournment.

- **File an action to challenge the foreclosure process after the sale.** This may invalidate the whole process and force the bank to start all over again. (If you know the bank erred in something that will cause the sale to be voided, contact an attorney. She may advise you to wait until later in the redemption period to challenge the sale.) This could force the bank to start all over again. Consult an attorney so you don't miss something important that could cost you everything.

- **During the redemption period (in judicial foreclosure or forfeiture), file an appeal or motion for a new trial.** This may suspend the redemption period and prevent the judge from issuing the writ of restitution.

- **Foreclosures by advertisement are subject to procedural challenges, so consider filing a challenge to the process.** You may lose if the bank followed proper procedure, but this may still give you a little more time.

Know the law and the rules of foreclosure where you live, exercise your rights, and challenge the bank when it doesn't follow the rules.

Filing for bankruptcy

Filing for bankruptcy may not be the perfect solution that many homeowners think it is. It can be costly, fail to solve the underlying problem, damage your credit, and fall short of saving your home anyway. However, we do recommend that you consult with a qualified bankruptcy attorney or at least read *Personal Bankruptcy Laws For Dummies,* 2nd Edition, by James P. Caher and John M. Caher (Wiley), to find out about your options before ruling out bankruptcy entirely. A good bankruptcy attorney may be able to fashion a plan with high odds of your being able to keep your house.

By filing for bankruptcy, you create an automatic *stay* that prevents creditors from attempting to collect on their loans. If you file before the sheriff's sale, your house can't be sold at auction.

Consult a bankruptcy attorney, preferably one who focuses on debtor representation, ask about costs, and find out the pros and cons of filing for bankruptcy. Most bankruptcy attorneys can review your situation and inform you of your options for $200 to $300. A few disreputable bankruptcy attorneys are what we call *mills* — they collect the filing fee and their fee, and then you may see the attorney only once when he firsts meets you and briefly goes through the benefits of filing. He doesn't take time to understand your situation, nor does he present the court with a plan that you can actually meet. Bankruptcy can be costly, so don't take it lightly. Enter it only with full understanding, commitment, and representation. For more about the bankruptcy option, check out Chapter 12.

Having your home sold out from under you

If you're living in a state that has no redemption period, the sheriff's sale is the beginning of the end of losing your home. As soon as a winning bid is accepted at the foreclosure auction, that winning bidder receives the sheriff's deed and can proceed to have you evicted if you don't move out willingly.

If you're living in an area with a redemption period, you can remain in your home and explore other options for retaining possession of the property, as explained in the following section.

Never assume that the sale is the end of the line. Contact your attorney to find out about any remaining options. If you can't afford an attorney, visit your county's register of deeds office and ask about your options.

In our area, where we have a 6- to 12-month redemption period, some unsavory characters visit distressed homeowners and tell them that they attended the sheriff's sale, they purchased the property, and the homeowners have to pack and leave immediately. These guys know that the homeowners have a redemption period, but they don't care — they rely on ignorance and fear. The best defense against these hooligans is to know your rights, verify everything someone tells you, and remain calm.

Seeking redemption: Buying back your home

At any time during the redemption period (assuming you're living in an area with a redemption period), you can "buy back" your home by paying the person who bought it at the sale the full amount that that person paid, along with interest (as stipulated in the mortgage or contract for deed) and any property taxes and insurance that the person paid and has the legal right to collect. In some cases, this means paying thousands of dollars more than the amount the buyer paid at auction.

During the redemption period, you have several options to retain possession of your home or sell it yourself:

- Refinance with a new mortgage.
- Borrow money from family and friends. (*Note:* This is easier to do before it goes to sale.)
- List your house for sale with an agent.
- Sell your house to an investor.
- Sell to an investor and then buy the house back on a contract for deed or via a lease-option agreement.
- Win the lottery and pay the house off in cash. (We haven't seen it happen yet.)

In some states, even though you have no right to redeem the property after the sale, you may be able to *cure the default* by paying all past due amounts several days prior to the sale.

We cover these options in greater detail in Chapter 5 and throughout this book.

The key is to do something to help yourself out of this mess. Better yet, do *everything* — put the house up for sale, contact an attorney, meet with a loan officer to find out about refinancing options, and meet with a private real estate investor. Knowing all your options empowers you to pick the best one or two or three.

Adjusting Your Strategy for Current Market Conditions

The foreclosure process is very clinical — at least for the bank that's foreclosing. What we mean is that the people you deal with may not be the most compassionate human beings on the planet. It kind of depends on the housing market in your area. If the housing market is in a meltdown and the bank stands to lose more through foreclosure than it stands to gain, people tend to be more compassionate and understanding. In a booming market, people tend to be more cutthroat.

In the following sections, we show you how to tweak your expectations and your strategy for different markets.

Surviving in a booming market

In a hot market, where homes are purchased the same day they're listed, you can expect the lender and its representatives to be fairly heartless. When you fall behind on payments, the first person you talk to may be helpful and understanding, but as you move further up the line, people generally become less patient and understanding. The collections department becomes more harsh, loss mitigation is more severe, and eventually the attorney or law firm handling the foreclosure may appear to be the most callous of the bunch.

Unfortunately, they aren't there to offer a solution, nor do they care how or why you found yourself in this situation. They care only about collecting the debt for their client (the lender) and abiding by the laws of your state to wrap it up.

 The good news is that in a booming market, your home is generally appreciating much more rapidly. You may be able to sell the home, pay off the debt, and walk away with some cash in your pocket to jumpstart your life. Refinancing your way out of foreclosure may also be a more realistic option. The more equity you have in your home and the more time you have to take action, the more leverage you have during negotiations.

Gaining the upper hand in a slumping market

In a slow market, particularly one that has been hard hit by dire economic conditions, you may find that the lender is more sympathetic. After all, the bank stands to lose out if nobody in the area can afford its mortgage payments. If the lender is smart, it'll try to work out a solution with you that enables you to stay in your home and eventually start making mortgage payments again.

It's kind of sad, but the reality is that the bank lends for interest. If it can't get the interest, then the bank wants its money back, and if the bank can't get its money, it wants the collateral. In a housing market that has tanked, that collateral may not be sufficient to satisfy the bank. The bank wants as much as it can get without the hassle of dealing with a loser piece of property. Taking back real estate in bad markets is costly for banks, and they don't want to do it if they can avoid it. This can be good news for you: In a down market, banks are more willing to strike a deal with you. Remain diligent, talk to everyone, and keep good records.

Chapter 3

Regaining Your Emotional Composure

- -

In This Chapter

▶ Acknowledging counterproductive emotions

▶ Sidestepping emotions that can make matters worse

▶ Taking positive steps

▶ Placing all options on the table

▶ Doing some damage control

- -

In foreclosure, negative emotions can shackle you and discourage you from taking action to fight the foreclosure. Angry outbursts can convince the lender to no longer cooperate or compromise with you. Shame and guilt can keep you from seeking help. And fear can shut down the communication needed to resolve the problem.

As soon as you begin missing payments and the bank starts sending you notices, the clock starts ticking and you can no longer afford to waste time on counterproductive emotions. You need to grab yourself by the shoulders, shake some sense into yourself, and start taking action to resolve the problem as soon as possible.

In this chapter, we identify the most common counterproductive emotions and reveal techniques for overcoming them and becoming more proactive in the process.

Understanding How Negative Emotions Can Sink Your Ship

Foreclosure is one big problem, and, like most problems, it requires clear thinking and hard work to resolve. Unfortunately, foreclosure can become a very emotional situation. You're unable to pay your bills, and you face the painful prospect of losing your home and all that the home may mean to you — self-respect, neighbors, shelter for your children, a future spent building memories in that home, and so on.

When you begin to think about all that, you can easily become overwhelmed by emotions, including anger, shame, fear, and a sense of helplessness — all of which are not only counterproductive but destructive. We want you to be well aware of just how destructive these emotions can be, so you're less susceptible to falling victim to them.

In the following sections, we reveal the most common negative emotions you're likely to have at some time during the foreclosure process. Later in this chapter, we show you how to begin to let go of the emotional baggage that may be dragging you down.

Yelling your way to the poorhouse

One of the most common and most destructive emotions we see in foreclosure is anger, which is usually borne from frustration. Everything starts piling up and you just can't take it anymore. The anger reaches a boiling point and then the lids start popping. If you're in a relationship, you start blaming your partner. If you're on your own, you start blaming everyone else.

Unless you stop playing the blame game, the crisis can continue to escalate, until nothing gets done and everyone loses. You can end up losing your home and all the equity in it, not to mention your relationships with the people who matter most to you — your family and friends.

In most relationships, there's plenty of blame to go around. Neither partner can really be blamed — as in the death of a spouse, the permanent loss of a high-paying job, or a debilitating illness. In any case, shouting at one another rarely does any good and can often worsen the situation.

Facing a possible foreclosure is like traveling the Oregon Trail in the 1800s. Nothing is easy, hardship is everywhere, and then the bandits arrive. You can't go off in different directions and hope for survival — you have to circle the wagons and fight together. This is just one battle, and you must not lose sight of all of the battles that you have fought and won together over the years.

A little emotional release may be good, and can actually clear the air and help you focus on the problem at hand, but be careful not to say something you can never take back. Someone once said that words are like toothpaste — they come out easy enough, but they're almost impossible to put back.

In order to work your way out of this tricky situation, you're going to need a clear and level head, focused on the task at hand. When emotions run hot as they sometimes do, take a break, cool off, and come back to it later. A walk

Who's really to blame?

Couples we assist are often caught up in the blame game. The partner who's in charge of the bookkeeping usually becomes the target. The other partner, in shock over what's happening, may say something like, "What have you been doing with the money I work so hard for?!"

Ralph has to keep Lois from jumping across the table and slapping some sense into the accuser. Although she has to keep from becoming confrontational, Lois wants to say, "Are you kidding?! You probably haven't been involved in the day-to-day responsibilities of making ends meet, because you didn't want to be burdened with such a distasteful and hard subject. Instead you decided to turn your head and be

Pollyanna. So, now your spouse has to take all the blame, when the blame should fall on your shoulders equally — or even more on you, because at least your spouse was in there trying!"

If you find yourself in a similar situation, you and your partner need to realize that what's past is past and that you're both responsible for correcting the situation moving forward. The only thoughts you should have about the past are that you won't repeat it. Budget carefully, and if you find that you have more month left than money, start cutting expenses or earning more money.

around the block can burn off some of that excess energy and stress, and put you in the right frame of mind to knuckle down and get to work.

The only thing worse than yelling at your significant other is yelling at the bank's representatives or the bill collectors. In most cases, these people are just doing their job and following company policies and procedures. Yelling at them rarely makes them work better or faster, and they're probably powerless to stop the foreclosure without your cooperation. However, if you communicate and cooperate with them, they may be more willing and able to work with you toward a better outcome.

Becoming paralyzed with fear

At some point in every good horror flick, the protagonist becomes paralyzed by fear and overcome with emotion. As a member of the audience, you're compelled to yell at the screen, telling her to run, telling her not to open that door, encouraging her to do something rational, but she simply can't do it. Instead, she freezes, only to be shot, slashed, burned, or otherwise abused and mutilated by the psycho villain.

Foreclosure can be a bit like that. Overcome with the situation and discouraged by the prospects of a bleak future of abject poverty, you feel defeated, as though you can't possibly do anything to remedy the situation. All of this is a nightmare beyond your control, so why bother?

What you should really be afraid of

People in foreclosure often fear the wrong things. They're afraid that everyone will find out, everyone will think they're a loser, only deadbeats don't pay their bills and get foreclosed, and so on. First of all, none of that is true. We see some pretty high-end houses end up in the sheriff's sale due to economic downturns. Highly educated people with fairly substantial incomes fall victim to foreclosure.

If you're going to be afraid of anything, let it be the fear of seeing all your stuff carried out to the curb on eviction day. Let it be the look in your child's eyes when he asks you what's going on when the court officer shows up to kick you out of your house. This is what you should really fear, and it is avoidable if you take control of the situation and take action. You can always shed yourself of a house and leave the bad situation in the past. Don't make it worse by letting your emotions control you.

A defeatist attitude, however, can be your worst enemy. It can cause you to lose everything unnecessarily. By keeping your emotions and fears in check, and taking a more proactive approach, you may be able to significantly improve the outcome. We don't mean to sound callous — foreclosure is an emotional event — but learning how to focus your emotions can liberate you instead of making you feel trapped.

Failing to act out of hopelessness

Foreclosure is one of those situations that commonly causes people to think in terms of black and white: "I can't pay my mortgage, so I'm going to lose my house." That kind of thinking is understandable, especially when you're trying to hold down a job (or find one), raise your kids, and deal with a hundred other things. Foreclosure can loom so large that you don't know where to begin. You don't know the process, who to talk to, who to trust, or whether you even have any options.

When you begin to feel helpless and overwhelmed, take a deep breath. If you're in tears, dry your eyes. Compose your thoughts, and take the first step — start learning about the foreclosure process in your area.

Chapter 2 provides a bird's-eye view of the different types of foreclosure processes. This can give you a pretty good idea of how foreclosures are handled in different areas of the United States and different situations.

After you have a fairly clear understanding of the overall process, start collecting more information about the foreclosure process in your state and county. Following are several sources where you can go to obtain additional information and guidance:

✔ **Search the Internet.** Use your favorite Internet search engine (type the name of your state or county followed by the word *foreclosure*) to find additional information specific to your state and county. The National Consumer Law Center Web site at www.consumerlaw.com offers some of the most accurate and reliable advice you can find on the Web.

Steer clear of any Web sites that offer quick-fix solutions to foreclosure. Many Web sites are actually fronts for con artists who want to steal your home or scam you out of even more money that you don't have.

✔ **Visit Freddie Mac's Don't Borrow Trouble Web site.** Go to www.dont borrowtrouble.com for reliable information about how to work with your lender to resolve the problem.

✔ **Visit your county courthouse.** In the county courthouse, track down the register of deeds office, where you can find people to explain the foreclosure process to you, along with your options. They probably won't have much time to walk you through every step, but they may know someone who can. If you find out nothing else, ask about the foreclosure timeline, so you know exactly when key events are going to occur.

Ask at the county courthouse for the names of any free or inexpensive legal services in your area that can assist you. These services exist in many counties across the United States and can be very valuable.

The key to a positive outcome is education. You may not need to know as much about the foreclosure process as the lawyers for your bank, but you should know your rights under the law and the timeline according to which events are going to unfold. After you've grasped the basics of what you're up against and the timeline for the process, you can begin sizing up your options and formulating your plan of attack.

Shaming yourself out of asking for help

Loser, you've always been a loser, and soon it's going to be official. In a matter of days or weeks, everyone in your neighborhood and your family is going to know that you failed to pay your bills and shelter your family.

If that's what you're thinking, stop right there. Plenty of people who've been far more successful than you have suffered greater failures. The only real losers are those who let others control the outcome. As long as you do your best to achieve the optimal outcome, you can hold your head high.

Foreclosure is humbling, yes, but insurmountable? No. In fact, most people facing foreclosure could avoid it by asking for a helping hand from a close friend or relative who has some money. You probably have people around you who know you, love you, and would like nothing more than to assist you, but if they don't know (and believe it or not, few people actually know you're in foreclosure), they can't help.

As Lois's father always told her, "A problem is something that money cannot solve." Death and terminal illnesses are problems; foreclosure is not. If your family is healthy, you can work together to get through this in one way or another and eventually come out on the other side a lot closer to one another.

Asking dad for help

Not too long ago, we met a couple who were facing foreclosure. The wife had contacted us and asked us to come out to the house to discuss the situation and explain their options. This was the couple's first home, and soon after buying it, they hit some hard times. The husband worked whatever hours he could find and was busting his hump to scrounge up side jobs, but nothing seemed to dig them out of the financial hole they had found themselves in.

When we met with them and discussed their options, we asked if they could ask anyone in their family for help. In fact, we asked several times, and the answer was always, "No." As time passed and their redemption period ticked away, we tried desperately to find a solution, but our options were running out.

Finally, just a few weeks before they were scheduled to lose their home for good, we thought we would ask one more time: "Is there *anyone* at all you can ask for help?" Again, the wife answered, "No." This time, however, the husband decided to give a different answer. He said, "Maybe." After all this time and frustration, we finally got a *maybe.* That *maybe* was music to our ears.

So, we asked the logical next question, "Who?"

"Well," the husband answered, "her father."

The wife still wasn't sold on the idea of calling her dad. She tearfully explained that they were trying to make it on their own, and she desperately didn't want to have to call her father and explain how they had failed. She was afraid that her father would be disappointed in her. After all, he had built a successful business of his own.

We understood, but we also put it into perspective for her. We asked, "What do you think would be more disappointing for your father — helping you out when you're trying so hard to make it work, or hearing about his grandchildren, his daughter, and his son-in-law being evicted when he was only a phone call away and could have stopped it all?"

Well, that rhetorical question was enough to convince the wife to call her dad, right then and there. Her dad was sympathetic, and you could hear the genuine love and concern he felt for his daughter and how hard it was for her to call him.

As it turns out, her dad is a very wealthy New England businessman. He cosigned for them and handled the financing with payments they could afford until they could get back on their feet. At their insistence, he charged them interest (after all, they were determined to make it on their own and just needed a little help right now).

All's well that ends well, but they were willing to lose everything because they were too embarrassed or proud to ask for help. Don't let the same mistake lead to the loss of your home and the eviction of your family. We wouldn't have wanted to be on the other end of that line when she was forced to call her dad and explain that they had lost everything and were being evicted. His only response at that point could have been, "Why didn't you call before it was too late?" Granted, you may not have a wealthy relative standing in the wings waiting to bail you out, but if you don't ask, you won't know what help *is* available.

We're not saying that you should plant a sign in your front yard that says "FREE FORECLOSURE HELP WANTED," but you should certainly talk to close friends and loved ones — especially if they're in a position to help you. Even if they aren't in a position to help, they may know someone, or know someone who knows someone who can point you in the right direction, as demonstrated in the "Asking dad for help" sidebar.

When you're reluctant to ask a close friend or relative for help, consider this: How would you feel if you were in a position to help this person, and he didn't come to you? You'd probably feel as though he didn't love you enough to ask for help or he was afraid you would judge him. You probably wouldn't want to feel that way, and neither do your loved ones. Don't do a disservice to your closest friends and relatives by not asking for help when you need it.

Shaking Any Counterproductive Emotions

Emotions are funny things — one moment, you're on top of the world, and the next you feel like you've been run over by a Mack truck. When you're in foreclosure, the emotional swings can be just as wild and even more so. Just when you think you've made a breakthrough, you encounter a setback, and all the positive thoughts in the world don't seem to be able to pull you out of your despair.

Despair is dangerous. It can cripple you and convince you to give up even when you're making great progress. Despair is real, though, and you're going to experience it, so prepare yourself. Know upfront that you're going to experience disappointments, so you can recognize those disappointments early and get over them more quickly.

Some days, you may find it nearly impossible to get out of bed and step into the boxing ring one more time, but you have to force yourself to do it. The alternative is always much worse. Many people give up when they're closest to success — don't quit prematurely.

Facing your fears

In our business, we take a lot of risks. When we're considering a risky business decision, we always ask ourselves, "If we do this, what's the worst that can happen? Can they skewer us and roast us over a pit?" Of course, the answer is usually, "No," and we can then proceed to overcome our fear and jump right in.

This approach is exactly the same one you should take to overcome your fear. The worst thing your bank can possibly do to you is evict you from your home, and they can't even do that if you move out prior to eviction day. They certainly cannot skewer you and your family and roast you over a pit.

Anything you encounter by trying to remedy the situation cannot possibly place you in a worse position than the one you're already in — assuming, of course, that you don't go along with some quick-fix con-artist scheme. The realization that you can't make things any worse may be enough to liberate you, so you can start taking positive steps in the right direction.

Try one solution. If the solution doesn't work, try it again or try something else. Remain diligent — you never know when the big break will come, but it will *never* come if you don't try.

Some solutions are better than others — that's why you need to educate yourself so you can chose the solution that's best for you. Know the pitfalls, be able to recognize the scammers when they come calling, know your rights and options, and then develop a plan of attack that will put you on the path toward renewed success or, in some cases, moving on. (The chapters in Parts II and III of this book can bring you up to speed in a hurry.)

Getting over guilt

Guilt can be a positive or negative emotion. If it drives you and other family members to stop doing something that resulted in the foreclosure, and then inspires you to take the action necessary to resolve the problem, it can be a very positive force. If it simply turns the situation into a blame game and makes the guilty parties feel so terrible that they have no desire to do anything, then guilt can be terribly destructive.

If you did or failed to do something that eventually triggered the onset of the foreclosure process, the best way to overcome the guilt is to come clean. Lay your cards on the table. Get whatever happened out in the open, deal with it, and then let it go.

You cannot change the past. You can apologize, you can feel horrible, and you can even beg for forgiveness, but it doesn't change the past. What's done is done. After you own up to the mistakes that caused the problem, you can begin to focus on the solution with a clean slate and a lot less emotional baggage.

Denial and blame are killers. To solve the problem you're facing right now, you have to forgive yourself and the people who are going to be in the trenches with you. The lies, the cover-ups, the deceit — they all hurt, but to get through this you have to be able to get over the past. Sometimes the hardest thing to get over is the feeling that you've let down someone you love.

This may sound a little sappy, but it's true: If you save your house but you lose your relationships in the process, you've really lost something. A house is just wood, bricks, and mortar, but a home is where families and loved ones live. Focus on saving your home. You may still lose the house, but if you save your home, you're going to be much happier in the end.

Side-stepping shame

"What will the neighbors think?"

That is the single most common question we hear from people facing foreclosure. They're worried that the neighbors are going to think less of them for not being able to afford their house and not being able to keep up with the Joneses. Most people feel some shame over letting other family members down — perhaps their spouse or their children.

The best way to overcome any shame you may be feeling is to put foreclosure into perspective. The fact is that most Americans are fairly deep in debt. We live on income that we're not guaranteed and spend money we don't have. According to some estimates, most American households are really only three to six months away from foreclosure, and that includes your neighbors.

Take away one of their dual incomes and see what effect it has. Cut the breadwinner's overtime or hourly wage and see who spirals into foreclosure. Have the engine blow up on the family car that costs $3,000 to replace, or bury a loved one at the cost of $5,000 that you just don't have right now, and guess who will suffer. Saddle one of the happily married couples across the street with an alcohol, drug, or gambling addiction and see how long they can keep it all together.

If you begin to feel shame, keep the following important points in mind:

- **Every family has its secrets.** Your foreclosure may be mild compared to some of the secrets in the neighbors' closets.

- **Most of your neighbors are never more than a few months away from foreclosure themselves.**

- **Keeping your head above water is not as easy as it looks on TV.** Life can throw you a lot of curves, and you and others can make poor choices that make it even more challenging.

- **Confronting difficult issues that life presents you with is more honorable than never having anything in life test you.**

Letting go of your anger

How could this happen to me? What was my spouse thinking? The bank screwed us! My boss or company screwed me! I'm mad as hell and I'm not going to take it anymore!

Okay, so how's that working for you? It could be working *for* you or *against* you, depending on your approach.

Bag that energy and emotion and focus it on a positive solution. When you're upset and angry, you tend to make lousy decisions — that's true for all of us. So, find a way to direct your anger at the problem; otherwise, you may as well add a bailiff to the list of people you hate when he shows up to evict you.

Maintaining your composure

Cooler heads usually prevail, and for good reason — because they are *reasonable*. People who maintain their composure think more clearly and usually make sound decisions.

If you're trying to work out something with the bank and you're irate, or all over the place, how far do you think that will go with the hourly employee on the other end of the line? How willing do you think he'll be to assist you if you sound irrational and make unreasonable demands?

The bank's employees are just doing their job, too. You have to help yourself by working within the system, and that includes maintaining your composure so you can get something accomplished.

Accepting that you may lose this house

In Chapter 7 of this book, we lead you through the process of reviewing your options, many of which can assist you in retaining possession of your house. Sometimes, however, keeping the house isn't possible or feasible, in which case, preparing yourself emotionally to lose this house is often necessary. This is particularly difficult if you recently experienced another significant loss — the loss of a loved one, the loss of control because of substance abuse, the loss of a job, the loss of your car, and so on. Looking beyond the loss to the future may be difficult when your final loss is your castle.

When we tell clients to prepare themselves to lose this house, we always stress the word *this*. You may lose *this* house, but you can rent a place or even buy another house later. You may be losing the place where you and your family built fond memories, but you'll find a new place where you can build new memories. And by taking control of the situation, you won't add the really bad memory of being evicted.

We always explain to people who are stuck in this seemingly dead-end situation that it's only a house. Of course, that's easier for us to say than for distressed homeowners to accept. After all, it's not *our* house. But if you think about it, losing a house is not the end of the world, although it may seem that way to you. It's okay to feel that way for a while, but eventually, getting beyond the grief will deliver more positive results.

Taking Control of a Bad Situation

When you fall behind on paying the bills, it begins to feel as though you're in the middle of a forest fire. As soon as you put out one fire, another one pops up right beside you. But you never get ahead just putting out one small fire after the other. You have to attack the root cause of the problem and hit it with everything you've got. At the same time, you have to make sure that you put the fires out for good, so you don't set yourself up for future failure.

In the following sections, I offer two suggestions for how you can become more proactive and immediately begin to take steps to improve your situation.

The more proactive you are and the more you stay ahead of the game, the less likely you are to become subject to circumstances beyond your control.

Lawyering up with a foreclosure attorney

If you're going to hire an attorney to assist you, do it early. If you try several options on your own first and then turn to an attorney at the very last minute, the foreclosure process may be so far along that the attorney wouldn't be able to do anything for you. You may have already sealed your fate. You have to contact an attorney when you still have options.

An attorney once told us a story that a client of his asked him to sit in on the closing for a piece of property he was buying. Of course, that's pretty normal, but what bothered the attorney was that his client hadn't asked him to be involved earlier in the process, when he was negotiating with the seller. The attorney told his client, "There isn't much I can do for you at a closing. You've already negotiated the purchase agreement, the title work has already been done and analyzed, the inspections and disclosures have already happened, and you're already bound under the contract. What do you want me to do — sit in the room and watch you sign your name?" That sounds a bit harsh, but his point was that his client didn't contact him early enough when he could have offered something of value.

Consult a bankruptcy attorney early in the process to find out about available options. You don't need to file for bankruptcy. For a few hundred dollars, however, you can determine whether bankruptcy is a viable option. If the idea of consulting a bankruptcy attorney doesn't appeal to you, at least pick up a copy of *Personal Bankruptcy Laws For Dummies,* 2nd Edition, by James P. Caher and John M. Caher, to check out the pros and cons of bankruptcy.

Sticking up for yourself

A highly qualified foreclosure attorney can certainly take many of the hassles and headaches out of the process for you, but if you can't afford your house payments, you probably don't have a lot of cash lying around to hire a top-notch attorney. The other alternative is to advocate for yourself. Most people have the general qualifications required to do the job:

✔ Ability to keep good records

✔ Ability to do a moderate amount of research

✔ Assertiveness (most people need to work on this)

In the following sections, we show you the basics of how to become your own best advocate.

Keeping impeccable records

The single most important foreclosure self-defense maneuver consists of keeping detailed and accurate records. That means recording everything that happens from start to finish. Why? Because if you ever have to appear in court, a complete record of what happened is your best defense whenever the hearing turns into a he-said-she-said event. The person with the most complete and accurate records, with each event recorded at the time it happened, receives the court's favor. And believe us when we say that the bank and its attorneys are recording everything.

The following sections describe the events and happenings that you should be recording or keeping track of.

Conversations

Use a tape recorder or digital recorder to record all the conversations you can. When it's not possible or not lawful for you to record a conversation, take detailed notes. Keep a notebook or legal pad along with a couple pens or pencils next to your phone, so you don't have to search for them when the phone rings. After you hang up, fill in the details of what you talked about and clean it up.

Jot down the date and time of the conversation. That way, if you need to reference what was said or call someone on it in court, you can say something like, "On January 14, at 3:30 p.m., we discussed this issue. At that time, you said x, now you're saying y."

Documentation

Keep every document (or at least a copy of it) that you send or receive. Put a date on every letter, form, and other correspondence you send out, and write the date and time on every document you receive to note when you received it.

Keep the envelopes you receive, too; staple the envelope to the document — postal stamps can verify dates pretty well. Also, keep photocopies of the envelopes you use to send documents to prove that you sent them to the correct address. If possible, send out everything with a return receipt requested, especially when you're sending something important like reinstatement funds or redemption funds. If you send a fax, do so from a fax machine that prints out a confirmation receipt to prove it went through and was delivered. If you're required to send certified money, keep the stub of any monies sent. All this information can really help your attorney, or you, in the event that you need it in court.

Verifications

To the greatest extent possible, verify everything that the bank or the bank's attorney tells you. If the sale was adjourned, go to your county's register of deeds or sheriff's office and make sure it really was adjourned. If the sale was supposed to be canceled, make sure it wasn't just adjourned but was truly canceled. If the sheriff's deed was redeemed, get a copy of the redemption certificate stating it was redeemed.

This is really just a measure to cover you in case something that is supposed to happen doesn't, or, even worse, something that is *not* supposed to happen *does*. Sometimes not finding out about something for a few days can really cost you, so the sooner you know about issues and can address or correct them, the better.

Checking out some useful Web sites

The Internet is packed with sites about foreclosure, most of which cover foreclosure investing and dubious foreclosure-rescue techniques. We do know of a few reputable sites, however, that offer reliable information:

- ✓ **HUD's Foreclosure Index (`www.hud.gov/foreclosure/index.cfm`):** This site offers a broad overview of the foreclosure process, with some helpful answers to commonly asked questions. You may also find additional information that applies to the state in which you live by selecting your state from the State menu on HUD's home page.

- ✓ **The page for your state's attorney general:** Go to your favorite search engine and type the name of your state followed by *attorney general foreclosure*. You're likely to find a link to foreclosure information from your state's attorney general.

- ✓ **FreeAdvice (`http://forum.freeadvice.com`):** FreeAdvice is a collection of online discussion forums related to various legal issues, including foreclosure. When you reach the site, scroll down to the section on real estate and click the link for the foreclosure forum.

    Always be careful in discussion forums to confirm any information you read with your attorney before accepting it as valid.

✓ **Freddie Mac's Don't Borrow Trouble (`www.dontborrowtrouble.com`):**
Why go to a site about borrowing money when you can't afford payments
on the loans you already have? Because one of the ways to avoid foreclosure is through refinancing, and this site offers a good collection of tips
on how to select a loan that's less likely to get you into trouble again
somewhere down the road.

✓ **Stop Foreclosure (`http://stopforeclosure.com/Foreclosure_`
`Laws.htm`):** Although we cannot recommend any of the programs listed
on this site, the site includes a list of foreclosure laws for all 50 states
that function as a fairly good reference. (Be sure to follow the capitaliza-
tion in the Web address, exactly as we list it — otherwise, you'll get an
error message.)

Confirm all information you obtain from any source on the Web to make sure
it applies to your local jurisdiction and your situation. Working with bad
information is often worse than working with no information. Be especially
careful of any site that makes promises of quick-fix, easy solutions. Stopping
and recovering from foreclosure is rarely easy.

Taking assertiveness training

Most people in the world need a little assertiveness training — not to become
pushy and overbearing, but simply to get what they want and deserve. People
in foreclosure often require a double-dose of assertiveness training to keep
them on track when the going gets tough.

Being assertive basically means not giving up until you resolve an issue. It
means asking pointed, relevant questions and then follow-up questions, until
you're sure you understand what's going on or the issue has been resolved. It
means that you follow up on everything and you push the envelope of your
comfort level, and the comfort level of the people with whom you're dealing.

If your lender's representative tells you that she'll get back with you in a
couple days and she doesn't, for example, call her back, and politely say that
you haven't heard anything and wanted to follow up. Explain to her that you
want to get this matter worked out and behind you, and you don't want to
miss any deadlines or cutoff dates.

Don't make promises you can't keep. If the bank offers some sort of arrangement in which you would pay $3,000 a month for two years to catch up on
missed payments, and you can't afford that, don't say you can. Simply say
something like, "I can't afford $3,000, but I can afford $2,200. Can we make
that work?" Banks are often willing to negotiate if you offer a reasonable
solution, so don't simply dismiss the initial offer your bank makes.

Being assertive may also mean being forceful when necessary. When you have
a legitimate right or a justifiable position, defend it. Don't let other people
push you around or dismiss legitimate claims. Take as much control of your

situation as you can without being a pushy pain in the neck — although sometimes that's required, too.

Weighing your options rationally

One way to keep the emotions of foreclosure from overwhelming you is to begin listing and evaluating your options. In Chapter 7 of this book, we explain the most common options in detail, but here we discuss how to approach the process of listing and assessing your options:

1. **Lay all options on the table, no matter how unrealistic they may seem right now.**

2. **Arrange the options in order, from the ones that sound most attractive to the ones that sound least attractive.**

3. **Move any options to the bottom that are likely to land you right back in the same place where you are now (or worse).**

   Be realistic. Your budget may challenge you, but you don't want it to bankrupt you.

Here are a few questions to ask yourself when evaluating your options:

- ✔ **Can I afford to fund this plan with my current income?**

- ✔ **What cutbacks can I make to help fund this plan?**

- ✔ **Can I afford this house, or should I take an honest look at downsizing?** Affording the monthly payment doesn't account for the monthly utilities and extra expenses of a larger home.

- ✔ **What are my priority debts?** Priority debts are things like your house, car, gas, water, and electric — but probably not 500 channels of 24/7 NHL hockey for $49.99 a month, or that KISS concert for $150 a ticket.

- ✔ **Can I do anything to boost the household income?** Could you work extra hours or take a side job, for example?

- ✔ **How long will the plan be?** Three months or three years?

Teaming up with your partner

Perhaps the most important part of evaluating your options consists of getting on the same page as your partner, if you have one. Your plan and execution of that plan is going to be most effective if you present a unified front. You both need to get with the program, agree not to fight (too much), and join forces to develop a solid plan and put it into action.

In many of the situations we encounter, one spouse is lying to the other. If that's happening in your case, put an end to it — no more secrets:

- ✔ **Be open and honest with one another (and with yourself).** The minute that communication breaks down or the lies start, all the negative emotions return and derail any progress you've made.

- ✔ **Work together.** Pay bills together, so you both know exactly what's been paid. Balance the checkbook together, so you can each see where the money is going and how much you have left. Fill out paperwork together, or at least share copies with one another.

- ✔ **Talk about the issues that affect your financial situation.** Maybe that vacation you take every year will have to be put on hold this year, but you can plan a day trip instead that will cost a small fraction of your traditional vacations.

Never make and implement a plan without informing your significant other, and never assign all the responsibility to one partner. The more the two of you sacrifice and work together, the more successful the plan will be.

Reducing collateral damage to you and your loved ones

Homeowners are often most distressed about the fact that their children may suffer. How do I tell Jacob he can't go to that weeklong soccer camp this year? How do I break it to Emily that she can't buy a new dress for the prom?

You have a couple options when dealing with children:

- ✔ **Shield the kids.** You and your partner may be able to hammer out a solution that keeps the kids in the dark about everything. Discuss the foreclosure in private, steer the kids clear of any unnecessary anxiety, and let the adults handle the situation.

- ✔ **Use this as a learning experience.** Break the news to the kids. Simply lay out the cold, hard facts of life. If you lost your job, explain the loss and the fact that it now means you need to cut expenses — only temporarily. Some families who take this approach find that it builds stronger bonds among family members. If not handled properly, however, the children may suffer unnecessary anguish.

Which option is best? That's for you to decide as a family. Every family is different, and parents have different ways of dealing with these issues. You have to decide what's best for you and the other members of your family.

Chapter 4

Touching Base with Key People Who Can Assist You

. . . .

. . . .

*W*hen you're facing foreclosure, you may be inclined to withdraw into your own little shell until the problem goes away. Although that is certainly one way to handle this difficult situation, asking others for assistance almost always produces better results. You just need to be a little careful about choosing the right people.

In this chapter, we introduce you to several people who may be able to offer valuable assistance, which may be enough to save your home.

Laying Your Cards on the (Kitchen) Table

The absolute worst-case foreclosure scenarios we encounter always involve someone who hides or attempts to hide the problem from the people who are closest to him. The person in the know either feels so afraid and embarrassed to disclose what happened or is playing the hero and trying to resolve the issue by flying solo. For whatever reason, this approach, if allowed to run its course, almost always ends with the loss of the home and relationships on the rocks.

Full disclosure, although initially painful, is almost always the best option. In the following sections, we offer some suggestions on how to break the news to your significant other, your children (if you have them), and your extended family.

Your spouse or life partner and most of your extended family are going to find out about the foreclosure eventually. The sooner you tell them about it, the more they can do to assist you, and the less of a burden you have to carry. The process of trying to keep a secret, in and of itself, can drain your energy.

Breaking the news to your spouse or partner

If you've been married for several years and have kids, you may not consider your relationship to be "romantic," but it still needs some level of intimacy to keep it going. And *intimacy* means an in-depth knowledge of one another's strengths and weaknesses. In an intimate relationship, challenging situations enable you to get to know one another more deeply.

Foreclosure can actually strengthen your relationship if you're open with one another and work together to overcome the challenge. If you haven't already done so, we strongly encourage you to break the bad news to your spouse or life partner as soon as possible.

If you're afraid that your partner is going to go ballistic and perhaps even become violent, you may want someone else present as you disclose the problem and the details. This is where another family member, an attorney, a minister, close friends, a foreclosure expert, or a family therapist or marriage counselor can come in handy.

How do you break the bad news to your partner? Here's one approach that we've found to be successful:

1. **Gather any and all letters and notices you've received, along with some basic financial information, including outstanding bills, credit card balances, and the amount of money (if any) you have in your savings and checking accounts.**

2. **Schedule a meeting with your partner so you can discuss the situation without interruptions or distractions.**

   Tell your partner that you want to discuss the family finances.

3. **During the meeting, provide full disclosure.**

   Explain the current situation and how you believe your family reached this point. If you did or failed to do something that brought you to this point, admit it — get everything out in the open, so you can deal with it.

Ralph's foreclosure fiasco

In 1979, I was a young hot shot real estate agent who was going to set the world on fire. I was so sure of my impending success that I began living way beyond my means. I bought whatever luxury or convenience caught my eye, confident that I would soon make enough money to pay off the credit I took on to finance my purchases.

I soon became overextended and was making so many payments on so may things that I couldn't keep up with my monthly living expenses. I wasn't overly concerned, though, because I knew that very soon, things would turn around. At least that's what I told myself.

Unfortunately, things *didn't* turn around. I fell behind on my bills. My home insurance lapsed. I had to hide my car in the backyard to keep it away from the repo man. Despite the harsh Michigan winter, the snow that had drifted into the corner of my bedroom, and the fact that you could see your breath inside my house, I still refused to ask anyone for help or even tell anyone about the trouble I was having.

Not surprisingly, I finally lost the house, but I still refused to tell anyone about what I was going through. In fact, I didn't even tell my family about my predicament until 5 p.m. on the day I had to be out of the house. My parents were actually moving that same day. After they were moved and we sat down to eat, I finally told them what was going on. My brothers pitched in and helped me move with mom and dad's rental truck. As we were loading the van, my dad took me aside and said, "Ralph, why didn't you tell us about this sooner? We could have helped you."

Like most people who face foreclosure, I was embarrassed, scared, upset, angry, frustrated, and in denial. Many times, I considered asking for help, but my pride got the better of me. I sabotaged my own best interest by repeatedly telling myself that I could make things better on my own — that I could get out of this mess without having to tell anyone about my financial problems. Boy, was I wrong!

You don't have to learn a costly lesson from your mistakes. Learn from *my* mistakes: Acknowledge the problem and share it with people who can help.

4. **Share this book with your partner and go over some of the options for dealing with the situation.**

   Also consider sharing your initial, preliminary plan for how you think that the situation can be solved. You can then work out the fine details together.

If your partner gets angry with you, let her know that you're upset about the situation, too, but that neither of you can undo what has brought you to this point. What's done is done — you can't go back and change the past. Your best hope is to work toward a solution together.

Shielding the children . . . or not

You have two options when it comes to breaking the news of the foreclosure to your kids — tell them or keep it a secret (see Chapter 3). We can't tell you which option is right for your family or the situation you're in — only you can decide that. We *can* tell you, however, what *not* to do: Do *not* have bitter arguments within earshot of the kids, and remember, they have keen hearing.

Feel free to disclose the foreclosure to your children, but always shield them from any negative emotions or hateful words that situations like this often stir up. Kids can deal with almost anything, as long as their mom and dad aren't at each other's throats or yelling at them. Demonstrating to them how two adults in an intimate relationship resolve their issues in a mature manner can often be a valuable life lesson.

If you decide to disclose the foreclosure situation to your children, let them know how the situation is likely to affect them:

- ✔ **Discuss sacrifices that your children may be able to make to help the family.** Kids often take pride in contributing when the family needs it. Asking your children to pay for their own cellphones or give up summer camp is not too harsh.

- ✔ **Don't increase your child's anxiety any more than necessary by discussing the worst possible scenarios.** Until you've had time to assess the situation and explore your options, you don't really know what the outcome is going to be.

- ✔ **As soon as you know what you're going to do and have a schedule in mind, let your children know.** Like most people, if you leave a vacuum, most kids are going to fill it with their worst thoughts.

Be honest and reassuring. Let your children know, both through your words and the way you handle the situation, that this is not the end of the world. Sticking together as a family is what's most important.

Bringing your extended family into the loop

We always ask homeowners facing foreclosure whether they have any close family members who are in a position to assist them financially. Most of them think the question is absurd. "Tell my mom? My dad?! My in-laws?!! Are you nuts?!!!" This is a perfectly normal reaction, of course. Nobody enjoys admitting defeat or failure to loved ones, especially if they've spent their entire lives proving to these loved ones that they can stand on their own two feet.

The reality, however, is that the reason we have families is never more evident than in times of crisis. Family members are supposed to support one another through thick and thin, and when foreclosure strikes, it's time to round up the troops.

Family members are often willing to assist you as long as they know exactly what you need. Write down the type of assistance you need from each family member — money, a car, someone to watch the kids, a drive to and from work, whatever it may be.

When it comes to breaking the bad news to your extended family, the first step is the toughest. Just making the call or asking the person to come over and discuss a problem you're having can be a major hurdle. When working with clients, we often sit with them while they call their loved ones and answer any questions the loved ones may have.

Taking a direct approach is usually best. Come right out and say what the problem is. Your family members are going to want to know how this happened — unless it's obvious, such as a job loss or extended illness. If you made some bad financial decisions, let them know about it. Say something like:

> _____ and I have made some mistakes with our money. We did _____, when we should have been doing _____. We're working to establish a budget and a plan to correct the situation and we'd like your help in two ways: 1) We need $_____ to pull the house out of foreclosure and reinstate, and 2) We'd like you to help us develop a budget, because you've always seemed to have the ability to do that well.

It can also help to let your family members know that you're terribly embarrassed that you even had to come to them, but you didn't know who else could help or who would be so understanding and yet able to keep this quiet.

Seeking Relief If You're in the Military

When you serve your country in the military, you're eligible for a few well-deserved perks, including mortgage payment relief and foreclosure protection. The Servicemembers Civil Relief Act (SCRA) of 2003 (formerly the Soldiers' and Sailors' Civil Relief Act of 1940) provides this protection for eligible service members.

According to the Federal Housing Authority (FHA), under the SCRA, upon your written request, the interest rate that your mortgage lender charges you cannot exceed 6 percent per year during the period of your active military service. Your lender must then recalculate your monthly payments to reflect the lower rate. The provision applies to both conventional and government-insured mortgages. However, this is not automatic; you must submit a written request to your lender no more than 180 days after the date of your release from active military duty. When contacting your lender, provide the following:

- A letter indicating that you have been called to active duty
- A copy of the military orders you received, calling you to active duty
- Your FHA case number
- Evidence that you took on the mortgage debt before being called up to active duty

The SCRA also protects service members from foreclosure. Your mortgage lender is prohibited from foreclosing on your mortgage while you're on active duty or within 90 days after your service without court approval. In order to foreclose, the lender needs to prove, in court, that your ability to make payments has not been compromised by your military service.

What makes you eligible? First, you have to be on active duty and have had your mortgage prior to enlistment or before being ordered to active duty. Next, you have to be one of the following:

- A member of the Army, Navy, Marine Corps, Air Force, or Coast Guard
- A commissioned officer in the Public Health Service Commissioned Corps or the National Oceanic and Atmospheric Administration Corps, engaged in active service
- A reservist ordered to report for military service
- A citizen ordered to report for induction (training) under the Military Service Act
- A guardsperson called to active service for more than 30 consecutive days

Contacting Your Bank Instead of Screening Calls

Caller ID really pays off when the bill collectors start calling, but when you're facing foreclosure, screening your calls may not be the most prudent move. The longer you put off dealing with the problem, the less time and the fewer options you have, so stop screening calls and start making them.

The problem is yours, so take the initiative to solve it. The best defense is a great offense. The more responsibility you take, the more control you have over the outcome.

In the following sections, we introduce you to the people you need to talk to who are affiliated with your bank. Get in touch with them as early as possible. When you call, jot down the following information for your records:

- The current date and time
- The person's name and job title
- Notes describing what you discussed, particularly what you or the other person promised to do — what actions need to by taken, by whom, and by what deadline

Dealing with your loan servicer

In most cases, you don't have the bank's phone number, because you don't actually make payments to the bank. Another company *services* the loan. In other words, you make your payments to the servicer, and the servicer processes your payments and keeps your payment records.

If you received a letter or other type of notice from your bank, you can safely skip to the next section and talk directly to your bank. If, however, you don't even know which bank yours is, track down the phone number for your loan servicer — it should be on your payment book or on any statements you received from the servicer. You usually talk to your servicer first; the servicer may or may not be able to offer assistance. If your loan servicer can't provide the information you need, ask for the bank's phone number.

A loan servicer or a collection agency may be able to work out a solution involving one or two missed or late payments, but these folks do not generally have the authority to negotiate a long-term solution or payment plan. You need to get in touch with the bank directly.

Contacting your bank

As soon as you track down the contact information for your bank, call the bank and ask for someone in the loss mitigation department. Your bank either has its own loss mitigation department or outsources this job to an attorney. In any event, this person is in charge of coming up with a solution that's in the best interest of the bank, whether that consists of moving forward with the foreclosure or working out a deal with you.

If your mortgage loan is through a local bank, request a personal meeting with the loss mitigator. This serves two purposes:

✔ It shows that you're responsible and committed to taking ownership of the problem.

✔ It places a human face on the foreclosure, giving the loss mitigator an added incentive to work out a solution that's in the best interest of all parties.

In your first meeting, you're simply gathering information and letting the bank know why you've been missing payments. In subsequent meetings, you can explore various options and pitch your plans (see Chapter 11).

Coming clean with your bank's attorney

When discussing your situation with the loss mitigator at your bank, ask the person whether an attorney is involved with the case. If an attorney is involved, find out the person's name and contact information, and give the person a quick call to introduce yourself. Let the attorney know the following:

✔ Your name

✔ Your contact information

✔ An overview of what's going on

✔ Actions you're taking to resolve the matter

Let the attorney know that you're available to answer any questions or address any concerns. By proving yourself to be proactive, rational, and organized, you may be able to win over the attorney or at least convince the person to cooperate with you more closely.

Working Out a Deal with Another Lender

The best-laid plans of mice and men often go awry, especially in foreclosure, so always have a backup plan (or two or three) in place. Put your home up for sale, look into refinancing, talk with a private investor, seek assistance from family members, and do everything else we tell you to do in this book. That way, if one solution falls through, you have a couple other options to pursue.

This advice applies to banks and other lenders, as well. The bank that holds your mortgage is not the only bank in town. Plenty of other banks and individuals loan money and may be more inclined than your current bank to float you a loan:

> ✔ A separate loan or second mortgage, in addition to your current mortgage, to reinstate the loan
>
> ✔ A new refinance mortgage that pays off your current mortgage, taking your current bank completely out of the picture

In the following sections, we suggest various lending institutions and individuals to contact for loans. In Chapter 12, we go into more detail about how to borrow your way out of foreclosure.

Asking a mortgage broker or loan officer for assistance

One of your best options is to work through a trustworthy and reliable mortgage broker or loan officer. Your bank may be able to recommend someone, but ask your friends and relatives for recommendations, too. Real estate agents are also excellent sources for recommendations.

Select a mortgage broker or loan officer carefully. Some are nothing more than loan sharks — they sell you a loan that earns them a big fat commission, and have little concern for whether you can afford the payments or whether a particular loan is best for you. Find someone with a solid reputation. They may not feed you the answers you want to hear, but you really don't want someone selling you a loan you can't afford.

Borrowing from traditional lenders

Lenders compete for business, so other lenders may be a little more eager than your current lender to work with you, especially if you're recovering from a temporary financial setback and you have some equity built up in your home.

A mortgage broker or loan officer can assist you in tracking down traditional lenders who offer loan packages that may be suitable for you. You can also try tracking down these lenders yourself, either online (at Web sites like LendingTree.com and eLoan.com) or by calling your local banks and credit unions.

Local banks may be more understanding, particularly if they've witnessed a rash of foreclosures in your area. They have a vested interest in the community and may be more willing to accommodate the right candidates. Keep in mind, however, that you can't expect them to approve risky loans. Have a reasonable plan in place before you go shopping for a loan.

Exploring nontraditional loan options

Private lenders and real estate investors may be willing to work out a solution with you. A *private lender* is usually an individual with money who is willing to loan it at an attractive interest rate. Your jurisdiction may set a cap on the interest rate that private lenders can charge. Private lenders may want to secure the loan by placing a second mortgage on the property, but in a tight spot, when the banks refuse to approve your loan, a private individual may come through for you.

Most private lenders, however, require that you put up some collateral — usually in the form of your home.

The best private lenders and investors work only with people they believe have the resources to repay the debt. If you're only a couple months behind on your payments and you have sufficient income, they may be willing to loan you the money you need to reinstate the mortgage. To secure the loan, they place a lien on your property, which they remove as soon as you repay the loan in full. Before meeting with a private lender, gather the following materials and information to streamline the process:

- ✔ Recent bank statements and other financial records
- ✔ Your credit report
- ✔ Payment history
- ✔ A recent appraisal, if you have one
- ✔ Title work
- ✔ Any other information that pertains to your situation

Be very careful when dealing with private lenders and investors. Read the contracts carefully. Most of them contain a forfeiture clause (see Chapter 5), giving the private lender or investor the rights to the property if you fail to make your payments on schedule or fail to repay the debt by a given date. In some jurisdictions, however, even if the loan agreement contains a forfeiture clause, the lender may not be entitled to forfeiture and may be required to work through the foreclosure process. (We explain all this in Chapter 5, and show you how to steer clear of disreputable investors and other unsavory characters in Chapter 9.)

Taking the Legal Route

One of the first questions distressed homeowners have is whether they have any legal options. There ought to be a law against taking someone's home away from them, right? Fortunately, several laws are in place to protect the rights of homeowners. Of course, plenty of laws are in place to protect lenders, as well. The key is to know your rights, figure out when those rights are being trampled on, and then take action to protect your rights.

In the following sections, we highlight the most common legal options you have at your disposal and then explore the question of whether you need an attorney's assistance in presenting your case.

Brushing up on your legal options

We've witnessed many cases in which attorneys have dropped the ball and left wide-open loopholes that our clients have taken advantage of. Although these legal strategies probably won't spare you from having to catch up on your payments and ultimately repay the debt, they can buy you more time for pursuing other options. The following list describes the most commonly abused homeowners' rights:

- ✔ **Public notification:** Most states have strict rules governing notification of the foreclosure. If the bank is supposed to advertise the foreclosure for five weeks prior to the sale and it advertises for only three weeks prior to the sale, you have a case against the bank.

- ✔ **Redemption:** Know the redemption rules in your state. Redemption periods may vary depending on the size or value of your property and whether the home is abandoned. If the bank informs you that the redemption period is only three months, but the law gives you six months, you have a strong case that may force the bank to start over from scratch, giving you even more time.

- ✔ **Forfeiture:** In some areas, investors and private lenders either knowingly or unknowingly abuse the forfeiture clause in contract for deed and lease-option agreements. Either they word these agreements in a way that makes it impossible for the homeowner to honor the agreement, or they try to enforce a forfeiture clause in a jurisdiction where foreclosure is required. By being aware of the rules and regulations in your area and consulting an attorney, preferably before signing such agreements, you can protect yourself.

- ✔ **Truth in lending technicalities:** According to the Truth in Lending Act (TILA), you may have up to three years to cancel a contract with a creditor who did not follow the TILA guidelines. In order to file a claim against the lender, your loan must be secured by your principal dwelling and the credit must be for consumer purposes (but not for the acquisition of the property or dwelling). If you succeed in rescinding the loan agreement, the court may also force your lender to refund all closing costs and finance charges, and perhaps even award damages.

TILA also provides the right of rescission for some loans under certain conditions. The right of rescission gives you the power to cancel a loan agreement within three days, which gives you some protection in the event that a disreputable loan officer pressures you into taking out a loan. If you feel as though you've been pressured or conned into taking out a bad loan, consult an attorney immediately; the sooner you act, the better your chance of winning the case and having your agreement canceled.

✔ **The waiver defense:** If your lender has accepted late payments in the past, some courts would say that it can't start foreclosure without first warning you that it would not accept late payments. If your lender tries to foreclose without providing you with a fair warning, the court may stop the foreclosure immediately. Check your mortgage or deed of trust; it may contain a phrase such as "acceptance of late payments does not constitute a waiver," in which case, the waiver defense is not an option. However, you may still be able to raise the question in court and buy yourself some more time. A reputable and competent foreclosure attorney can inform you of your rights.

The mother of foreclosure self-defense is bankruptcy. When you file for bankruptcy, you receive an automatic *stay* that prevents the bank from moving forward with the foreclosure. This gives you the time you need to cure the default, typically through Chapter 7 (liquidation) or Chapter 13 (debt restructuring) bankruptcy. (For more about playing the bankruptcy card, check out Chapter 10 of this book.)

Do you need an attorney?

In the United States, the courts are intended to be set up in a way that allows equal justice for all. Anyone is welcome to stand before a judge (or jury in some states) and plead a case. But as the old saying goes, "He who represents himself in court has a fool for an attorney." In other words, if you plan on going to court, hire an attorney to represent you. The bank is going to have its own experienced attorney in its corner. To make this a fair fight, you really need your own attorney.

How much is this going to cost?

We can't quote you attorney fees, but suffice it to say that you can expect to pay a lot if you hire a private attorney. Most legal eagles charge by the hour, and they don't get a whole lot done in an hour. Expect to pay at least a few hundred dollars, probably more in the range of thousands of dollars.

The following guidelines can help you come up with a ballpark figure:

- ✔ **If the attorney charges by the hour, you can expect to pay anywhere from $125 to $300 per hour depending on location and experience.** An attorney in New York City is going to charge a lot more than one who works out of Okemos, Michigan. Likewise, a 25-year senior partner is going to charge more than an attorney who's fresh out of law school.

- ✔ **If the attorney charges by the task, she should be able to give you a fairly accurate estimate of what the whole process is going to cost you.** This should be spelled out in the retainer agreement; if it's not, ask.

Make sure you get what you pay for. Your attorney should be available for you and responsive to your timeline. That foreclosure clock is ticking. You don't have time to waste waiting for your attorney to return phone calls.

You may be able to score some free or very affordable legal assistance through federal, state, or local organizations. Also some worker's unions, such as the UAW, have attorneys available for their members. If you don't know where to turn for legal assistance, head down to your county courthouse; sometimes they have a toll-free number you can call.

The cost of an attorney is usually less than the cost of not having an attorney.

Tracking down a foreclosure specialist

When you find yourself being dragged into court over a foreclosure issue, you don't want a general practitioner, a divorce attorney, or your brother-in-law who wants to be a lawyer someday representing you. You want a foreclosure specialist.

So, how do you go about finding a foreclosure specialist? Here are some suggestions:

- ✔ **Contact local real estate brokers or investors.** They should know attorneys in the area who deal with real estate and landlord-tenant issues, which is a kissing cousin to foreclosure.

- ✔ **Call the local branch of your state bar association.** They can direct you to an attorney who deals with foreclosure issues from a consumer side, or at least point you in the right direction.

- ✔ **Ask down at the public auction for a referral to an attorney.**

- ✔ **Ask a bankruptcy attorney for a referral.** The two fields seem to overlap quite often.

- ✔ **Go online and search within a larger firm's practice groups for the real estate practice group.** Browse the names of the attorneys listed there and their area of practice. Shoot them an e-mail message asking if they handle foreclosure cases from the side of the mortgagor (the one being foreclosed on). Even if they don't handle such cases, they probably know someone who does.

Interview at least three candidates before choosing one. Be sure to ask the following questions:

- ✔ **Is this first meeting free?** Most attorneys will let you interview them for free, but be sure to ask so you don't get hit with another unexpected bill.

- ✔ **How long have you been an attorney?** All other things being equal, someone who's been in the business for five to ten years is likely to have seen more situations and may be better than an attorney who's fresh out of law school.

- ✔ **How long have you been working with people in foreclosure in this area?** Again, the longer the better. Make sure the attorney has experience in your state and county. An attorney who just moved in from another state may not be up to speed on state and county laws.

- ✔ **Are you familiar with the foreclosure laws in this state?** If she says she is, follow up by asking how familiar she is with the laws and the role she plays in the courts. Does she usually represent banks or homeowners? If she says she isn't familiar with the foreclosure laws in your state, move on to another candidate.

- ✔ **How many foreclosure cases do you deal with in an average year?** The more, the better. Someone who deals mostly in divorce and handles foreclosures on the side may not be the best candidate, but he may be able to refer you to a good foreclosure attorney, because the fields tend to be complementary.

- ✔ **Are you familiar with the judicial foreclosure process and not just the sale-by-advertisement process?** Some attorneys deal mainly in foreclosure-by-advertisement. If your state allows judicial foreclosure, you want an attorney who has experience in court.

- ✔ **What's the nature of your representation?** Look for a full-service attorney who's not only going to file paperwork but also assess your situation, talk with your lenders, and represent you in court, if needed. What exactly is your attorney going to do for you?

- ✔ **What are your rates and fees?** Comparison-shop for both services and costs. An attorney who charges you $100 per hour may seem like a bargain, but if all she's doing in filing papers, that may not be the best deal. Likewise, $300 an hour may seem steep, but if the attorney is efficient and can save your home, she may be the real deal.

- ✔ **When are the best times to call you?** Make sure the attorney's schedule matches yours. If you work from 9 to 5 and can't take phone calls at work, can you get a hold of your attorney in the evening or early morning?

Sometimes all you need is to have an attorney draft a few letters on her fancy law-firm letterhead for you. If this is all you need because your issues are not complex enough to warrant hiring an attorney for much else, discuss that with the candidates during your interview.

Striking a Deal with a Real Estate Agent to List Your Home for Sale

A local real estate agent can be your best resource person when you're facing foreclosure. Real estate agents know the local market, are usually well versed in foreclosure rules and regulations, and should have an address book chock-full of names and contact information for other real estate professionals in your area who can assist you. More importantly, a real estate agent can list and sell your home for you and find you more affordable accommodations.

According to our estimates, the best option for 90 percent of homeowners facing foreclosure is to sell their home and purchase a more affordable house.

A big myth in the real estate industry is that real estate agents cannot or will not negotiate their commissions. This is simply not true. A real estate agent who is committed to her marketplace is often willing to negotiate the commission, particularly if she knows that you're facing foreclosure. Assisting people in foreclosure builds positive PR that generates future business for the agent. (For additional details on finding and teaming up with a real estate agent for optimum results, check out Chapter 13.)

Leaning on Your Government

In the midst of the great mortgage meltdown of 2007, President George W. Bush held a news conference announcing that the federal government was taking action to assist homeowners in foreclosure. He announced that the Federal Housing Authority (FHA) would be given more flexibility in insuring mortgage loans so that some people in foreclosure could refinance high-interest loans. He also announced that if banks forgave some of the amounts due, homeowners would not be excessively taxed on those amounts.

The point here is that the government — from your local government all the way up to the president of the United States — does not want to see people lose their homes. Much of the U.S. economy is driven by home ownership, and if too many people start defaulting on their mortgage loans and losing their homes, retail sales sink and the national economy sinks along with them.

It is in the government's best interest to assist you in retaining possession of your property, and the government knows it. As a result, assistance is available at every level of government: county, state, and federal.

Starting at the county level

One of the best places to begin rounding up assistance is at the county level. Your foreclosure is going to be processed by the county register of deeds and the sheriff's office, so they know all the local players. Contact the county register of deeds and ask whether they know of any homeowner assistance programs in your area. Also ask whether they're aware of any free or affordable legal services for people in your situation.

If you have a community center in your area, check it out to determine whether it has any legal assistance available. Many communities offer legal assistance for those in trouble who cannot afford to hire an attorney.

Moving up to the state level

Every state has a state housing authority that deals with homeownership and leasing issues in that state. Your state's housing authority may be able to assist you with securing a loan or steering you toward local resources.

The National Association of Realtors (NAR) has an excellent directory of state foreclosure assistance programs at www.realtor.org/home_buyers_and_sellers/foreclosure_assistance_programs_by_state.html.

Not all real estate agents are Realtors, but all Realtors are real estate agents. Basically, in order to use the trademarked designation of Realtor, a real estate agent has to be a member of NAR and adhere to its code of ethics. We strongly recommend that you choose a Realtor to represent you, particularly one who has experience in foreclosure situations. (See Chapter 13 for additional tips on selecting a top-notch real estate agent.)

Going straight to the top: Federal assistance

The U.S. Department of Housing and Urban Development (HUD) funds free or very low-cost housing counseling nationwide. Housing counselors can help you understand the law and your options, organize your finances, and represent you in negotiations with your lender if you need this assistance. To find a HUD-approved housing counselor near you, visit www.hud.gov/offices/hsg/sfh/hcc/hcs.cfm or call 800-569-4287 (TTY 800-877-8339).

Chapter 5

Deciphering Your Mortgage and Other Documents

In This Chapter

▶ Exploring and understanding your mortgage

▶ Seeing what your deed has to say

▶ Remembering your promise to pay

▶ Dissecting a contract for deed

▶ Surveying a lease-option agreement

When most people buy a house, they do it with someone else's money, usually a bank's, and sign an agreement to pay off the loan by a certain date, usually by signing a mortgage and note. The *mortgage, deed of trust,* or *contract for deed* or *lease-option agreement* (if you financed the purchase through the seller) and the *note* (a promise to pay) contain language stipulating what exactly constitutes a default situation and what the lender is legally allowed to do to you if you default on the loan. Most people don't read these documents thoroughly (or at all) when they purchase a home, but when you're facing foreclosure, you'd better know what you agreed to when you signed on the dotted line. It could save your home, or at least buy you some extra time.

Unfortunately, because these contracts are written in legalese, they're very difficult to decipher and understand. In this chapter, we highlight key clauses in a sample mortgage, deed, contract for deed (also known as a land contract), lease-option agreement, and promissory note. We translate these clauses into plain English, so you're well aware of your rights and the power that these documents grant to your lender.

Your *note* is your promise to pay. Because lenders aren't typically convinced by a promise alone, they have you sign a mortgage that provides the property as collateral and backs up your promise. The good news is that if you signed a loan agreement that places another lien on the property (not to purchase the property, but to buy stuff) and your lender wasn't completely forthcoming as to what you were getting into, you may be able to rescind that agreement. (See "Knowing Your Rights Under the Truth in Lending Act," later in this chapter.)

Decrypting Your Mortgage

Your mortgage may have the look and feel of a book, but it's not exactly the type of book you want to curl up with on a stormy night. The clauses and provisions are enough to make you bleary-eyed . . . and that's just on the first page. When you're in foreclosure, however, knowing exactly what your mortgage stipulates can get you out of a serious jam and buy you some extra time.

The bank wrote your mortgage to protect itself, not to protect you. Most of what the mortgage contains are clauses and provisions that protect the bank's interest and give its lawyers the ammo they need when it comes time to foreclose on your home.

Understanding power of sale

If your mortgage contains power-of-sale language and your jurisdiction allows for power of sale, then the bank does not have to go through the courts to foreclose on your property. All the bank needs to do is advertise its intent

---

What exactly is a mortgage?

The origin of the word *mortgage* is intriguing. It's a French word generally believed to be derived from two Latin words — *mort* (meaning "death") and *gage* (meaning "pledge," or something of value that's forfeited if the debt is not repaid). Mortgages just give Americans one more thing to blame on the French.

Although you may feel as though you're signing your life away when you take out a mortgage, that's not really what the word means. The part of the word dealing with death applies to the passing away of the agreement. When the homeowner eventually pays off the loan, the lender's claim to the property is dead. If the homeowner fails to make payments in accordance with the mortgage, the homeowner's rights to the property cease to exist (or die).

A mortgage is a contract that enables people to purchase property without paying the full value upfront. In essence, a mortgage pledges the property to the lender (the *mortgagee*) in the event that the borrower (the *mortgagor*) fails to repay the debt according to the conditions stipulated in the note. In other words, in the note, you promise to repay the debt, whereas the mortgage secures the loan by offering the home as collateral.

to foreclose and notify you (or at least try to notify you) prior to the sale (auction). The number of days or weeks the advertisement must be posted prior to sale varies by state. (For the differences between judicial and nonjudicial foreclosure, check out Chapter 2.)

One of the first items you should look for in your mortgage is a power-of-sale clause. In the following sections, we show you where to find it, what it says, and how it can affect the foreclosure process.

If you're dealing with a contract for deed or lease-option agreement instead of a mortgage, check to see if your jurisdiction allows a power-of-sale provision with those contracts. Some jurisdictions require judicial foreclosure on land contracts (meaning the person must file a lawsuit against you). If the person tries to take your home without filing a lawsuit, you can take her to court and win. Know your rights. (See "Picking Apart Other Contracts," later in this chapter, for additional details.)

Where to find it

The power-of-sale provision is usually in the mortgage, but if your jurisdiction uses a deed of trust, then it will be in the deed of trust. Skim through the document looking for the words *power of sale*. It's easy to miss, as shown in the following section. (For more about the deed of trust, check out "Deconstructing Your Deed of Trust," later in this chapter.)

What it says

The power of sale is a diminutive phrase that packs a wallop. It's very easy to overlook, even upon close reading. Some lenders include the language in bold or as a separate paragraph to call attention to it, but don't count on it. Here's one example (we italicized *power of sale* to make it stand out):

> This security instrument secures to the lender: (1) the repayment of the Loan, and all renewals, extensions and modifications of the Note; and (2) the performance of Borrower's covenants and agreements under this security instrument and the Note. For this purpose, borrower does hereby mortgage, warrant, grant, and convey to KRAYNAK MORTGAGE CORPORATION and to the successors and assigns of KMC, with *power of sale*, the following described property, located in the County of Who, City of Whoville. . . .

Did you miss it? The three words *power of sale* effectively grant power of sale to the lender. Instead of filing a claim against you in court, the lender simply has to post a notice for a few weeks and notify you.

Take a look at another example. This one is at least located in a section that talks about remedies:

> KRAYNAK MORTGAGE CORPORATION has the right: to exercise any or all of those interests, including, but not limited to, *the right to foreclose and sell the property under power of sale;* and to take any action required of Lender, but not limited to, releasing or canceling this security instrument.

This time the clause was a little more obvious, but not much more. You have to pay close attention when reading your mortgage.

Don't expect your mortgage to contain a clear presentation of the power of sale — some do, some don't. If you're in a jurisdiction that allows foreclosure by advertisement via power of sale, and you don't see the language in your document, ask your lender, your attorney, or someone else who's more accustomed to reading these documents whether your mortgage contains a power of sale. If the answer is yes, have him point out where it is. If the answer is no, you know that the only foreclosure remedy the bank has is a judicial foreclosure.

How a power of sale can affect the foreclosure process

Banks love power of sale, because it generally shaves six to eight months off the foreclosure process and saves them a ton of money in attorney fees. With a judicial foreclosure, the bank has to file a lawsuit, wait for the judge to enter an order allowing the bank to sell the property at auction, and then wait even longer before it can advertise and sell the property. With foreclosure by advertisement, the bank advertises the sale, notifies you, and within a matter of weeks can have the property up on the auction block.

In a nonjudicial foreclosure, you have to take the initiative to file a lawsuit to stop the foreclosure and bring the case to the attention of a judge. In judicial foreclosure, the lender files a lawsuit against you. Be sure to file your answer to any lawsuit promptly; otherwise, the court is likely to grant a default judgment in favor of your lender, and you'll have a tough time stopping the foreclosure after that's done. Always respond to requests from the court, including any requests for you to appear in court; otherwise, you're at the mercy of the court.

Deconstructing the acceleration clause

Almost every mortgage on the planet has an acceleration clause — wording that makes you pay off the loan in full under certain conditions, like missed or chronically late payments. Without an acceleration clause, the bank can only collect on missed payments. If you miss three payments of $1,000 each, for example, the bank cannot file a claim to collect the entire mortgage balance;

it must file a claim for each of the three missed payments. With an acceleration clause, the bank can declare a default after you miss one or two payments and call in the entire balance of the loan.

Where to find it

Like the power-of-sale provision, the acceleration clause is usually in the mortgage, but if your jurisdiction uses a deed of trust, then it will be in the deed of trust. Skim through the document looking for the words *acceleration, balance immediately due,* or *payable in full.* Anything that suggests repayment of the balance immediately and in full indicates the presence of an acceleration clause. We can almost guarantee that your mortgage or deed of trust has an acceleration clause.

The best place to look is under any heading that deals with *remedies* or *default,* but it doesn't have to be under either of these headings.

What it says

The acceleration clause basically says that if you default on the mortgage loan, the entire balance of the loan becomes due immediately. Here's one example of how the acceleration clause may be worded:

> **Remedies.** On the occurrence of any default, Mortgagee *may, at its sole option, declare the entire Indebtedness immediately due and payable.* On the occurrence of any such event of default and *Mortgagee's election to accelerate the Indebtedness,* Mortgagee shall be authorized and empowered to sell or cause to be sold the Premises and to convey them to a purchaser.

This is an example of an acceleration clause that's triggered at the lender's discretion. When default conditions exist, the lender has the right, but not the obligation, to accelerate repayment and make the full balance due. When you have an acceleration clause that is enforceable at the lender's discretion, you're usually permitted to cure any default prior to enforcement of the acceleration clause and avoid the full balance becoming due. In cases such as these, the bank usually must notify you that it's accelerating repayment.

An acceleration clause can also be triggered automatically, in which case whenever default conditions exist, the full balance is due immediately. You have no ability at this point to cure the default and avoid the acceleration of the balance. When an acceleration clause is triggered automatically, the bank is under no obligation to notify you.

We can come up with dozens of examples of acceleration clauses from both traditional mortgages and contracts for deed. Some go into great detail, defining exactly what a default condition is, others explain what the borrower can do to cure the default, and some are very basic and open to interpretation.

A *default* can be whatever the mortgage document says it is. An obvious default is failure to make payments, but default isn't limited to that. Default can also occur for failure to pay property taxes or insurance premiums, death or insolvency of a cosigner, violation of a deed restriction or covenant, and even the failure of the borrower to maintain the premises (jeopardizing the mortgage collateral). These *non-monetary defaults* usually give the borrower a chance to cure the default, but not always.

How an acceleration clause can affect the foreclosure process

An acceleration clause makes foreclosure possible. It calls the entire balance due, so the lender can proceed with foreclosure and sell the collateral described in the mortgage at auction to satisfy the debt.

If you're in an area that allows for judicial foreclosure exclusively, be aware that some jurisdictions frown upon acceleration clauses. You're likely to encounter differing schools of thought on this topic, ranging from "always enforceable" to "almost never enforceable." Most courts consider the answers to the following three questions to determine whether acceleration is enforceable:

- Is the potential hardship to the borrower great?
- Was the default minimal or accidental in nature?
- Was the borrower at all times attempting to act in good faith?

If the court examines the case and sees that you've acted in good faith, fell into this predicament by no fault of your own, and stand to suffer greatly if the repayment is accelerated, then the court may decide that the acceleration clause is unenforceable at this time. You could then reinstate the mortgage without having to come up with the full balance all at once.

Checking out the due-on-sale and due-on-encumbrance clauses . . . just in case

The bank can't control what you do with your house, but it can control what happens to the money it loaned you to purchase that house. This is what the due-on-sale clause and its kissing cousin, the due-on encumbrance clause, are all about.

Watch out for foreclosure rescue scams that ask you to sign over your property to them, so they can catch up on your missed payments and save you from foreclosure. Many of these scams are possible because homeowners believe their mortgages are assumable — that someone else can take over the mortgage and make the payments. The fact is that most mortgages after about 1989 are not assumable. (Any loans closed before 1989 through the Federal Housing Authority [FHA] and any closed before 1988 through Veterans Affairs [VA] are assumable.) In any event, check with your bank and your attorney to ensure that any foreclosure rescue arrangement is legitimate and that it will release you completely from any liability.

Due-on-sale clause

The due-on-sale clause essentially states that as soon as you sell the home, you have to pay the balance of the mortgage loan. The idea behind this clause is to shut down *assumable mortgages* (letting someone take over your mortgage) and prevent homeowners from profiting off low-interest loans.

For example, say you have a mortgage at 5.5 percent interest, and the current interest rate is 7.5 percent. The bank doesn't want you to be able to finance the purchase of the property at 7 percent and keep the extra 1.5 percent interest for yourself, or simply let the buyer assume your mortgage at 5.5 percent. The bank wants to write a new mortgage, so it can raise the rate to 7.5 percent and keep it all for itself.

Following is an example of a due-on-sale clause:

> **Due on sale.** Lender, in making the loan secured by this Mortgage, is relying on the integrity of Borrower and its undertaking to maintain the Property. *If Borrower should (a) sell, transfer, convey, or assign the Property or any right, title, or interest in it, whether legal or equitable; voluntarily or involuntarily; by outright sale, deed, installment sale contract, land contract, contract for deed, leasehold interest (other than leases to tenants) with a term greater than three years, lease-option contract, or any other method of conveyance of real property interests; (b) cause, permit, or suffer any change in the current ownership . . . as of the date of this Mortgage, then the Lender shall have the right at its sole option to declare all sums secured and then unpaid to be immediately due and payable even if the period for the payment has not then expired.* If the ownership of the Property becomes vested in a person other than Borrower (with or without Lender's consent), Lender may deal with the successor or successors in interest with reference to this Mortgage and the Obligations in the same manner as with Borrower.

This due-on-sale clause is not automatically enforced. The lender is free to waive the enforcement and may choose to do so in a slow or declining market or in exchange for some upfront interest in the form of points. The lender may also waive the due-on-sale clause if it accepts payments knowing that the clause has been violated. In other words, this is an area that may offer technicalities you can exploit or negotiate.

The due-on-sale clause may or may not become relevant during foreclosure, but if you choose to sell your home, be aware of this clause. You may not be able to sell the home on contract, for example, and then use payments you receive from the buyer to make your mortgage payments. After you sell the home, the entire loan balance becomes due.

Certain types of transfers are exempt by federal law, such as transfers due to divorce, death, certain living gifts to relatives, and long-term leases that do not contain an option to purchase. Another important exception is that the foreclosure of a junior mortgage may not trigger the due-on-sale clause. This means that if a lender forecloses on a second mortgage and you manage to keep making payments on the first mortgage, you may have time during the redemption period (if your area has a redemption period) to redeem the second mortgage without fear of foreclosure on the first mortgage.

Due-on-encumbrance clause

The due-on-encumbrance clause is designed to keep homeowners from borrowing their way into a default situation. The clause essentially states that if you take out another loan on your property, you have to pay off the balance of the first mortgage in full. This clause may be sandwiched inside of the due-on-sale clause, or it may be a stand-alone provision, as in the following example:

> **Secondary financing.** *Borrower will not, without the prior written consent of Lender, mortgage or pledge the Property as security for any other loan or obligation of Borrower.* If any such mortgage or pledge is entered into without the prior written consent of Lender, the entire Obligations may, at Lender's option, *be declared immediately due and payable without notice.*

> **Against further encumbrances.** *Borrower shall not,* without Lender's prior written consent, *permit any lien, security interest, encumbrance, or charge of any kind to accrue and remain outstanding against the Property,* any part, or any improvements, irrespective of *whether* the lien, security interest, encumbrance, or charge is *junior to the lien of this Mortgage.* If any such encumbrance is created without the prior written consent of Lender, the entire Obligations may, at Lender's option, *be declared immediately due* and payable.

The problem with an encumbrance clause in foreclosure is that it can prevent you from taking out another loan against your property to reinstate your first mortgage. This clause, however, is not set in stone. A bank may be willing to waive it. If your mortgage includes an encumbrance clause, be sure to ask your bank about it and whether it would enforce the encumbrance clause if you took out another loan against the property.

Some mortgages include a provision that calls the loan due in the event of "waste" being committed on the property. In plain English, this means that if you're trashing the joint, the bank may be able to declare you in default and initiate foreclosure proceedings, so it doesn't get in even worse shape by the time the bank tries to sell it.

Investigating your right to reinstate

Whether your bank wants to allow you to reinstate your mortgage may not be up to your bank to decide. If your mortgage contains a Borrower's Right to Reinstate clause, you have the right to reinstate no matter what your bank has to say about it. Reinstating consists of making up all missed and late payments and paying any interest, fees, and penalties that have accrued as a result of those late or missed payments (see Chapter 7 of this book).

Examine your mortgage for a Borrower's Right to Reinstate clause, as shown in the following example:

> **Borrower's Right to Reinstate.** If Borrower meets certain conditions, Borrower shall have the right to have enforcement of this Security Instrument discontinued at any time prior to the earlier of: (a) 5 days (or such other period as applicable law may specify for reinstatement) before sale of the Property pursuant to any power of sale contained in this Security Instrument; or (b) entry of a judgment enforcing this Security Instrument. Those conditions are that Borrower: (a) pays Lender all sums which then would be due under this Security Instrument and the Note as if no acceleration had occurred; (b) cures any default of any other covenants or agreements; (c) pays all expenses incurred in enforcing this Security Instrument, including, but not limited to, reasonable attorneys' fees; and (d) takes such action as Lender may reasonably require to assure that the lien of this Security Instrument, Lender's rights in the Property and Borrower's obligation to pay the sums secured by this Security Instrument shall continue unchanged. Upon reinstatement by Borrower, this Security Instrument and the obligations secured hereby shall remain fully effective as if no acceleration had occurred.

Deconstructing Your Deed of Trust

In some jurisdictions, you're more likely to find a *deed of trust* than a mortgage, but both documents essentially serve the same purpose: They name the property as collateral for the loan and provide the lender with some security for repayment.

What's different about a deed of trust is that it enables an unbiased third party (the trustee) to act as an intermediary. The trustee holds the deed until the mortgage is paid in full. If you default on the mortgage, then the trustee has the power to sell the property and disperse the proceeds of the sale to the lien holder(s). Initially, banks loved the deed-of-trust arrangement, because it allowed for a faster recovery of the property in the event of a default, but the power-of-sale clause in most mortgages has the same effect.

Even though a trustee is handling the sale, you may still have redemption rights. Rights vary depending on your jurisdiction.

Knowing Your Rights Under the Truth in Lending Act

The Truth in Lending Act (TILA) was enacted to prevent lenders from feeding borrowers misleading information about personal loans and other forms of credit. Under TILA, lenders are required to present consumers with clear and accurate information.

A skilled bankruptcy attorney can often leverage the power of these technicalities to convince the courts to cancel certain loan agreements, but the defense of such cases can be very complicated. If you feel as though you've been the victim of unfair lending practices, we recommend you consult an attorney.

Explaining the technicalities of TILA is beyond the scope of this book. We can, however, highlight a few important points about TILA:

- TILA generally does not apply to residential mortgage transactions (meaning, it probably won't help you regarding the mortgage you took out to purchase your home). It may, however, offer some protection for second mortgages and other such loans.

- TILA gives the borrower the *right of rescission* (the right to cancel a loan within three days).

- You may have up to three years to cancel a contract with a creditor who did not follow the TILA guidelines.

- Bankruptcy attorneys often use TILA to help their clients avoid paying credit card debt.

Delving into Deeds

When you purchased your home, you received a deed, which grants you ownership, guarantees, and certain rights to the property.

Several types of deeds are used to transfer ownership of real estate. In the following sections, we introduce you to the different types of deeds, including the general-warranty deed, limited-warranty deed (or bargain-and-sale deed), quit-claim deed, and sheriff's deed. By understanding some of the basic language included in these documents, you can develop a clearer understanding of your rights and obligations.

Checking out the general-warranty deed

The general-warranty deed is probably what you received when you purchased your home. It transfers ownership of the property from the seller to the buyer and guarantees that the title is free from any encumbrances. If anyone shows up later with a valid claim to the property or has a lien against the property, the seller is responsible. This is why people buy title insurance. The title company makes sure the title is free and clear, and if the title company misses something, then it has to pick up the tab for its error. Otherwise, the seller is responsible for providing a warranty of the title.

A general-warranty deed contains some fairly basic language, as the following example illustrates:

> On **[date]**, **[husband's name]** and **[wife's name]**, husband and wife, whose address is **[address of sellers]** (Grantors), *convey and warrant to* **[name of buyer]**, whose address is **[address of buyer]** (Grantee), the real property commonly known as **[address of property]**, in **[village/city/township]**, **[county]**, State of **[state]**, and described on exhibit A (the Premises) for $**[amount] or good and valuable consideration,** *subject to any easements and building and use restrictions of record and the lien of taxes not yet due and payable.*

Two sections are important here. First, the very simple language *convey and warrant to* transfers official ownership of the property from the seller to the buyer. Second (at the end), the *subject to* clause limits what the seller guarantees. On some deeds, you see a list of specific restrictions, but here you see a blanket statement freeing the sellers from any obligations related to conditions outside their control or knowledge.

The general-warranty deed has very little to do with foreclosure. If you sell your home, however, some of the restrictions stated in the deed may come into play. Consult your real estate agent, attorney, or title company for additional details.

Scoping out the limited- or special-warranty deed

A limited-warranty deed is almost identical to a general-warranty deed, except for the fact that it guarantees the title only for the period of time that the seller owned the property. In other words, it says, "I can vouch for the 15 years I owned the property, but I won't be held responsible for anything that occurred prior to those 15 years." Here's an example of the wording that limits the seller's liability:

This deed is given for good and valuable consideration (a transfer valuation affidavit is filed with this deed).

Grantor will warrant and defend the Premises against the lawful claims and demands of all persons claiming through Grantor but against no other claims and no other person, including predecessors in title.

Again, the limited-warranty deed is not something that is going to directly affect the foreclosure, but it may come into play if you decide to sell the property.

Getting up to speed on quit-claim deeds

A quit-claim deed is a powerful piece of paperwork that allows you to sign all your ownership rights over to someone else. Following is an example of the wording you're likely to find in a quit-claim deed:

On **[date]**, **[husband's name]** and **[wife's name]**, husband and wife, whose address is **[address of sellers]** (Grantors), quitclaims to **[name of buyer]**, whose address is **[address of buyer]** (Grantee), the real property commonly known as **[address of property]**, in **[village/city/township]**, **[county]**, State of **[state]**, and described as [insert legal description and tax identification number] for $**[amount]** or good and valuable consideration, *subject to any easements and building and use restrictions of record and the lien of taxes not yet due and payable.*

Using a quit-claim deed, you can only relinquish rights to property that you own. For example, Ralph Roberts could hand you a quit-claim deed to the Brooklyn Bridge, but all that would do is *cloud* the title — add to the confusion of who really owns the property. It doesn't actually quit or convey property unless Ralph Roberts owns it.

Con artists often slip quit-claim deeds or other types of deeds into stacks of other documents or try to trick homeowners into signing over their property (see Chapter 9). Before signing any documents, read them carefully and make sure you fully understand what you're giving away. By signing a single sheet of paper, you could be giving away your home.

Discovering redemption in a sheriff's deed

If your property ultimately ends up on the auction block, the sheriff's office issues its own deed to the property, cleverly called a *sheriff's deed.* The most important wording (for you, anyway) in the sheriff's deed talks about the redemption period, if applicable. If your area has a redemption period, obtain a copy of the deed from the sheriff's office and read the redemption clause. The redemption language is likely to look something like this:

I DO HEREBY CERTIFY that the *last day to redeem is August 20, 2009,* after which the within Sheriff's Deed will become operative, unless determined abandoned in accordance with Michigan statute 123.4567, or unless redeemed according to the law, in such case made and provided.

This example is from a sheriff's deed in Michigan, where redemption periods range from 30 days to one year, depending on the amount of acreage and whether the property has been abandoned or the current balance of the loan is more then 50 percent paid. The typical redemption period for a residential property is six months. This date (August 20, 2009) is six months from the date the property is sold at public auction. This means that you either come up with the money necessary to redeem your home by the specified date or lose your home, and the new owner can have you evicted. It's as simple as that.

Not all states have a redemption period. To determine whether you have redemption rights and the length of the redemption period, if any, consult your attorney, the register of deeds, or someone else who is well-versed in the foreclosure laws in your area.

How much money do you have to come up with? That varies over time, so check with the sheriff's office or the party who purchased your property at auction to determine the exact amount you'll need on a specific date and where you need to make the payment. The total you owe is going to include the full amount the buyer paid at auction, along with interest and any qualifying expenses the buyer incurred and filed an affidavit for.

Extending your redemption period with creative counting

If you count the days in six months from August 15 to February 15, you come up with 185 days, but if you count from February 15 to August 15, you come up with 182 days. So what?

The point here is that the definition of six months can vary, so you may be able to question it in court. You may also want to question whether the date of the sale counts. If you can show that you've been diligently pursuing redemption and that your financing came through right at the last minute, the court may just give you an extra day or two to redeem the property. Don't count on this, but it is worth noting.

You may also be able to wring a little extra time out of the system if your redemption period expires on a weekend. How can you possibly redeem your property on Saturday at the county building if the county building is closed? If you can walk into court on the following Monday with the full amount needed to redeem, show when you acquired the funds, state that the county building was closed, and are willing to deposit that money with the court, the court may just allow you to redeem. Of course, you should try your best to keep from cutting it this close, and we offer no guarantee that the judge is going to rule in your favor, but it's worth a try.

Settling out of court

In addition to assisting homeowners in foreclosure, we've been purchasing foreclosures for almost 20 years. In one case, we purchased a foreclosure, and the homeowner hired a savvy attorney. The attorney filed a suit to challenge the foreclosure redemption period based on the fact that the homeowner had the ability to secure financing, which would allow her to redeem the house.

Prior to the court date, we spoke with the attorney, who explained to us that his method of counting six months differed from ours. Although we considered six months to be 182½ days from the date of sale, his method resulted in a count of 185 days. He was planning to argue that his client didn't receive the full six months as was allowed by law and was, therefore, denied her ability to redeem (not by us, but by the system).

He wasn't exactly sure what the judge would rule, but he was pretty certain that he could cite prior cases to prove his argument and that the judge or jury may very well err on the side of the homeowner and allow her to redeem. He didn't want to have to take the case to trial. What he wanted was for his client to have the right to redeem.

We ended up settling the issue between ourselves, because we didn't want to incur the expense of court or the time it would take to see this issue resolved in a overburdened legal system. It worked out for the both of us, but his client was really fortunate to have hired the right attorney and to have dealt with foreclosure investors who chose not to pursue the matter.

Clogging of the equity of redemption

One thing you need to watch out for concerning redemption is any attempt by a lender to *clog the equity of redemption* (limit or eliminate your right to redeem). Commercial lenders don't generally do this, but private lenders or real estate investors may try to pull this on you.

Here's how it works: Say you need some money for whatever reason (son's college education, medical bills, reinstating your mortgage, whatever), but you can't qualify for a loan from a commercial lender. A private lender agrees to loan you the $25,000 you need, but instead of using a mortgage to secure the loan, the private lender demands a *deed absolute* (a deed for the property that goes into effect if you fail to repay the debt). If you default on the loan, instead of having to foreclose on the mortgage, the private lender receives a deed to the property, and you have no right to redeem.

As you may have guessed, clogging the equity of redemption is not allowed and is against public policy, but people still get away with it, primarily because homeowners are unaware of their rights. A court would most likely hold that the deed is not a deed but, in fact, merely a security instrument and would force the private lender to foreclose as if he had been granted a mortgage and not a deed.

If someone tries to take your home (and equity) from you by clogging the equity of redemption, take him to court. If your jurisdiction allows for a redemption period, that's your right, regardless of any attempts to skirt the law. Some jurisdictions do not offer a redemption period.

Taking Notes on Your Note (or Promise to Pay)

A promissory note is your contractual guarantee to make timely payments. It is literally your personal promise to repay the debt, as shown in the following example:

> **Borrower's promise to pay.** In return for a loan that I have received, *I promise to pay* U.S. **$[amount]** (this amount is called "Principal"), plus interest, to the order of the Lender. The Lender is **[lender name]**. I will make all payments under this Note in the form of cash, check, or money order.
>
> I understand that the Lender may transfer this Note. The Lender or anyone who takes this Note by transfer and who is entitled to receive payments under this Note is called the "Note Holder."

This first provision simply tells you what the *principal balance* is (the beginning amount that you borrow) and who the lender is. The second clause allows the lender to assign your note, which is very likely to happen. In other words, the lender named on your promissory note may not be the lender you need to contact to work out a solution.

Your note also includes language explaining actions that the lender can take if you send in late payments or default on the loan (note the acceleration clause at the very end):

(A) Late Charge for Overdue Payments

If the Note Holder *has not received the full amount* of any monthly payment *by the end of* **[number of]** *calendar days* after the date it is due, I will pay a late charge to the Note Holder. I will pay this late charge promptly but only once on each late payment.

(B) Default

If I do not pay the full amount of each monthly payment on the date it is due, *I will be in default.*

If I am in default, the Note Holder may require me to pay immediately the full amount of Principal that has not been paid and all the interest that I owe on that amount.

Note that the first clause provides for a grace period, typically to allow for mail delays and other holdups. Your note may say that payments are due on the fifth of the month, but you have up to ten days after that to make the payment before it is considered officially late. The second clause simply explains what is considered a default condition. Unlike the mortgage, which has a default provision for more than failure to pay, a note is defaulted only when you fail to pay.

The note is your promise to pay. The mortgage is the security instrument that pledges the property as collateral.

Another area that could limit your options is a *prepayment penalty* clause. To discourage borrowers from refinancing, some banks include a prepayment penalty in their notes. The following example shows wording that you're likely to find if no prepayment penalty is in effect:

> Borrower has the right to make payments of Principal at any time before they are due. A payment of Principal only is known as a "Prepayment."
>
> *Borrower may make a full Prepayment or partial Prepayments without paying a Prepayment charge.* The Note Holder will use Prepayments to reduce the amount of Principal owed under this Note.

If your note contains a prepayment penalty, you have to take this into consideration if you're thinking about refinancing your way out of foreclosure. A substantial prepayment penalty could make refinancing a lousy option. Fortunately, prepayment penalties are fairly rare in traditional residential mortgage loans, and even when they are included, they are often phased out over two or three years. They're much more common, however, in subprime loans.

The promissory note is packed with additional details you should be aware of but that do not necessarily affect you in foreclosure:

- ✔ **Interest:** The percentage interest that's applied to the principal.

- ✔ **Payments:** The payments section explains the date on which you are expected to make your monthly payment, the payment method (check, cash, money order, and so on), and the amount of your monthly payment.

- ✔ **Cosigners:** Everyone who signs the note is usually held *jointly and severally* (individually and as a group) responsible for repayment of the debt. In other words, if the lender forecloses, the lender can seek repayment from any or all of the people who signed the note. This is why it's generally a bad idea for parents to cosign for their kids' loans.

- ✔ **Due-on-sale clause:** Like your mortgage, your promissory note is likely to include a due-on-sale clause that calls in the entire balance of the loan when the property changes hands. (See "Due-on-sale clause," earlier in this chapter.)

Picking Apart Other Contracts

The mortgage and note are the most common contracts used for financing the purchase of real estate, but they aren't the only ones. If the person you purchased the property from also financed the purchase, you may have a *contract for deed* (commonly called a *land contract*) or a *lease-option agreement,* instead of a mortgage and note.

Both of these contracts commonly include a *forfeiture clause,* stating that if you default on the terms of the contract, you forfeit the property. In some jurisdictions, this means that the seller/lender has the right to take immediate possession of the property. In other jurisdictions, the seller/lender must initiate formal foreclosure proceedings, just as if she were holding a mortgage and note.

In the following sections, we highlight the key points of contracts for deed and lease-option agreements, pointing out areas that may affect you in the event that the seller/lender claims that you breached the contract.

Skimming your land contract (or contract for deed)

In a land contract, the seller is essentially taking on the role of the bank. Sellers typically use land contracts for sales of property that a bank isn't comfortable financing, such as vacant farm land or other agricultural land, but they can also be used when the buyer is unable to secure traditional financing. A typical land contract includes language such as the following:

> The consideration for the sale of the above-described premises to Buyer is $**[amount]**, of which $**[amount]** has been paid to Seller. The balance of $**[amount]** is to be paid to Seller, with interest at the rate of **[percentage]** per year. This balance of purchase money and interest shall be paid in monthly installments of $**[amount]** each, or more at Buyer's option, on the **[number]** day of each month, beginning **[month and year]**. These payments shall be applied first on interest and the balance on principal. *However, the entire purchase money and interest shall be fully paid within* ***[number]*** *years from the date of this Agreement,* despite anything to the contrary in this Agreement.

The italicized text is fairly typical in a land contract and refers to a *balloon payment* (a lump-sum payment due on a specific date or a specific number of months or years following the date on which the contract is signed).

In foreclosure, you're likely to encounter a land contract in either of the following two scenarios:

- ✔ **You financed the purchase of your current home through the seller.** If you currently have a land contract rather than a mortgage or note, the land contract describes your rights and the rights of the seller in terms of foreclosure or forfeiture.

- ✔ **An investor has offered you a land contract as a way to prevent foreclosure.** An investor may purchase your home from you or at auction and offer to sell it back to you on contract.

If an investor has offered to sell your property back to you on a land contract, we strongly recommend that you have your attorney review the contract. In some cases, if you take possession of the property after foreclosure, any liens that the foreclosure erased are reattached to the property. In addition, you have to be careful of the forfeiture clause. Some land contracts are worded in a way that nearly dooms you to forfeiture. Your jurisdiction may also limit the amount of interest a seller can charge you. You really need to know all the details, which a qualified attorney can explain to you.

With a land contract, the seller doesn't transfer the warranty deed until the contract is completed. Often this deed is placed in escrow (as a buyer, you should insist on this for your own protection) to be released by the title or escrow agent when the contract is satisfied. The language looks something like this:

> *On receiving payment in full of all sums* owing under this Agreement, *Seller shall execute and deliver to Buyer* or Buyer's assigns a good and sufficient *warranty deed* conveying title to the land, subject to the specified restrictions and easements, subject to any then existing mortgages, and *free from all other encumbrances except* those set forth in this Agreement and those accrued or attached since the date of this Agreement through the acts or omission of persons other than Seller or Seller's assigns.

The land contract has two major remedies in the event of default — forfeiture and foreclosure. The language may look like this:

> If Buyer fails to perform this Agreement or any part of it, *Seller has the right immediately after the default to declare the Agreement forfeited and void;* to retain whatever may have been paid on the Agreement and all improvements that may have been made on the premises.

> If a default is made by Buyer and continues for 45 days or more *and Seller desires to foreclose this Agreement in equity, Seller has the right to declare the entire unpaid balance to be immediately due and payable.*

No matter what kind of agreement you have, if you don't pay, you don't stay. Know the steps you need to take in order to make staying put an option.

Studying your lease-option agreement (for rent-to-owners only)

A lease-option agreement is basically a rent-to-own deal. The owner of the property leases it to you for a certain number of months or years, at the end of which time you have the option, but not the obligation, to buy the property for a previously agreed upon price.

Lease-option agreements are very similar to land contracts, and they usually come into play when an investor purchases your property and offers to sell it back to you. The agreement should specify your rent amount and due date, the date by which you must exercise your option to buy, and the method for exercising the option:

> **Grant of the option.** Seller grants Buyer an exclusive option to purchase the real property described on the attached exhibit A. The option shall remain in effect for *one year* from the effective date of this Agreement, as defined below.

> **Purchase price.** The purchase price for the Premises under this option is $[amount].

> **Exercise of the option.** Buyer may exercise the option by giving written notice to Seller at its address stated above. The notice must be sent by certified mail and received by Seller before this option expires.

> **Failure to exercise the option.** If Buyer fails to properly exercise the option before this Agreement expires, the option shall terminate.

Make sure you know what you need to do to exercise the option. If you choose to exercise the option, make sure you follow the instructions in the contract exactly as described. If the option says you have to hand-deliver the notice to exercise the option, dressed as Little Bo-Peep, and you agree to that, then you'd better hand-deliver the notice dressed as Little Bo-Peep.

Part II

Confronting Foreclosure Head On

The 5th Wave   By Rich Tennant

"So, in anticipation of receiving a foreclosure notice from the bank, you buried your mailbox. Well, it's a start."

In this part . . .

Dealing with foreclosure is like confronting a strange dog when you're out walking or jogging. Dog trainers recommend that instead of running from a strange dog, you stop what you're doing and act as natural as possible. If you show anger or fear, the dog may be more prone to attacking you.

Likewise, with foreclosure, remaining calm and rational is the best approach. In this part, we show you how to slow down, get a handle on your finances, examine your options and exit strategies, stop the financial bleeding, and avoid any con artists and opportunists who are looking to capitalize on your current vulnerabilities.

Chapter 6

Getting a Handle on Your Current Situation

*T*he path you take out of foreclosure often depends on your current situation and the resources you have at your disposal. If you have no equity built up in the house and no future prospect of making enough money to catch up on your payments, your best option may be to sell the house or give it away. If, on the other hand, you have some equity in the house and a temporary job loss led you to this point, you may be able to refinance your way out of foreclosure.

This chapter guides you through the process of assessing your current situation and setting a steady course (financially speaking), so you can more effectively deal with the situation without making matters worse. By the end of this chapter, you should have a list of all your financial resources and a pretty clear idea of how much money you have to live on monthly. The information you gather here is critical for exploring your options in Chapter 7 of this book.

Calculating Your Net Worthiness

If you sold everything you currently own and paid off all your debts, how much money would you have? That's your net worth, and when you're facing foreclosure, that amount is key in assessing your options. One of the first questions your lenders or future lenders are going to ask you is, "What's your net worth?" So grab a pencil and a piece of paper, and do the math. Officially, the equation goes like this:

Net Worth = What You Own – What You Owe

In the following sections, we step you through the process of calculating your net worth and analyzing the numbers.

Adding up what you own

People who are experiencing foreclosure shock often overlook the bountiful riches they have locked up in all the accounts and material goods they own. We're not talking about all those nickels in your car's cigarette ashtray and the change that's collected under the couch cushions. We're talking about things of real value, like your home, retirement accounts, and even your 2005 Jaguar.

Estimate the value of everything you own, and then add it all up. The following list can assist in preventing you from overlooking some of your most valuable assets.

Total the current value of everything you own, including:

- Savings account balance
- Checking account balance
- Retirement savings — IRA, 401(k), and so on
- Cash value of any life insurance policies
- Cash
- Savings bonds
- House
- Car
- Boat
- Jewelry
- Personal belongings — art collection, model trains, jewelry, antiques, and so on
- Furniture
- Appliances
- Valuable equipment, like a riding lawnmower

Don't overestimate the value of your assets. If you paid $20,000 for a new car three or four years ago, that car has depreciated. To account for depreciation, look up the Kelley Blue Book value of the car at www.kbb.com. You may need to hire an appraiser to estimate the value of jewelry, antiques, and collectibles, but if that's not an option, at least be realistic about their value.

Adding up what you owe

You already know that you owe some money on your house, but who else do you owe money to and how much? Add up all your debts — everything you owe. Think about it this way: If you died, who would be in line to get paid off? The following list can assist you in identifying your debts:

✔ Amount owed on the house

✔ Any second mortgages or other loans (such as student loans)

✔ Amount owed on your car

✔ Property taxes

✔ Unpaid income taxes due

✔ Outstanding bills

Calculating what's left: How bad is it?

After you've totaled all your assets (what you own) and all your debts (what you owe), subtract your total debts from your total assets. The resulting number is your net worth, which is useful in assessing the foreclosure options described in Chapter 7 of this book:

✔ **Zero:** A net worth of zero means you're broke. You're pretty much starting from scratch. You may have trouble obtaining loan approval, but if you can get out of your current situation and establish a decent cash flow, you can begin anew.

✔ **Negative value:** The more negative your net worth, the less likely that you're going to be able to refinance your way out of the foreclosure. You need to develop a plan to reduce your personal debt (see Chapter 8).

✔ **Positive value:** A strong positive net worth delivers the most options. You can sell stuff or borrow against it to buy yourself some time or refinance out of the foreclosure. If you have a healthy net worth and you run into financial hardship, you can always sell everything and start fresh with fewer expenses.

A zero or negative net worth doesn't necessarily seal your fate. It just means that you're going to have a tougher time qualifying for credit and financing. When it really becomes a problem is when it's coupled with a lack of steady income. When you have a zero or negative net worth and your monthly income doesn't cover your monthly bills, you can't even sell all your stuff and walk away with a little seed cash to start all over. You still have options, but you may need some additional assistance.

Taking the Pulse of Your Current Cash Flow

Imagine that your house is a big bucket with a garden hose pouring water into it from the top and a spigot at the bottom where the water flows out. The flow of water into and out of the house is like your cash flow. As long as cash flows in fast enough to keep up with the cash that's flowing out, your finances are stable. If more cash flows in than flows out, you can sock away some money. If more cash flows out than flows in, however, you begin losing your financial footing.

Now that you know what cash flow is, you may not quite be ready to enroll in the University of Chicago and start working on your PhD in economics, but you know enough to realize the importance of a budget. To establish a healthy, positive cash flow, the household needs to be bringing in more money (from wages, salaries, bonuses, odd jobs, and so on) than it's spending (on groceries, utilities, mortgage and car payments, gas, and so on). The formula for calculating cash flow is fairly easy to remember:

Cash Flow = Income – Expenses

By income, we mean steady income you can count on. We're not talking about the million dollars you're going to win in the lottery or the $10,000 a month you'll be earning as soon as your online auction business takes off. We're talking about dependable income, like salaries or the $100 extra a week you always earn by moonlighting as a server at the local restaurant.

Add up all your monthly income and then subtract all your monthly expenses. The resulting number is your household's cash flow, and it falls into one of the following three categories:

> ✔ **Zero:** Zero cash flow means that you're just scraping by, living from hand to mouth. Because you're facing foreclosure, you probably cannot regain your financial footing without increasing your income or reducing your expenses.

- ✔ **Positive:** A positive cash flow indicates that you have the financial resources to begin steering more money in the direction of solving your foreclosure problem. The more positive your cash flow, the better.

- ✔ **Negative:** When you're spending more than you're earning, you're in serious trouble. Your first order of business is to stop the financial bleeding (see Chapter 8). You need to draw up a budget and then stick to it.

Cash flow is an area where couples often get into spats. One partner, who doesn't quite know how much a gallon of milk really costs, starts accusing the other partner, who does all the grocery shopping, of overspending. If you don't do the grocery shopping, you may be shocked at just how much it can cost to feed a family of four or five, especially if you have a baby in diapers. You really need to sit down together, so you both are fully aware of exactly how much money is flowing in and how much is flowing out.

Cash flow fuels your plan. Without a positive cash flow, any plan you develop is doomed to fail.

Checking Out Your Credit Report

Access to loans can often buy you time and enable you to restructure payments in such a way as to make them more affordable. To gain access to loans, however, a fairly clean credit history can help both in obtaining loan approval and in securing loans with lower interest rates.

If you apply for a loan, one of the first things a loan officer is going to look at is your credit history, so make sure yours is accurate and do what you can to remove any blemishes and boost your credit score, as explained in the following sections. No irregularity is too small to correct.

Obtaining a free copy of your credit report

You can obtain your credit report through any of the following three credit reporting services, but because lenders may report to only one service, ideally, you should check all three:

- ✔ **Equifax:** 800-685-1111 or www.equifax.com
- ✔ **Experian:** 888-397-3742 or www.experian.com
- ✔ **TransUnion:** 800-916-8800 or www.transunion.com

For the complete picture of your credit history, request a *tri-merge report* that compiles information from all three credit reporting agencies. Some creditors don't report to all three agencies, but when lenders check your credit history, they're probably going to look at everything, so you should, too.

As of September 1, 2005, the Federal Trade Commission has made it mandatory for the three major credit-reporting companies to provide you with a free credit report once every 12 months. To obtain your free credit report, do one of the following:

✔ Submit your request online at www.annualcreditreport.com.

✔ Phone in your request by calling 877-322-8228.

✔ Download the Annual Credit Report Request Form from www.annual creditreport.com/cra/requestformfinal.pdf, fill it out, and mail it to Annual Credit Report Request Service, P.O. Box 105281, Atlanta, GA 30348-5281.

Picking out key details

When you receive your credit report, inspect it carefully for the following red flags:

✔ **Addresses of places you've never lived**

✔ **Aliases you've never used,** which may indicate that someone else is using your Social Security number or the credit-reporting agency has mixed someone else's data into yours

✔ **Multiple Social Security numbers,** flagging the possibility that information for someone with the same name has made it into your credit report

✔ **Wrong date of birth (DOB)**

✔ **Credit cards you don't have**

✔ **Loans you haven't taken out**

✔ **Records of unpaid bills that you either know you paid or have good reason for not paying**

✔ **Records of delinquent payments that weren't delinquent or you have a good excuse for not paying on time**

✔ **Inquiries from companies with whom you've never done business** (When you apply for a loan, the lender typically runs an *inquiry* on your credit report, and that shows up on the report.)

An address of a place you've never lived or records of accounts, loans, and credit cards you've never had may be a sign that somebody has stolen your identity. Contact the credit-reporting company immediately and request that a fraud alert be placed on your credit report. For tips on protecting yourself against identity theft and recovering from it, check out *Preventing Identity Theft For Dummies,* by Michael J. Arata, Jr. (Wiley).

Patching bruised credit

Your credit report should contain your credit score. (If it doesn't, contact the credit-reporting agency and request your score.) Credit-reporting agencies often assign you a credit score that ranges roughly between 300 (you never paid a bill in your life) and 900 (you've had a credit card for a long time, borrow small amounts often, always pay your bills on time, and don't carry any huge balances). Each credit reporting agency may use a different scoring method and range of scores, so you can expect some variation.

Your credit score determines not only whether you qualify for a loan, but also how much you're qualified to borrow and at what interest rate. A high credit score lets you borrow more money at a lower interest rate.

A credit score of 700 or higher is superb. Anything below about 680 raises red flags. If your credit rating dips below 700, take steps to improve it, such as the following:

- **Dispute any erroneous items on your credit report.** Most credit-reporting agencies supply you with an address to submit a letter of dispute.

- **Apply for fewer loans and credit cards.** Applying for several loans or credit cards in a short period of time can make you appear financially desperate and significantly lower your credit rating.

- **Pay off your credit card balances, or at least pay off enough so the balance is 50 percent or below your available credit limit.** If you have sufficient equity built up in your home, you may be able to refinance or take out a home equity loan to pay down your high-interest credit card debt. Of course, if one of your creditors has already initiated the foreclosure, you may have trouble getting loan approval.

For additional tips on boosting your credit score, check out *Credit Repair Kit For Dummies,* by Stephen R. Bucci (Wiley).

Digging Up Other Stashes of Cash

The foreclosure process can be so emotionally devastating (as explained in Chapter 3) that you just want to crawl into a dark cave and hide from the world, but that's not going to solve anything and is almost guaranteed to make it worse. In times of need, you need other people, particularly friends and family members who have the resources to lend you a hand.

Finding cash under the floorboards

Our resident attorney, Paul Doroh, who contributed a great deal to the contents of this book, tells the story of one of his friends who purchased a run-down property from someone who apparently did not have the financial resources available to properly maintain it:

"The house was out in the country, and the broker had listed it as 'In Need of TLC,' which is a broker's way of saying that the house is a piece of junk.

"The owner was an old man, and nobody could tell whether he failed to maintain the property because he didn't care or couldn't afford to. My friend, the buyer, actually dealt more with the man's daughter. She was helping her father sell the house, so her father could move in with her family just down the road. The father's memory was fading, and he required a little extra attention. Well, the father didn't exactly think so, but he was going along with the plan anyway.

"When the day came for my friend to move in and start repairing the house, he discovered something a little odd. The old man was sitting in the living room. My friend called the daughter and then sat down next to her father. The old man told him some stories that only old men know, and when the daughter arrived she was apologetic. My friend said there was no need to apologize — they had just been talking. The daughter said, 'I know dad can tell some tall tales sometimes — he claims he's a millionaire, but look around you. . . . Is this how millionaires live?'

"A few hours later, the old man rushed into the house again, carrying a crowbar and shouting, 'Why didn't someone tell me we were moving? I forgot all my stuff!' The daughter was fairly close behind him and didn't know what to make of it.

"The old man went straight to the backroom, threw an old beat-up rug out of the way, dug his gnarly finger into a hole in the pine floorboard, and pulled it up. He then took his crowbar and revealed more and more of his 'stuff.' Underneath that floor was probably better than $2 million dollars' worth of old rare coins, gold items, paper money, bonds, stock certificates, and collectible rare guns.

"The old man literally wheelbarrowed all his 'stuff' out of the house and into his beat-up 40-year-old pickup truck. The daughter stood there with a more dazed look on her face than my friend had.

"My friend actually called me while it was all going on and said, 'You'll never believe this, but that old man I thought was a little crazy . . . turns out he's a millionaire! He buried it all in the floor. He's wheel-barrowing it all out of the house right now!' As it turns out he lived through the Great Depression and didn't trust banks, so he just kept all his valuable items right where he knew they'd be safe — under the floor of his falling-down farmhouse."

Now that's "another stash of cash" for the record books.

In the following sections, we reveal the two primary sources for extra cash — friends and family members. We also provide some tips and cautions on how to borrow money without compromising your relationships.

Hitting up your relatives for gifts or loans

If you need a one-time cash infusion to set you on the straight and narrow, consider asking a relative for assistance. Tread carefully when borrowing from relatives — you want to make sure that whatever arrangement you agree to does not jeopardize your relationship:

- ✔ **Borrow only from relatives who are not going to need the money back right away.**

- ✔ **Offer to pay interest, but explain that you may not be able to make payments for some time.**

- ✔ **Don't agree to an arrangement in which you're going to be in no better shape several months down the road.**

- ✔ **If you can make immediate payments, do it; if you can't, tell them that upfront.** If you come into some money, such as tax returns or work bonuses, consider paying off the loan or at least a chunk of it as a demonstration of your intention to pay them back as soon as you can. If you demonstrate that you want to pay them off and you do pay them off, they'll be willing to loan you money again if you need it; if you don't, it'll be a one-time-and-never-again loan.

- ✔ **Explain that you're borrowing the money because things are tight, and you have every intention of repaying them.**

- ✔ **Make wise decisions with the money you borrow.** If you appear to be living high on the hog with borrowed money, your relative may get a little tense, and you're certainly not doing yourself any favors, either.

Use the money wisely to resolve your current financial situation. Don't use it in a way that causes more problems later.

Asking your friends to pitch in

Friends can be great resources for cash and other forms of support, but unlike family, friendship is a choice, so you have to be particularly careful. Don't ask a friends for assistance and then burn them. Treat their money better than you would treat your own, and pay it back as soon as possible.

Your repayment plan should be similar to the plan for paying back your relatives (see the preceding section): Pay when you can, make arrangements upfront, and be honest with your friend. Make realistic promises that you're likely to keep.

The great thing about friendships is that friends often ask for very little in return — the friendship itself is that valuable. If you need your friend to watch your kids three nights a week, so you can work a double shift and earn some extra money, you can usually repay your friend by returning the favor or taking her out for a relatively inexpensive night out on the town. If your buddy loans you the $200 for materials you need to complete a side job, you can simply repay the $200 when you finish the job and collect your money — telling the story over a couple of cold beers about what you had to do to get the job done is an added bonus. We know a guy who built a two-story pole barn on his property, with all the labor being done by a few of his closest friends. The payment — cold beer and hot pizza.

Reciprocate when you can. You have to be ready, willing, and able to do unto others what those others have done unto you. You may not always be able to help the same person in the same way he helped you, but by making giving a habit, you begin to find that good things come your way.

Keeping a Bad Situation from Getting Worse

As soon as you begin to sense that your financial situation has taken a turn for the worse, you and the rest of your household need to work together to prevent the problem from getting any worse. The situation is as though you're in a boat that's taking on water. Before you start bailing out the water, you want to find the holes and plug them.

In the following sections, we show you how to stabilize your current situation so you can begin taking the necessary steps to improve it.

Freezing your finances

The number-one thing you can do to put yourself and your household on the road to financial recovery is to buckle down and stop the financial bleeding (see Chapter 8). You and everyone else who has a stake in the matter needs to identify areas where you can cut expenses. Here are some ideas to get you started:

- ✔ Instead of dinner and a movie out, eat in and watch something on TV or do something else, like taking a walk or reading together.

- ✔ Instead of ordering in Chinese and renting videos, cook a meal and have a family game night.

- ✔ Put off that weekly trip to the salon for a manicure, pedicure, facial, and hair appointment. Do it yourself.

- ✔ Scale back on this year's vacation. Instead of flying to Aruba, head to somewhere that's within driving distance or take day trips and pack a picnic lunch.

- ✔ Instead of treating your friends and family to dinner, invite them over for a pitch-in.

If you have children, trimming the fat is more stressful, because you may fall into the trap of thinking that you're depriving your children or letting them down. Keep in mind that the one thing your kids want and need most is *you,* not the stuff you buy them. You can give your kids what they need most without spending a lot of money — you may just have to be a little more creative. An afternoon picnic at the county park, teaching your kid how to hit a curve ball, and taking a nature walk with your little ones are all priceless. Spend enough quality time with your kids and they may never even feel the financial pinch.

Catching up on property tax payments

Part of the process of stabilizing your current situation consists of prioritizing your bills, and one of the bills you never want to overlook is the property tax bill. Even if you can't afford to make a house payment, you should be paying your property taxes.

Why? Because every penny counts, and if you fail to pay, not only do you make it easier for someone to buy your home right out from under you, but you also make yourself vulnerable to having to pay additional interest and penalties. Your county probably charges a stiff interest on late property tax payments. If you're like 90 percent of the population, the county is already charging you an arm and a leg for property taxes, so why pay more?

Plus, if you don't pay your taxes, your bank or the person who purchases your mortgage at auction may pay them and add it to the payoff amount required to redeem the property. That's not bad, except for the fact that they may have the right to charge you interest at the rate set forth in the mortgage, which may be even more than what the county would charge you.

Finally, by not paying your property taxes, you may lose the home to a property tax foreclosure before the redemption period of the mortgage foreclosure expires. This isn't likely to happen, because the bank or whoever purchases your home at auction is likely to pay the taxes to protect their interest, but it could happen.

Part of advocating for yourself (see Chapter 3) and part of successfully working through your recovery plan is to pay attention to details and make sure that nothing falls through the cracks. Know when your property taxes are due and pay them on time, so you don't have to cover a fat property tax bill later.

Maintaining your homeowner's insurance

One of the most critical bills you should be paying is your homeowner's insurance premium. After all, if the house burns down, is washed away, or is torn up by a tornado or hurricane while you're still the owner, you want to make sure that you receive the insurance proceeds, so you can pay off the bank and keep any money that's left.

If you fail to obtain insurance coverage, the bank steps in and obtains its own insurance policy on the house. This is called *force placed insurance,* which isn't the greatest deal for several reasons:

- ✔ **Force placed insurance can be substantially more expensive than your average homeowner's policy.** The bank pays the premium and then adds it to the amount you owe.
- ✔ **The policy typically protects only the bank, not you.** In the event of a loss, the bank receives the insurance proceeds, and you get nothing.

You can prevent the bank from ordering a force placed policy by paying your homeowner's insurance premiums. Your policy should list the bank as an insured party. You may need to supply your bank with some sort of proof of insurance, either by faxing them a copy of the policy or having your agent fax a proof of insurance letter to your bank. As with everything, document the date and time you submitted the document — if your insurance company submitted it for you, have the company fax you a copy for your records. That way, if you see a fee for force placed insurance on your next mortgage statement, you can dispute it with evidence.

Keep thorough and accurate records of every conversation you have with someone involved in foreclosure, every document you send or receive, and every meeting you have. Double-check everything you're told, so you know that you're basing your decisions on accurate information. (For more about record-keeping and advocating for yourself during foreclosure, check out Chapter 8.)

The follies of the self-insured

Insurance is not an optional accessory. Our resident attorney, Paul Doroh tells the story of one of his friends, an investor who refused to purchase insurance for his properties, so he could trim the fat and boost his bottom line:

"I'm always advising my friend to purchase homeowner's insurance on the foreclosed homes he buys, but he never does. His response is that he 'self-insures.' He tells me that most every house needs work, and that he can put the money he saves on premiums back into the house. As he reasons, 'Why spend more just so that an insurance adjuster can try to deny my claim if that claim is even over my deductible?' Well, that line of reasoning does have some logic to it, but I tried to warn him that someday he just might encounter a home that had more than run-of-the-mill damage to it, and he would live to regret not having insurance.

"That day arrived. My friend bought a very nice house in an exclusive neighborhood and expected to be able to turn it for top dollar. The owner had spared no costs when building the house — everything was top of the line — granite countertops, built-in appliances, $150 light fixtures, the works.

"The problem was that the owner decided not to leave without a fight. He declared war and dragged my friend through a long, drawn-out court battle. My friend ultimately ended up with the house, but that's not the end of the story. When the owner moved out, he took everything with him — everything that wasn't bolted down

and 99 percent of everything that was. My friend actually invited me to witness the devastation. The previous owner had literally cleaned house, removing the granite countertops, built-in appliances, ceiling fans, furnace, every light fixture, every light switch, the gas logs from the fireplace, the shower fixtures, everything. It was truly amazing that someone could accomplish such a feat.

"While at the house I said to him, 'Thank goodness for insurance, eh?' Then I looked at him. He was just looking blankly back at me. So I said, 'Please tell me you didn't self-insure this one.' He did."

Okay, so this is a great story and all, but how does it apply to you? The moral of the story applies to anyone who owns a valuable piece of property: Have it insured. You never know what can go wrong, and if you don't have insurance in place, you could lose everything. Keep paying your insurance premiums, even if you can't pay some of your other bills.

According to Paul, "The one redeeming thing for my friend in all this is that he decided to file charges against the former homeowner for malicious destruction of property. If it all works out, he should be able to get a judgment for the value of the damages and be able to see the previous homeowner spend some time in jail, which could be good news for him, too — after all, he just lost his house and could really use a place to stay."

Chapter 7

Sizing Up Your Options and Exit Strategies

In This Chapter

▶ Buying time with bankruptcy and other legal options

▶ Keeping your home and working out the details

▶ Selling your home and starting fresh with a little cash

▶ Walking out on your house

▶ Deciding to do nothing — the worst approach

*W*hen you're facing foreclosure, slipping into panic mode is far too easy, and panic can often blind you to the many options you have at your disposal. The earlier in the process you begin to consider your options, the more options you have available.

This chapter reveals an entire menu of options from which to choose, some of which may be available to you and others of which may not. Your options generally fall into four categories:

✓ **Stay in the home.** Work with your lender and others to resolve the problem, or sell to an investor and buy or rent the home from him.

✓ **Sell your home.** Put the property on the market, sell it, pay whatever you owe on it, and then take the rest of the cash and move into more affordable accommodations.

✓ **Take a hike.** Move out and let the bank deal with the mess.

✓ **Stall.** Take advantage of your rights as a homeowner, and put off the foreclosure for as long as possible while exploring your options.

The people coming by and offering to "help" you out of your current dilemma may not present you with all your options, so be careful when a self-proclaimed philanthropist shows up to offer a helping hand.

This chapter lays out all your options — options that your bank or others may not be letting you in on. You can then choose which strategy is best for you and your family.

Filing for Bankruptcy

Filing for bankruptcy sounds like the ultimate sure thing, and it may very well be the best option for many homeowners buried in debt. Most of the people we deal with who eventually play the bankruptcy card go about it all wrong. They try every other option, or simply sit around twiddling their thumbs and then, at the very last minute, when all other options have disappeared, they decide to file for bankruptcy. They usually end up in what we call the "bankruptcy mill," where a hack attorney takes their money and provides little or nothing of value.

The right way to approach bankruptcy is to explore your options early. Even if you have no plans to file for bankruptcy, schedule a meeting with a reputable bankruptcy attorney (see Chapter 10), and see what she has to say about your situation. This initial consultation may even be free; if it's not, it should cost no more than about $300, which is money well spent.

Is bankruptcy the right option for you? Well, that depends on several factors. Generally speaking, however, if you owe just a few thousand dollars in back payments, don't have a lot of other debt (such as credit card debt), and can catch up on your payments, then filing for bankruptcy may be a little drastic. If you're drowning in debt and doubt that you'll ever have the resources to catch up, then we strongly encourage you to consult a bankruptcy attorney.

Holding Onto Your Home: Is It Possible?

Homeowners who receive a foreclosure notice often automatically assume that they're going to lose their home. They don't have the cash to catch up on the payments, they're falling behind on their other bills, and they can barely afford groceries. How can they possibly expect to keep their home?

Well, several options can keep you in your home, and you may want to consider them. Moving out may not be something you want to consider, particularly if the home has been in your family for some time or you don't want to uproot your children and move away from their schools and friends. Whatever the case, if moving out and moving on are options that you don't want to consider, then look at some options that can keep you in your home.

Working out a deal with your lenders

Most lenders have a lot to lose by foreclosing on homes. In addition to losing you as a customer, your bank has to take possession of the property, fix it and clean it to place it back on the market, hire a real estate agent to sell it, and pay the agent a commission. The bank also has to declare that it has a bad loan on its books, which can draw the scrutiny of bank regulators. In short, your bank doesn't want to foreclose on your house.

This is good news for you, because it gives the bank more motivation to work out a deal with you, especially if you have little, no, or negative equity built up in the property — in other words, you owe more on the property than what it's worth.

In the following sections, we describe two options that your lender may be willing to consider — reinstating the mortgage or agreeing to a *forbearance* (a payment plan).

Reinstating your mortgage . . . with a little help from your friends

Reinstating a mortgage consists of catching up on your past payments, paying any additional interest and penalties your bank levied against you for those missed payments, and then picking up where you left off as if nothing every happened. This is usually the most attractive option, assuming that you:

- ✓ **Have a mortgage with a low enough interest rate to make this option attractive.** If banks are currently offering mortgage loans at much lower interest rates than your current loan, refinancing may be a more attractive option, reducing your monthly payments. However, if you're in foreclosure, you probably have bruised credit and may not be able to qualify for a loan to refinance your existing mortgage. (See "Borrowing from Peter to pay Paul: Refinancing," later in this chapter.)

- ✓ **Can obtain a the chunk of money you need to catch up on past payments (usually by borrowing from relatives or friends).**

- ✓ **Are able to increase income or slash expenses enough to start making your mortgage payments again.**

The good thing about reinstating your current mortgage is that you pick up where you left off. The bad thing is that you pick up where you left off. In other words, it may solve the problem temporarily but set you up to repeat the same scenario three or four months down the road. Reinstating the mortgage has several drawbacks:

- ✓ **You may not be able to borrow a sufficient amount of money to reinstate the mortgage, in which case, the option is off the table.**

- ✔ **The bank may refuse to reinstate your mortgage,** if you're unable to prove that you can continue to make your monthly mortgage payments after reinstating the mortgage.

- ✔ **Reinstating usually requires you to borrow *more* money (unless your rich aunt decides to give you the money).** You now have to make payments on two loans — your original mortgage and the loan you took out to reinstate the loan. Are you going to be able to cut expenses and boost your household income enough to cover the additional payments?

- ✔ **Reinstating could result in throwing good money after bad.** You may put yourself in a better position by stopping payments and saving your money in preparation for a move to more affordable accommodations (see Chapter 13).

Reinstating usually requires an influx of cash from family members or friends. If you're getting others involved, make sure you handle the situation appropriately, so you don't end up losing valuable relationships in addition to losing your house. (See Chapter 4 for details on how to borrow money from relatives and friends to get back on your feet.)

If reinstating the mortgage is simply going to buy you some time and put off the inevitable loss of your home, don't do it. Instead, consider one of the other options discussed in this chapter.

Negotiating a forbearance: Payment plan, anyone?

If you've experienced a temporary financial setback, you may be able to work out a solution with the bank to restructure your payments and get back on track through a *forbearance* (payment plan).

In a forbearance, the bank can agree to accept just about any agreement and structure it however it sees fit. The restructuring may be held to certain good-faith restrictions and usury laws, and you may find a standard "reasonable" forbearance agreement with national lenders, but otherwise the bank can set it up however it wants. National lenders have formulas set up, and your plan must fit into that formula.

A forbearance arrangement is similar to reinstating the mortgage except for the fact that, with a forbearance, the bank may not require you to come up with a chunk of cash to catch up on missed payments and pay penalties and interest. Instead, the bank allows you to make up the missed payments over time (typically 24 months or less). If you owe $1,500 in missed payments and penalties, for example, the bank may allow you to pay an extra $150 per month for ten months until you're caught up.

If you've fallen way behind your payments and your prospects of getting back on track look bleak, the bank is unlikely to agree to a forbearance, and you should be happy about that. You don't want to place yourself in a situation in which you'll ultimately end up right back in the foreclosure pit. If you can't afford the monthly payments required by whatever repayment plan the bank offers, forbearance isn't the solution for you.

Although you may be able to negotiate with the bank and leverage your poor financial position for a more attractive deal, the bank is pretty much in charge. Your bank is going to ask you to provide financial information and prove that you're going to be able to honor any repayment agreement it draws up. When negotiating a forbearance, tread lightly — if you come across as someone who's difficult to deal with, the bank may wash its hands of the whole thing and cease to work with you. (For additional advice on how to work with your lender, check out Chapter 11.)

Working out a mortgage modification

A forbearance agreement allows you to catch up on missed payments over time (see the preceding section), but your mortgage remains unchanged. As soon as you catch up on the missed payments and any penalties, you pick up where you left off.

To give you even more time to make up missed payments or to make your monthly payments more affordable, your bank may be willing to negotiate a *mortgage modification* — an entirely new mortgage that replaces your current mortgage. With a mortgage modification, the bank has much more flexibility and can modify the mortgage in any of the following ways:

- **Adding to the principal the amount due:** Your bank may agree to roll the amount owed in missed payments, penalties, and interest into the total loan amount, enabling you to pay off the past due amount over the life of the loan.

- **Lowering the interest rate:** If you have a mortgage with an interest rate that's much higher than the going rate, your bank may be willing to lower your interest rate. A 1 percent to 3 percent decrease could save you hundreds of dollars per month.

- **Changing the terms of the loan:** The bank agrees to adjust the terms of your loan to meet your financial situation. For example, the bank may tack on several months to the end of the term in order to recoup missed payments along with penalties and interest.

Unfortunately, a mortgage modification isn't always an option. When a bank sells your mortgage, the loan servicer who processes your payments may not have the power to negotiate a mortgage modification. However, it can't hurt to ask.

Borrowing from Peter to pay Paul: Refinancing

Depending on your situation, you may be able to refinance your way out of the foreclosure swamp, assuming, of course, that your credit is not so damaged that you can't qualify for a fairly attractive loan. Following are some conditions that make refinancing a more attractive and realistic option:

- ✔ You have equity in the home that you can borrow against.

- ✔ You can reconsolidate all your debt so that the new monthly mortgage payment is less than the total you currently pay each month on all your other loans and credit cards combined.

- ✔ You have sufficient income to cover the new monthly mortgage payments.

Consult a reputable loan officer in your area to discuss your refinancing options. Prior to the meeting, gather the information described in Chapter 6, so you know your net worth, the amounts of all outstanding debts, and your cash flow. Your loan officer can use this information to determine the best refinance package for you. (See Chapter 12 of this book for more about refinancing.)

Don't take the bait if some mortgage lender who specializes in foreclosure bailouts dangles a high-cost loan in front of your face. The lender may charge you 8 points (8 percent of the total loan amount upfront), 14 percent interest, and your firstborn baby. The loans are usually sold off and you never hear from that mortgage company again. These loan sharks, er, lenders serve a purpose — the loan can solve the current crisis and buy you time to work toward a more permanent solution. But be careful: When people are desperate, they're often willing to sign anything, and the con artists know it — as do the banks that specialize in high-risk loans.

Before you jump at the chance to refinance your way out of foreclosure, do the math. Say your house is worth $125,000, and you owe $95,000 on your current mortgage — a $100,000 loan you took out a few years ago at 8 percent interest. A lender offers to refinance the mortgage for you with a loan for $125,000 at 13 percent interest. That $30,000 or so you would get at closing would sure make life great right now, but it would also boost your monthly mortgage payment (principal and interest) from $723 to $1,380 — almost double what you were paying. How long could you sustain that? Maybe you would be better off selling the home and using the proceeds to buy something more affordable.

Bottom line: Refinancing is a great solution if you have the equity to borrow against, and the lender offers you a reasonable interest rate and requires you to pay no or very few points upfront. Don't set yourself up for failure, and don't let someone else do it for you, either. If you can't swing it, you may be better off putting the house up for sale and walking with your equity instead of giving it all to a bank in refinancing costs.

Selling your home and buying it back: The ol' give and go

Some real estate investors who invest with integrity may be willing to purchase your home directly from you or at auction, and then sell it back to you either on a land contract or via a lease-option agreement. We spell out these two options in the following sections.

Before entering into a land contract or lease-option agreement, run it past your attorney for review. Both of these types of contracts usually contain a *forfeiture clause* (see Chapter 5), which enables the investor to declare the agreement null and void if you fail to honor your end of the agreement. For example, if you miss a single payment, the investor may have the legal right to evict you, retain possession of the property, and keep your deposit and any down payment or rent you already paid. If the investor tries to talk you out of seeking legal counsel, you should be doubly careful.

Land contract (or contract for deed)

With a *land contract* (also called a *contract for deed*), the investor buys the property and then sells it back to you. In some cases, the investor may be able to offer you lower payments than your bank is currently charging.

However, you have to be careful with this option. The investor must buy the *senior lien* (first mortgage) at auction, or have the lender assign the senior lien to him and proceed with the foreclosure in order for the *junior liens* (claims that are lower on the pecking order) to be erased. If the junior liens are not erased, and you buy back the property, these liens could reattach to the property, and you'll be responsible for paying them off.

Lease-option agreement

With a lease-option agreement, the investor buys the property and leases it to you for a fixed period of time, after which you have the option to buy back the property. Normally, the investor requires 5 percent to 10 percent down, which should be applied to the purchase price, along with monthly rent equivalent to about 1 percent of the purchase price.

A lease-option agreement can be a great solution, assuming you're working with an investor with integrity and you have a great plan in place for getting your finances in order by the time your option to buy the property rolls around. The lease option is typically most useful for homeowners who need more time to secure financing or fix something on their credit report, or who are waiting for an insurance check or some other payment. (See Chapter 5 for details about lease-option agreements.)

Selling your home and renting it back

Another way an investor can assist you through the foreclosure process is to buy your home and then lease it back to you for several months or even years until you're ready to move. This option is especially attractive for couples who have children in school. If the foreclosure occurs in the middle of the school year, you may be able to rent the property until summer break. Or if your children are nearing their high school graduation, the investor may agree to lease the property to you until your kids graduate.

Many real estate investors are willing to wait if they know they can earn long-term profits by renting out the property, assuming they believe that you'll take care of the property. Make sure the investor knows that you're willing and able to properly care for the property for the duration of the lease. Otherwise, the investor may think that reselling to someone else is in her best interest.

Watch out for shady investors and other people who show up at your door offering assistance, especially those who show up at the eleventh hour. These wolves in sheep's clothing may be out to fleece you. The information we provide in Chapter 9 can steer you clear of these shysters.

Getting Out from Under It: Selling Your Home

For about 90 percent of homeowners facing foreclosure, selling their home is the best option — assuming, of course, that they have some equity built up in the house. By selling the house, you can cash out the equity instead of giving it to a bank in refinance charges or to an investor who buys the property for pennies on the dollar at auction. You can then use the proceeds from the sale to secure more affordable accommodations, such as a smaller house in a neighborhood that's not so pricey.

Unfortunately, most homeowners facing foreclosure put off doing anything about it until the option of selling their home is no longer available. An excellent real estate agent may take as long as three to six months to sell your property, depending on the market, so if this is an option you want to consider, read through the following sections in a hurry, and then put the book down and find yourself a great agent to list the property for you. (Chapter 13 gives you some pointers on selecting a qualified real estate agent.)

If you need more time to sell, you may be able to file a special type of Chapter 13 bankruptcy (see Chapter 10) that allows you to sell your home in a reasonable amount of time (for example, 18 months) and use the proceeds to buy another home. This strategy is becoming quite popular. The downside is that you have to pay an attorney to file for bankruptcy, and the bankruptcy trustee earns a 6 percent to 7 percent commission on the sale.

In order to even break even by selling their homes, most homeowners who are forced to sell usually need to negotiate short sales with any lenders who have liens against the property. A short sale requires the lender to accept less than the full amount owed. (See "Selling your lender short with a short sale," later in this chapter, for details.)

While interviewing people facing foreclosure, we ask the following question: What do you have in your savings account? The answer is usually a humiliated chuckle. By the time they get to us, they've usually drained that account. If the house has equity, we point out that they do have a savings account — in their house. Determine the real value of the house, minus the costs associated with selling, to arrive at the amount in your "savings account." Then determine whether you're willing to use some of that savings to save your home or whether it would make better financial sense to sell and move to a more affordable dwelling. Take the emotions out and deal with cold hard facts. As detective Joe Friday used to say on *Dragnet*, "Just the facts, ma'am."

Planting a FOR SALE sign on your lawn

When you're facing foreclosure, you usually need to unload the home in a hurry for as much as you can get, and to accomplish that, you have to do three things:

- **Hire a great real estate agent.** Hiring a top-producing agent is the best move you can make. Real estate agents, on average, sell homes twice as fast for more money than homeowners who try to sell on their own. Choose your agent carefully — you want the person whose name is on the most SOLD signs in the neighborhood.

- **Price it right.** Setting a competitive price not only sells the home faster but can also generate enough interest to drive up the price. Don't get greedy. Set the right price the first time. Your real estate agent can assist you and is well aware of the importance of pricing the home right the first time.

- **Spruce up the place.** To command a higher price, your home should be properly *staged* — uncluttered, tastefully furnished, and impeccably clean. You may not have the money to do major repairs and renovations, but you need to invest enough sweat to make the house look as nice as possible.

You're in foreclosure, so don't be afraid to ask your real estate agent for a reduced commission or for a listing that allows *you* to find the buyer and pay a reduced commission or avoid the commission all together. The worst that can happen is that the agent refuses, but some real estate agents are happy to assist knowing that their assistance is going to generate positive PR. Don't select an agent on commission alone, however — you want the very best, even if you have to pay the going rate.

For additional information about placing your house on the market, check out Chapter 13.

Selling quick to an investor

As soon as real estate investors, con artists, and other opportunists catch wind of the fact that you're facing foreclosure, they begin to circle like vultures. You can expect to receive plenty of phone calls, letters, and even personal visits from people who want to "help" you out of your current dilemma. Some of these folks may be legitimately interested in assisting you and earning a fair profit in return, while others may simply be out to con you out of your house or at least any equity you may have in it.

Selling to a legitimate investor who simply wants to make a fair profit has its benefits. An investor can offer the following:

- ✔ **Cash for your home,** allowing you to shed yourself of the home much more quickly

- ✔ **Additional perks,** such as money to cover moving expenses or one or two month's rent

- ✔ **Special deals,** such as buying the house and then selling it back to you with a lease option or land contract (see "Selling your home and buying it back: The ol' give and go," earlier in this chapter)

If you decide to sell to an investor, be very careful. Choose an investor who's less likely to take you to the cleaners. Here are some tips to protect yourself from those who are seeking to take advantage of your misfortune:

- ✔ **Choose an investor who has a platinum reputation in your area for following through on what she says she's going to do.**

- ✔ **Make sure the investor has an office address, not just a P.O. box.** You're always safer working with people from brick-and-mortar establishments. Be sure to verify that the office exists and that the person works there.

- ✔ **Keep excellent records and record all conversations.** (See Chapter 3 for details on how to keep good records and advocate for yourself.)

✔ **Verify everything the person tells you** by contacting your attorney or someone else who should know the foreclosure laws in your jurisdiction.

✔ **Don't give the "investor" or "foreclosure rescue" person any money upfront.** An investor who's asking for money upfront is probably not the real deal.

✔ **Never sign your home over to the investor using a *quit claim deed* before consulting your attorney.** When you sign a quit claim deed, you relinquish all rights to the property, and give the "investor" license to do whatever he wants.

Be very careful to avoid phony foreclosure rescue scams. One of the most common methods that con artists use to steal houses is to promise distressed homeowners that they can fix the problem — all the homeowners have to do is sign a quit claim deed, and the con artist will take care of the rest. What these con artists end up doing is ripping off the homeowners through one of the following schemes:

✔ Charging the homeowners rent and then failing to redeem the property, so the homeowners get evicted

✔ Redeeming the property, taking a loan out against it to strip all the equity out of it, and then disappearing, leaving the homeowners in much worse shape

✔ Kicking the homeowners out and taking possession of the property

In Chapter 3, we talked a little about the importance of becoming fully aware of the situation. Check out some of the government Web sites and your attorney general's site to determine which scams are going on in your area, or to report a suspected scammer who came to your door. This is where your documentation can come in handy.

If you have the good fortune to meet an investor with integrity, pick his brain for more information. This person is probably as close to a foreclosure expert as you're going to get. Just make sure you verify everything he tells you. If you decide to sell to the investor, realize that he needs to be able to resell the property and make some money, so don't expect top dollar for your home. Selling to an investor may be your best option if time is running out on other options and you don't have the money to make your property marketable.

Selling your lender short with a short sale

If you decide to sell your property, either by listing it with a real estate agent or selling to an investor, you may need to negotiate a short sale with the bank and other lenders so you can clear all your debts and perhaps even walk away with a small amount of cash.

With a *short sale,* the bank agrees to accept a payment of less than you currently owe on the loan as payment in full. Why would any bank agree to this? Well, if it's staring a big fat loss in the face if it moves forward with the foreclosure, a short sale may be in the bank's best interest. If, for example, you owe the bank $100,000 on a house that's worth $105,000, the bank is probably going to lose money by foreclosing. It has to hire an attorney to take the house back, pay to fix up and clean the house so it can be placed on the market, and then pay an agent to list and sell the house. By accepting a payoff of $90,000 (more or less), the bank could be saving itself the time, money, and hassle inherent in foreclosure.

Banks are almost never willing to agree to a short sale if it's going to put money in your pocket. If a short sale allows you to sell your home and salvage your credit but otherwise walk away empty handed, the bank may be willing to offer you a discount. If the lender suspects, however, that the $10,000 discount it gave you is going to end up in your pocket, it won't agree to a short sale — and understandably so.

Negotiating a short sale is often most effective with second mortgages or junior liens, in which the lender stands to lose the entire loan balance if the situation culminates in a foreclosure. If an investor purchases the first mortgage at auction, the proceeds are used to pay the first mortgage holder, and then any excess funds are used to pay second mortgage and other junior lien holders. If the proceeds from the sale cover only the amount owed on the first mortgage, the second mortgage and junior lien holders receive nothing. This makes them more motivated to agree to a short sale.

A short sale case study

Your house is valued and really worth $100,000, but you owe $102,000. The house may have been worth $110,000 a year ago but the market turned and gobbled up all your equity. You're behind and facing a foreclosure.

You decide to list your house and try to sell it. You get an offer on the house (which you took great care of) for $97,000. You call the bank and explain that you have an offer, but in order to sell and close you need to negotiate a short sale. You need the bank to discount its position by almost $11,000. Why so much? You owe only $102,000 and you're selling for $97,000, so shouldn't a discount of $5,000 be enough? No, because you still

have to pay your real estate agent a 6 percent commission for selling the house:

$$\$102{,}000 - \$5{,}000 - (\$97{,}000 \times 0.06) = \$91{,}180$$

If the bank sees some reason to accept $91,000 of its $102,000, you have a deal; if not, you're back to the drawing board. The bank may want to talk to the agent, and may try to get the broker to take a bit of a discount as well. You may have to jump through some hoops and do a little more wheeling and dealing of your own, but if you can make it happen, you can sell, relieve yourself of the debt, and move on.

If you convince a bank or any lien holder to accept a short sale, make sure they accept the short sale amount as payment in full for the debt. You don't want them to hold you accountable for the deficiency or have any recourse to pursue other assets for the amount they agreed to discount. Get everything in writing and have your attorney review it.

Always consider what the bank stands to lose if your house ends up on the auction block. The worse it's going to be for the bank, the more power you have to negotiate. The bank may be willing to discount the total amount you currently owe on the loan if it's staring at a lengthy redemption period, the market is forecasted to get worse, the house isn't in a great area or in great shape, or for a host of other reasons.

Now, you can understand why a bank may agree to a short sale, but why would *you* agree to a short sale? After all, you walk away with little or nothing in your pocket and you lose the house. Well, you're not exactly walking away with nothing. By negotiating a short sale and then selling your house, you gain the following benefits:

- ✔ Relief from your debt
- ✔ A clean slate — no record of the foreclosure in your credit history
- ✔ Pride in having erased your debt

Some people can't get over the fact that they paid for ten years on a home and then have to walk away with nothing. They blame the banks for charging so much interest and feel entitled to profit from the sale in some way. We recommend that you avoid this bitterness. First of all, it doesn't improve the situation. Second, you didn't receive any money when you bought the house — the entire mortgage amount was applied to the purchase, and the bank took a risk by loaning you the money. Sure, the bank probably earned some profit from the interest you paid, but it earned that profit by taking a risk. If you choose the short sale option, use it to put the foreclosure behind you, including any lingering bitterness you may have toward the bank. Regardless of where you were living for those ten years, you would have had to pay to live there, and you never have a guarantee that the value of your investment is going to increase.

Getting taxed on your loss

The funny (or not so funny) thing about short sales and other deals you may work out with your lender is that the federal government may actually try to tax the money you never received from the transaction. For example, if the bank forgives $10,000 in debt (as a short sale), so you can sell your home and break even, the IRS may count that $10,000 as capital gains and hit you with a tax bill!

During the mortgage meltdown that began in 2007, the government discussed providing some temporary relief from this taxation to allow homeowners to refinance or sell their homes without facing this tax penalty. In any case, if you stand to have any portion of your debt "forgiven" for any reason, we suggest that you consult an accountant or tax specialist to determine how this could affect you.

Rope-a-Doping with Delay Tactics

Foreclosure self-defense is always a race against the clock — in some states more than in others. In Michigan, for example, you have about 30 days from the first publication of the foreclosure notice to save the house from ending up on the auction block, but then you have a full 6 to 12 months from the date of the sale to redeem the property. In Mississippi, a state with no redemption period, you only have about a month to come up with a solution.

Having a little extra time to explore options always helps, but finding that time can be difficult. In the following sections, we reveal a few delay tactics. (In Chapter 16, we offer ten additional methods for slowing down the clock.)

Living in the home for free during redemption

If your state has a lengthy redemption period, your best option may be to remain in your home through the redemption period without making any more payments. When moving time rolls around, you can then move out with as much money as you were able to squirrel away during that time.

In some cases, you can even extend the redemption period through various loopholes and legal technicalities. If the bank didn't properly advertise your foreclosure, for example, and you can prove it in court, the bank may need to start the foreclosure proceedings all over from the very beginning. In the meantime, you have more time to squirrel away additional cash in anticipation of moving day.

Although you may be able to act *pro se* (as your own attorney), the old saying that someone who represents himself has a fool for a client usually holds true. If you can afford a good attorney, hire one — but consider the expense. We've yet to meet an attorney who works for free, so you have to decide whether the cost of the attorney is going to be offset by how much additional time the attorney could keep you in the house (and the money that saves you). Whether or not you use an attorney, however, you should always show up for your court dates.

The key to the stay-without-pay maneuver is saving every penny you can, so that when the time comes to move, you have a stash of cash to move with you. We've seen homeowners save money during the redemption period and then hold an auction, garage sale, or estate sale and pocket thousands of dollars to make a fresh start. It's certainly a more attractive option than getting evicted without a penny in your pocket and having the sheriff haul your stuff out to the curb where passersby can help themselves to it. (For additional details about this strategy, check out Chapter 13.)

Knowing the value of a good attorney

We bought a house at auction and got a pretty good deal on it. As we usually do, during the redemption period we tried to contact the owners and offer them the opportunity to buy the home back from us, but they managed to avoid us for almost the entire duration of the redemption period. About a week prior to the expiration of the redemption period, we received notice that the homeowners had filed for bankruptcy. We learned later that a mother and her adult daughter had lived together in the house; the mother had taken ill and, sadly, passed away, but not before she managed to file for bankruptcy.

Bankruptcy placed an automatic stay on all actions we could take and any issues surrounding probate. We weren't sure what we could do except to have the automatic stay lifted. The daughter, however, had found an attorney who really knew how bankruptcy worked and how to use it to his client's best advantage. He managed to drag out the case for weeks on end. While the daughter remained firmly planted in the house, we were footing the bill.

Just when we thought we would be wrapping the whole thing up, we were told that the homeowner would be seeking a jury trial. A jury would quickly see us as the big bad investors preying on the helpless homeowner. At the preliminary hearing, the attorney whispered to me that the judge scheduled to hear the case would be heading to China for a three-week vacation. We knew that this was going to lead to some major delays. (Of course, there's no right to a jury trial in relief-from-stay proceedings, but we didn't know that at the time.)

That night, we stewed the defensiveness right out of ourselves and decided to stop fighting the system. The next time the attorney contacted us, we asked him, "Does your client want to just buy back the house, so we can put this behind us?" The attorney responded, "I thought you'd never ask! We can probably wrap this all up before her honor goes on holiday."

The attorney was able to structure a deal for his client that allowed her to keep the house, and we were able to make a tiny profit on the buy-back price. We obtained court approval, and the whole fiasco disappeared as quickly as it had first surfaced.

The moral of the story is that a good attorney can wear down a bank or an investor and often negotiate a better deal on your behalf — assuming, of course, you have a pretty good case to start with.

Abandoning Ship Altogether

Some days, you may just feel like loading all your stuff into a moving van and driving away, leaving the house and all your troubles behind. Is that really a viable option? Sure, it is. Nobody can keep you living in your home. The trouble is that leaving may damage your credit and make it tougher for you to obtain loan approval later.

In the following sections, we reveal various ways to leave your home and discuss the pros and cons of each approach.

If you have equity built up in the house, simply walking away is never a good idea. Selling the property, refinancing, or exercising one of the other options discussed in this chapter enables you to cash out at least a portion of that equity rather than simply giving it to someone else.

Giving a deed in lieu of foreclosure

Your bank may agree to let you off the hook by handing over a *deed in lieu of foreclosure*. Ideally, you sign the house over to the bank, hand them the keys, and hit the road. The bank can then sell the house to recoup some or all of the remaining balance on your mortgage and you walk away without having a foreclosure posted to your credit history.

You have to be careful, though, so you don't end up giving the bank the power to pursue you later with a *deficiency judgment* — a ruling that allows the bank to sue you for the balance of the loan that the sale proceeds did not cover. Have your attorney draft an agreement that allows you to walk away without looking back. The agreement should state that the bank can use only the house to recoup its money.

Your bank may even offer you a small amount of cash to sign the agreement, and if you couple it with the stay-and-don't-pay strategy (see "Living in the home for free during redemption," earlier in this chapter), you may be able to sock away a good chunk of change. Keep in mind, however, that the longer you stay without paying, the less money the bank may be willing to give you for moving on.

Gifting the house (and your problems) to an investor

You may be able to shake yourself loose from that monkey on your back by deeding your home over to an investor. The investor may be in a better position to negotiate a short sale (see "Selling your lender short with a short sale" earlier in this chapter), to make the deal worthwhile to himself while providing you with a little cash to move on.

If you have little or no equity in the property, giving the property to an investor by signing a quit claim deed may be your best option. Again, you should consult with an attorney to make absolutely sure that your rights are protected and the bank cannot pursue you later for any losses it suffers.

Taking a hike . . . and leaving the house keys behind

If you're fed up with the foreclosure, don't care about how it's going to affect your credit history, and have little or no equity in the property, walking out on it is always an option. Simply pack your bags before eviction day rolls around and move on to your new life.

Is this a viable option for you? Well, it may be. The following list describes the conditions that may make this option worth considering:

- ✓ **You have little, no, or negative equity in the property.** Why throw good money after bad by trying to fix up the house and place it on the market, if you're not going to get anything out of it?

- ✓ **Your house would be more costly to maintain and sell than it would be just to move.**

- ✓ **You don't have enough time to execute a more attractive option discussed in this chapter.**

- ✓ **You have a family you want to save from the embarrassment of a forced eviction.**

What's the worst that can happen? Surprisingly, nothing terrible is likely to happen if you simply abandon ship:

- ✓ **Defaulting on the mortgage loan is going to damage your credit,** but that's going to happen if you lose your home in foreclosure anyway.

- ✓ **The bank can obtain a deficiency judgment against you** if the proceeds from the sale of your home do not fully cover the remaining balance on your loans. But again, this could happen if your home is sold at auction.

- ✓ **Junior lien holders may sue you on the note for the entire debt.** Instead of following through on their secured position, they may choose to abandon it and pursue full payment of the debt.

Time your move to reap the greatest benefits. If your state has a six-month redemption period, for example, stay in the home for 5 months and 29 days rent-free, save as much money as you can, and then move out. (See "Living in the home for free during redemption," earlier in this chapter, for details.)

Doing Nothing: The Lazy Man's Guide to Foreclosure Self-Defense

The absolute worst option is to do nothing. You simply continue on the same path you were on when you received the eviction notice. Your household doesn't earn any more money, spend any less, or try to work out a deal with the bank, and you allow the wheels of justice to roll over you and your family.

If you're single and you really don't care, this may be the option of choice. You wouldn't be the first person to choose this option, and you certainly would not be the last. But if you have kids or others who depend on you to put a roof over their heads and food in their bellies, this is really no option to consider. Eventually, your house is going to be sold at auction and if you don't leave by the end of the redemption period, you, your family, and your belongings will be moved out of the house for you.

The very fact that you're reading this book proves you're not really serious about this option. This book lays out your viable options and helps you develop a plan, so don't give up!

Chapter 8

Stopping the Financial Bleeding

. . . .

In This Chapter

▶ Stabilizing your situation with a strict budget

▶ Adding to the household income

▶ Obtaining the assistance of a credit counselor

▶ Trimming total monthly expenses by consolidating your debt

. . . .

*W*hether you choose to reinstate, refinance, negotiate a forbearance, or simply walk away, you have to stop the financial bleeding and resolve your cash flow problems immediately. A two-pronged attack usually works best — reining in your spending while finding ways to increase your household income. This two-pronged attack, if successful, keeps the situation from becoming worse, increases the number of viable options open to you, and improves your future outlook.

In this chapter, we take on the roles of credit counselor and financial advisor, providing some strategies and tips on how to put your financial house in order. However, we are not certified in these areas. For professional advice on dealing with your specific situation, we recommend that you seek the assistance of a certified debt or credit counselor. If you choose to do it yourself, you can find plenty of books to assist you, including *Personal Finance For Dummies,* 5th Edition, by Eric Tyson, MBA (Wiley); *Sorting Out Your Finances For Dummies,* by Melanie Bien (Wiley); *Frugal Living For Dummies,* by Deborah Taylor-Hough (Wiley); *Managing Debt For Dummies,* by John Ventura and Mary Reed (Wiley); and *Credit Repair Kit For Dummies,* by Stephen R. Bucci (Wiley).

Hire a reputable credit counselor — some may be out to capitalize on your misfortune. The Federal Trade Commission offers a free guide on how to select a credit or debt counselor, which you can read online at www.ftc. gov/bcp/conline/pubs/credit/fiscal.shtm. Don't be ashamed to look for or ask for help. As Lois's grandmother used to say, "There's no shame in getting lice — the shame is in keeping 'em." All kinds of unexpected situations jump into your life that just can't be helped, but the way you address them can help.

Slashing Expenses with a Tight Budget

Far too many households function like the federal government, embracing the notion of deficit spending. Unlike the government, you can't simply print more money when your stash of cash runs low. You need something like a line-item veto to control expenses, so you have at least as much money coming in as you have going out. You wouldn't believe how many people we meet whose foreclosure self-defense plan consists of buying more lottery tickets or hoping that their long-lost rich uncle is going to show up and bail them out. You have to plan, and every plan starts with a tight budget.

When budgeting, you can take either of two approaches:

- ✔ **Make payments.** If you decide to make payments, your budget must ensure that you're able to make the monthly payment each and every month, or your plan is doomed to fail. Be realistic. Are you going to be able to make the payments? If not, then Plan B is probably a better strategy.

- ✔ **Live in the house rent-free for as long as possible.** If you decide to live in the house rent-free until moving day arrives, then your goal should be to trim expenses to the max, so you can squirrel away as much money as possible. Chapter 13 reveals a 12-step plan for putting this strategy into action.

In either case, your goal is to minimize expenses at least to the point of being able to fund your plan, whatever that may be. Minimizing expenses isn't easy. You may already be operating on the bare essentials (or at least you think you are), and you may need to sacrifice a lifestyle that you've become quite accustomed to, which is very difficult, indeed. However, we often find that even a lean budget can be trimmed a bit.

Budgeting success relies heavily on cooperation among all household members. Everyone needs to make concessions. If your partner is going without lattes at Starbucks, and you're living large, er, Venti, your partner is going to resent you sooner or later. Some family members may need to sacrifice more, but everyone involved must be willing to do his share.

Covering the cost of bare essentials

Two pieces of dry white toast made from day-old bread, a glass of tap water, and dinner is served. Well, maybe your austerity program isn't quite that bad, but when you're drawing up a budget, focus on the bare essentials — food, shelter, and transportation. You can then add in the cost of nonessential items, assuming you can afford them.

Jot down a list of bare essentials. Say, "I need . . ." and then follow up with what you need to live, such as "I need a roof over my head," "I need food," and "I need a way to get to work."

After you have a fairly comprehensive list of everything you need to keep your household running, write down the monthly expense for each item and add them all up. If you're into deficit spending territory and you can't live without the items on your list, hope remains, but you're going to need to make a few additional adjustments.

Vetoing discretionary spending

Spending habits can become so ingrained that what you once considered a luxury item you now consider a necessity. When you're facing foreclosure, however, you may need to adjust the way you look at your finances and become a little more brutal when it comes to slashing expenses. This is a key step to righting your ship and putting it back on course.

Do you really need that car?

A car used to be more of a luxury than a necessity. In a typical town or city, you could walk or bicycle to work or take public transportation (the bus). A car was more of a status symbol that enabled you to take day trips and drive to your vacation destination.

Relatively recently, with the mass exodus from towns and cities to suburbs and other outlying areas, cars have become more of a necessity — at least in the minds of most Americans. A majority of us now drive to work, to pick up groceries (even if the grocery store is only a few blocks away), to drop our kids off at school and pick them up, and to run various other daily errands.

If you live and work in your town or city, however, you may be able to get around without taking on the financial burden of owning a car. You may be able to walk, bicycle, take a bus, or carpool to your desired destinations. Sure, it's inconvenient, but right now you're in a situation that's even more inconvenient — facing the prospect of losing your home.

If you can shed yourself of your car, you may be able to free up about $1,000 a month — $200 to $600 in car payments, $100 to $300 in insurance, $50 to $100 per week in gas, plus whatever you pay for oil changes and other maintenance and repairs.

This option may not work for everyone, but if your household has two or three cars, maybe you can shed just one of them and save enough to get yourself back on budget. Just because every other 16-year-old is driving himself to school doesn't mean yours has to during this time. It's a matter of adjusting your perspective so that you can keep your home.

In the following sections, we examine the spending categories that often sink the household finances and offer some suggestions on how to cut your spending to bring it more in line with your budget.

Trimming vacation expenses

If your family has become accustomed to lavish vacations, you may need to scale back this year, or perhaps even forego the family vacation for a little quality time at home. This may seem overly obvious, but we often see families who continue to take expensive vacations because they "worked hard and deserve it" or because "the kids would be *so* disappointed." Neither of these reasons is good enough for losing the roof over your heads and condemning your life and your family to a future of abject poverty.

Nobody is saying that you can't take a vacation with your family. What we're saying is that maybe renting a cottage for a week on a local lake can replace the two-week stay in a chalet in the Swiss Alps. Your goal isn't to torture yourself, but to be conscious about where the money is going and how you can achieve the same results on a more frugal budget. Extra planning and a sense of adventure can result in a very successful and memorable vacation for the entire family.

Another vacation expense you may need to trim is in the area of separate vacations. Many couples take personal vacations apart from their significant others, such as weeklong hunting trips in the country and weekend shopping sprees in a big city. These vacations should be the first to go, at least until you're back on your feet.

Spending in good times and bad

We know a guy in the automotive business who keeps spending like a king no matter what the market is like. When the market was booming, he was making money hand over fist. He lived a lavish lifestyle and socked away a considerable sum of money to protect himself and his family in the event of any market downturns, which is an excellent strategy.

The problem, however, is that during the most recent market downturn, he continued spending as he did when the money was gushing in. The gush is now down to a trickle, yet the guy keeps spending they way he was before. He's not in foreclosure, but the lavish family vacations, the expensive luxury automobiles, and the high-dollar extras, which were quite affordable before, are gobbling up huge chunks of his savings. If the market doesn't turn around sometime soon, we're afraid that he's going to be facing foreclosure and wishing that he'd spent his money a little more wisely.

When your financial landscape changes, you and your family may need to become more proactive and take the steps necessary to ward off a future fiscal crisis. Don't just keep spending as you did before, thinking that everything will be okay.

Hanging up on some phone services

Everyone seems to have a cellphone these days. We often encounter families in foreclosure in which every single family member has a cellphone — mom, dad, teenagers, and even grade-school kids are equipped. In addition, the family may even have a separate landline and a line for the Internet.

Are all these phones and phone lines necessary? Do you really need to call home from the movie rental place to find out which movie to rent? Does your teenager really benefit from spending hours on the phone every single day chatting with friends?

Paul has a friend he calls "Batman," because the guy's belt is decked out with just about every wireless communication device known to man. He has a cellphone, pager, BlackBerry, you name it. It looks like he's wearing a Bat belt. In his line of work, this can be considered a necessity, but most people can get by comfortably without all these gadgets.

Take a close look at your phone bills and decide what you can live without. If a device saves you more in convenience and productivity than the cost of having it, keep it. If it's just one more extravagance that you can live without, or if it's a major distraction that simply gobbles up time you could be spending earning some money, get rid of it. Many families decide to do away with their landlines and rely solely on the cellphone; this may be an option for you.

You may also be able to trim your phone expenses by looking into other plans, switching services, or having your teenagers cover the cost of having their own cellphones. You would be surprised to learn how many people just pay their bill without actually reviewing it. The plan you signed up for may not be the best and most cost-efficient right now.

Cutting the cable on premium TV

Big-screen HDTVs, satellite TV, and cable service are three luxuries that every family can do without, yet nearly all the families we visit who are facing foreclosure have cutting-edge entertainment systems. Most households outfitted with 10,000 channels of cable or satellite TV, plus premium sports channels and movies on demand, end up spending most of their time watching three or four free local-access channels anyway.

If you simply can't part with your cable or satellite service, then look for other areas to cut on your family entertainment budget. Consider cutting movie rentals or family trips to the local movie theater. Instead, stay home and explore those other 9,996 channels you've been missing out on. You can probably save enough by cutting one trip to the movie theater to pay for a whole month's worth of satellite TV. Also consider cutting back on your satellite or cable service, opting for one of the basic plans instead.

Eating in

How much do you spend eating out every month? If you're like an average family of four, every time you circle through the drive-through, you rack up a bill of $25 to $30. The average price of a combo meal is about $6. Biggie-size it, and you're looking at $7 to $8. Eat out three or four times a week, and over the course of a month, you're shelling out $300 to $500. If you're a careful shopper, that could cover an entire month's worth of groceries!

You can get a 2-liter of pop for less than it costs for a large soft drink, and that 2-liter isn't three-fourths full of ice.

Trim the fat by cooking your own meals at home; planning at least a few nutritional, but low-cost meals, like tomato soup and grilled cheese sandwiches; and brown-bagging it for lunch. You can even transform mealtime into family time, by involving all family members in the meal planning, grocery shopping, food preparation, and cleanup. It doesn't have to make you miserable — it just has to be affordable. Eating out is not a necessity.

Avoid impulse purchases. Plan your meals for the week, create your grocery list, and then go to the store just to pick up what's on the list. Whoever is best at getting only what's on the list should be the designated shopper. Prepared food is always more expensive, but if you find that you're buying fresh food and letting it spoil, then shopping in the frozen-food aisle may save you some money.

Chopping clothing costs (for the fashionably poor)

Everyone has a weakness. Some are cellphone junkies, others are fast food addicts, and more than a few are clothing fanatics, changing their entire wardrobes with every change in seasons or waist size.

You and other family members don't have to look like orphans to save a little money on clothes. You just need to watch your wallet, stick to your budget, and find less expensive duds. Here are a few tips for clothing your family on a budget:

- ✔ **Make that suit last another season.** Nobody's going to notice that the suit you're wearing is the same one you wore last fall.

- ✔ **Pass it down.** If you have children, don't toss the clothes as soon as your oldest child outgrows them. Save them for the next kid. Some kids are going to grumble about this, but they need to learn to make some sacrifices, too.

- ✔ **Buy gently used clothes or even new clothes at Goodwill or the Salvation Army store.** These stores often receive brand-new clothing, sometimes even designer fashions, that you can purchase for a few dollars. Shirts and jeans are real bargains!

> ✔ **Check out consignment shops and other stores that deal in hand-me-downs.** You can often find clothing with the original tags still on them, only instead of having to pay $47.50, you can now pick it up for $8.25 or less.
>
> ✔ **Watch your spending on accessories.** Shoes, belts, hats, and even purses and wallets can chip away at your budget fairly quickly.

If you simply can't resist the sales or that darling little item, stay away from stores until the urge to buy subsides. You may also want to steer clear of the sales inserts in the Sunday paper and pull the plug on the family's online shopping.

Expenses in the clothing category are a mix of necessity and luxury. Buy what you need, but pass over what you want, at least until you're back on your feet again. You can save a good chunk of money by focusing on necessities and slashing the luxuries.

Boosting Your Total Household Income

When you can't make ends meet with expense cuts alone, start looking at the other end of the cash flow equation — income. You, your partner, and any children you have may be able to generate just enough additional income to make it work — assuming, of course, that you're committed to retaining possession of your property. You can use the additional income to cover daily expenses or earmark it all for the house.

Everything is a trade-off. If you're committed to keeping your property, you need to work harder. If you're working as hard as you can (or want to) work, and you still can't make it happen, then you need to slash even more expenses and perhaps even sell the property and move into something more affordable. Nobody can tell you what's best for you and your family. We can only lay out your options.

In the following sections, we discuss two ways to increase the household income — taking on another job yourself and putting other family members to work.

Moonlighting

Assuming your current agreement with your employer doesn't rule out moonlighting as an option, this can be an excellent source for the extra cash you need. We know of many mechanics who do minor repairs in their garage for a fraction of the cost you would pay at a repair shop, and they earn a good chunk of cash doing it. Carpenters who frame houses by day may work nights and weekends building and installing cabinets. Photographers who take family portraits in the mall during the week can pick up some extra cash by photographing weddings and anniversaries on weekends. If you don't have a marketable skill, you can still earn some extra money by taking on a second job at a local restaurant or store. Do it regularly enough and you have a steady additional flow of income.

Moonlighting does have a couple drawbacks:

- ✔ **It can quickly sap your energy and distract from your day job.** We wouldn't want you to lose your primary occupation by taking on side jobs.

- ✔ **It doesn't always deliver a steady stream of cash.** You may get loads of work one month and nothing the next. Moonlighting is "extra" money and can be a great way to catch up on some delinquent bills, or throw a little extra at the payments you planned out in your program, but it's not always reliable.

Don't plan on the extra money unless you always get the extra work or are very confident that you'll be able to hustle up side jobs. Develop a plan that *doesn't* take into account the sporadic moonlighting money, but use that money to help you reach your goals earlier than the plan calls for.

If you have young children, you may need to draw up a work schedule that consists of one spouse working days and the other going to work when the first comes home in the evening. Depending on your family's goals, this can be a temporary arrangement until the family gets back on its feet.

Putting other family members to work

During World War II, when manpower was short in the United States, women made up a significant segment of the workforce. If you're a baby boomer or older, you probably remember the Rosie the Riveter posters. (If not, you can check them out at www.rosietheriveter.com.) When the United States was at war, everyone pulled together and contributed to keep the country running and our military overseas well equipped.

When your family is facing foreclosure, everybody of working age can pull together and contribute his or her fair share to get the family back on its feet. If you have young children whom you're trying to shield from the problem, that's fine, but older teenagers are certainly capable of earning their own spending money and enough to cover their cellphone bills. Simply explain what's going on, ask them to assist you and be part of the solution, and share your plan with them. The experience can be very valuable in the future, if they ever face a similar situation.

If an older child is extremely reluctant or refuses to help, tough love may be the order of the day. Older kids need to be paying their fair share. Obviously, we're not talking about asking your 15-year-old son to get a job bagging groceries and turn over his whole $87 paycheck each week, but you may ask your 17-year-old daughter to help offset the additional cost of auto insurance with a portion of her weekly check. Adult children should be working and contributing something toward the house payment, maintenance, and utilities; otherwise, perhaps *they* can find more affordable accommodations elsewhere.

Consulting with a Credit Counselor

When people have emotional or psychological issues, they turn to a therapist. When they have marital troubles, they turn to a marriage counselor. Yet, many people avoid seeking counsel when their finances are in shambles. Certain financially gifted individuals specialize in offering financial advice to those who struggle in this area. Don't hesitate to call on them for assistance.

Ask friends, family members, your bank, or a real estate or financial professional for references, or search online for a credit counselor. Choose at least three prospective candidates, and interview them thoroughly. Make sure you understand whatever program each person offers and its cost. Just because a credit counseling service claims to be a nonprofit organization doesn't mean that its services are free. You can find a list of government-approved credit counseling agencies at www.usdoj.gov/ust/eo/bapcpa/ccde/cc_approved.htm. Another useful site at www.debtadvice.org is maintained by the National Foundation for Credit Counseling (NFCC).

Choose a credit counselor carefully. Nonprofit organizations don't always offer free or affordable service, and some may not even be legitimate. Find out exactly how much it's going to cost you before you sign on the dotted line, and be less than generous if the organization asks for a contribution. Compare at least three services before choosing one. Look for a counselor who can meet with you in person. Universities, military bases, credit unions, housing authorities, and other institutions may be able to steer you toward a reputable credit counselor. Also ask family members and friends for referrals. For additional information, check out the Federal Trade Commission's "Choosing a Credit Counselor" article at www.ftc.gov/bcp/conline/pubs/credit/fiscal.shtm.

Some credit counselors have arrangements with credit card companies and other lenders who foot the bill. In exchange, the credit counselor assists the credit card company or lender collect on a debt that otherwise would be uncollectible. In many cases, counselors can work out a win-win solution for both the lenders and the debtors — but make sure the counselor is working

---

You're not alone

People in foreclosure often feel like complete losers and develop a defeatist attitude that can be very counterproductive. Whenever we meet with people in foreclosure, we let them know that they aren't the only ones facing a financial crisis. We show them the foreclosure notices in the weekly county legal news publication. During slow foreclosure periods, we see at least 50 notices a week. During the peak, it's not unusual to see over 200 foreclosure notices in a single publication.

Although foreclosure statistics can be a little depressing, those who are facing foreclosure may also find them a little comforting:

✔ Americans owe close to $13 trillion in mortgage debt.

✔ The number of foreclosed homes in the first six months of 2007 surged by 58 percent. That equals approximately 573,397 homes in danger.

✔ As of this writing, most analysts predict that the condition will worsen through the end of 2007, with 2.5 million first mortgages defaulting in 2007.

✔ Close to 50 percent of consumers whose homes face foreclosure never speak to their lender prior to foreclosure.

People who find themselves in foreclosure are often highly successful professionals. Bad things do happen to good people. What's most important is how you deal with those challenges when they arise.

---

for you and not just pretending to. Whatever the arrangement, take a moment to think about any plan before you sign up. Make sure that the company can deliver on any promises it makes — and that it's done so in the past.

A qualified and reputable credit counselor can:

✔ **Analyze your situation and present several options from which to choose.**

✔ **Negotiate payment plans with your creditors** that allow you to make payments, avoid repossession actions, and protect your credit score.

✔ **Negotiate short sales or discounted payoff amounts** that enable you to square away a debt for less than you currently owe. This can free up money to pay other debts.

✔ **Suggest debt consolidation refinancing** that may result in a single monthly payment that is less than what you currently pay per month on all your other payments combined. (See the "Consolidating Your Debts into One Low Monthly Payment" section, later in this chapter, for additional details.)

✔ **Assist you in drawing up a plan to prioritize your debts, schedule payments, and develop a budget.**

If you're staring off into space without a clue as to how to begin to put together a program to get you moving forward, think about contacting a credit counselor for guidance.

When teaming up with a credit counselor, keep good records of what you discuss and everything you give to and receive from the credit counselor. Verify whatever the person tells you with at least one other reliable source. See Chapter 3 for additional details on keeping records, verifying information, and advocating for your rights. For more about working with a credit counselor after foreclosure, check out Chapter 15, but remember that the earlier you get a credit counselor involved, the more options you have.

Consolidating Your Debts into One Low Monthly Payment

If you have credit card debt, second mortgages, or other loans in addition to your first mortgage, debt consolidation can take a huge chunk out of your monthly expenses, so you can pay down the principal more quickly, or simply free up some money to cover other bills.

Just sell it!

Lois and her granddaughter Emma like to watch *Antiques Roadshow* on PBS. People bring in possible hidden treasures that they discovered in a basement, in an attic, or while dumpster diving. Some people bring in very valuable items, and everyone is astounded at how much the items are worth. Usually between the *oohs* and *ahs* of shock come the words, "Oh I'll never part with it." At this point, Emma shouts out, "Sell it!" Like her practical father, she has picked up on the fact that the money would serve the family much better. These valuables are just objects. Take a picture to remember it by, and then sell it!

Recently, we consulted with a real estate professional who was facing foreclosure. The market in Michigan was in a slump and so was her business. She was fraught with worry and

hopelessness. She became physically ill, and her blood pressure skyrocketed. After we sat down, educated her on the foreclosure process, and began drawing up a list of income, assets, and expenses, we discovered that she and her husband had a barn full of antiques, including two antique cars. They began cleaning up and clearing out, and they were able to sell one of the cars for $31,000. They went from cowering to empowering.

According to the Self Storage Association, there are over 2.2 billion square feet of storage space in the United States. Much of that space is stuffed with personal belongings that just won't fit in today's massive houses. If you're a packrat, start selling that stuff. It just may bring in enough money to get you past your current financial crisis.

In the following sections, we reveal the potential benefits of debt consolidation, show you various ways to consolidate debt, and lead you through the process of determining the actual cost of a loan, so you can comparison-shop for debt consolidation loans. (For additional tips and tricks related to borrowing your way out of foreclosure, check out Chapter 12.)

Understanding the benefits of debt consolidation

When people are already in the position of not being able to pay their bills, they're often reluctant to take out yet another loan, but you have to realize that debt consolidation can be a valuable tool for reducing your overall debt and making life a little more livable:

- **You can transfer non-deductible interest (like the interest you pay on credit card debt) into tax-deductible interest (like the interest you pay on your mortgage).**

- **Consolidation often transforms high-interest debt into low-interest debt.** If you owe $20,000 in credit card debt at 18-percent interest, you're probably making payments of about $300 per month. Payments on that same amount at 8 percent would be around $136 per month.

- **If you apply the savings toward paying down the principal of the consolidation loan, you can pay off your debt much more quickly.** In the previous example, if you could afford to continue making the $300 monthly payment, you could apply the extra $164 to principal. And if you can't afford it, you have an extra $164 to cover other bills.

Choosing the debt consolidation option that's right for you

So, how do you go about consolidating your debt? The following are some options you may want to explore:

- **Refinance your mortgage.** You may be able to refinance and use the equity in your home to pay off your other debts and have a single monthly payment. Be careful with this option, however: Refinancing is costly — you usually have to pay some sort of closing costs upfront, which can add thousands of dollars to your total debt. (See Chapter 12 for more information on the refinancing option.)

✔ **Take out a home equity loan.** If you have equity in your home, you can take out a separate loan to borrow against the equity and use the money to pay off your credit card debt and other loans. You then end up with two payments — your mortgage payment and your payment on your home equity loan.

✔ **Take out a home equity line of credit.** With a home equity line of credit, you borrow what you need when you need it, against the equity in your home. You then have two payments — your mortgage payment and the payment on your home equity line of credit. The best part of the home equity line of credit is that you borrow only what you need and are charged interest on only the amount you borrow. If you pay off the loan, your line of credit remains in place in case you ever need it again. In most cases, the bank hands you a checkbook; as you write checks to pay your bills, each check amount is charged against your account.

Unfortunately, when you're already having trouble paying your bills, you probably have damaged credit, which makes it that much more difficult to obtain the loan you need to consolidate your debt. You may need to look at other means of consolidating, like getting an *unsecured* or *secured loan* from a lender:

✔ **An *unsecured loan* allows you to pay off the old debt and make one monthly payment to the bank.** This kind of loan may be difficult to obtain if your credit is bad and you're in trouble already. The bank may require a cosigner or some additional security.

✔ **A *secured loan* requires that you put up some form of collateral so the bank has something it can take from you and sell to cover the debt.** What the bank accepts as security varies from one bank to the next, but your bank may allow you to pledge stocks, bonds, rare coin or stamp collections, jewelry or other valuables, or vehicles. This may allow you to borrow money against items that you don't want to sell right away. When you pay off the loan, the bank releases its interest in your collateral, and you're on your merry way.

Which is best — a secured or unsecured loan? That really depends on your situation. Discuss your options with a qualified loan officer or mortgage broker in your area. (Chapter 12 offers some tips on finding and selecting a loan officer or mortgage broker.)

The loan, whether secured or unsecured, allows you to lower the monthly interest payment and give yourself a bit of a cash flow break. In Chapter 6, we ask you to imagine cash flow in terms of a hose pouring water into your house while a spigot at the bottom lets it out. Consolidating debt gives you a little more control over that spigot, letting you slow down the outbound flow, so your income can begin to catch up. You can always open the valve and make a larger monthly payment, but if finances are tight this month, you can make the minimum payment and still survive.

Whenever you're borrowing money and asked to sign on the dotted line, read and fully understand the documents before signing them. Know what the provisions are, when payments are due, what happens to surplus funds if collateral is sold for more than is required to pay off the loan, and so on. Have your attorney review the document and advise you of any potential issues before you sign.

Consolidating debts is a great rebuilding/restructuring tool. Use it if you can. If you're not in trouble quite yet, consider opening a home equity line of credit now in case you need to draw on it in the future. Many of these equity lines allow you to draw up to a certain capped amount, with the full amount backed by your house as collateral. If you don't draw on the line, you may not be charged, and when you do, the bank charges interest only on the amount you borrowed. You may be allowed to borrow and pay back as time goes on, depending on your loan. Ask around at a couple of banks and pick the program that works best for you and your situation.

Comparing the costs of loans

Although you can select from hundreds of loan types, the bottom line is how much the loan is going to cost you in the long run. The best way to compare loans is to determine the total cost of each loan over the life of the loan:

1. **Add up the fees charged to process the loan, including the loan origination fee, points, and closing costs.**

2. **Multiply the monthly payment times the number of months it will take you to pay off the loan in full.**

3. **Add the amounts from steps 1 and 2 to determine the total cost of the loan.**

4. **Subtract the total amount you expect to pay toward principal over the life of the loan.**

    Ask the bank for an amortization worksheet for each loan, so you can see how much principal you'll have paid at the time you expect to sell the house and pay off the loan.

The result is the total cost of the loan to you. Now, you simply choose the loan that costs the least.

Don't focus only on the "low monthly payments." Consider how much you're going to end up spending over the life of the loan.

Chapter 9

Steering Clear of Quick-Fix Schemes and Scams

As soon as word gets out about your foreclosure, the carpetbaggers and con artists pick up the scent of blood and begin circling your home. They know full well that you're probably very weak and very vulnerable — afraid that the neighbors will find out, afraid to call your bank, afraid to ask for help, and probably willing to try anything to get out of this jam. All of this fear and desperation make you highly vulnerable to a host of scams and schemes designed to separate you from your home and any equity you have in it.

As Franklin Delano Roosevelt said in his first inaugural address, the only thing we have to fear is fear itself. Con artists are experts at using fear, desperation, greed, blind trust, and other human weaknesses against their victims and to their own advantage. The key is to know exactly what makes a person more vulnerable and then be able to spot the early warning signs of a scam.

This chapter begins by pointing out exactly the types of emotions that make you and your family high-profile marks. It then reveals common scams cleverly designed to cheat distressed homeowners out of their homes and steal money that rightfully belongs to the homeowners. Here you discover how to spot the signs of a scam and protect yourself from the bad guys.

Understanding Why Your Vulnerability Makes You Easy Prey

Have you ever seen the wild dogs of Africa in action? The way they hunt is very similar to the way foreclosure con artists operate. When a pack of wild dogs spots a herd of wildebeests, they don't try to catch the herd by surprise. Instead, they fan out and make their presence known, so the herd panics and starts running. At first, this may seem a bit strange. After all, why would the wild dogs want to give the wildebeests advance warning?

Unlike lions or leopards, the wild dogs of Africa can't make the kill on their own, and they certainly can't go head to head with a healthy adult wildebeest. To level the playing field, they get the herd moving and then use their keen vision and discriminating taste to pick out the ones that don't keep up for one reason or another. Maybe a particular wildebeest is old, ill, or crippled. Whatever it is, the wildebeest stands out from the rest of the herd as being more vulnerable. The wild dogs then focus in on that one animal, try to cut it off from the rest of the herd, isolate it, wear it down, and kill it.

Real estate con artists do the same thing. They often hunt in packs of two to five people to make themselves appear more credible. They have a keen, yet twisted, ability to pick out the vulnerable homeowner, and then they work toward isolating that homeowner, wearing him down, and stealing everything of any value.

By knowing what the con artists are looking for, you can employ some evasive maneuvers to make yourself a less attractive target:

- **Desperation:** Anyone who has no money, has fallen behind on her bills, and owes everyone with no end in sight is an attractive mark. Desperate for a way out, these people often make quick, impulsive decisions, which play right into the hands of the con artists.

- **Pride:** An overwhelming desire to solve the problem before your spouse, other family members, or friends hear about it often works in favor of the con artists. This is how they manage to separate distressed homeowners from the herd. They want to be the only ones who feed you information, false information that other people may encourage you to question. Con artists often tell homeowners, "We can solve this problem, and your friends and family, wife, or husband won't even have to know. You can fix this before anyone finds out."

✔ **Trust:** Being a trusting person is generally a good thing, but not when you're approached by a foreclosure con artist. They know that people generally trust what others tell them. Be skeptical. Don't believe anything anybody tells you until you have at least one other independent source of information that verifies it. Con artists often single out the more trusting member of the household and use that person to convince everyone else to go along with the deal.

Con artists often use religion as a diabolical tool — they pray with you, so they can prey upon you. They may present themselves as guardian angels sent from heaven, but by the time they get done with you, you're going to feel as though you've been dragged through hell and back. Don't fall for slick words, false compassion, and feel-good solutions. Carefully scrutinize *anyone* who isn't willing to answer your questions or who operates out of his car and has no business card, phone, or office.

Avoiding the Empty Promises of Quit Claim Deeds

How would you like to simply make all your problems go away? Someone shows up at your door, offering you this option: "Sign this deed, and I will take care of everything for you." You sign the deed, and for a couple months, at least, it seems as though all your problems have disappeared — you haven't received a letter or a phone call from the bank in several weeks. All is well.

A few months down the road, however, you receive a foreclosure notice from another bank that you'd never heard of. You call the bank to find out that you took out another mortgage on the house! Furthermore, you happen to owe much more on the new mortgage than what you owed on your previous mortgage. What happened? You've just been taken to the cleaners by a foreclosure con artist.

This is only one of several ways you can be duped out of your home. In the following sections, we reveal the two most common ways con artists use quit claim deeds to steal homes, so you can defend yourself against these scams.

A quit-claim deed is the easiest deed for con artists to use to steal your home, but it's not the only type of deed that can pose a problem. They can also use a warranty or a bargain and sale deed. Before signing any deed, consult your attorney and have her explain the ramifications of signing.

Using sleight of hand with the bait and switch

The bait and switch is as old a tactic as the "profession" of con artistry. In the foreclosure arena, con artists use it, along with the quit claim deed, to fool distressed homeowners into giving away the rights to their homes.

Here's how it works: The con artist shows up and tells you that he knows private investors with a lot of moolah and big hearts for people in foreclosure. The investors want to loan money to help people save their homes and at the same time earn some interest. (The "investors" are usually the ringleaders. The con artists selling the bill of goods to the homeowner are the bird dogs who are out trying to identify vulnerable homeowners.) The con artist interviews you and informs you that you're a perfect candidate for the investor's National Foreclosure Rescue Program. Lucky you!

Over the next day or so, the con artist explains how the program works and sets you up with a new mortgage that refinances you out of all your problems. The program that was explained to you is clear and it is, indeed (pardon the pun), exactly what you need to correct the situation.

The bait and switch happens when you go to sign the documents. The con artist shows up with a stack of 15 to 20 official documents representing the new mortgage. In some cases, the con artist explains each document in great detail, so you feel comfortable signing them. The con artist then informs you that she needs to have a second, and perhaps a third, identical set of documents signed as well — one for her files and one for each investor, or whatever the story happens to be. The papers are exactly the same as the stack you just signed, but in the middle of the second or third stack is one extra document — a deed to your home. Because the documents are complex, you don't pay much attention to what each page looks like, and eventually they all look the same. You sign all the documents, signing over your legal rights to the home to the con artist.

The con artist then tells you that she'll send you a full copy of the documents after they're recorded, or she'll drop them off to you. You thank her and she leaves. You sleep peacefully, believing everything has been taken care of.

Now that the con artist has the deed to your home, she can record it at the county register of deeds to make the transfer of property official. After the deed has been recorded, the con artist is ready to cash out in one of three ways:

- **Refinancing:** The con artist refinances for as close to the full value of the property as possible, pays off the existing mortgage, and pockets the remaining cash (the equity that you had in the property).

✔ **Taking out a second mortgage:** The con artist takes out a second mortgage, cashing out as much of the equity as possible. This can cause some serious hassles. You'll have to cancel the deed, recover the property, and explain to the bank why you're not responsible for paying off that second mortgage. You may even end up with two mortgages to pay.

✔ **Selling the property:** The con artist places the home on the market and explains to anyone who's interested in the property that you're a tenant, or she makes up some other story. She sells the property and pockets the proceeds. A complete stranger shows up at your door, explaining that he just bought this house and is ready to move in. Little does he know that both you and he are the victims of a clever scam.

A deed is a legal document, and after it's recorded, it's highly enforceable. Going before a judge and claiming that you didn't realize what you were signing is rarely sufficient in proving that you are the rightful owner. Whenever you sign documents, you should *read everything you sign,* and insist on receiving identical copies of the originals immediately. Never leave empty-handed.

Stealing equity with the alternative financing scam

Alternative financing is a perfectly legitimate way to save your property, assuming you're dealing with a trustworthy investor. Using a deed, you sign over your rights to the property to the investor, who pays off the mortgage or redeems the sheriff's deed for you. You make regular monthly payments (sort of like rent) to the investor for 3 to 24 months, building your credit rating. After you've repaired your credit, you can then qualify for a mortgage to pay off the investor, who then signs the rights to the property back over to you — problem solved and you're back on your feet. All is well.

Foreclosure con artists often use this same technique with any of several variations to steal homes:

✔ **The con artist fails to redeem the property as promised, simply collecting your monthly payments.** At the end of the redemption period, the bailiff evicts you.

✔ **The con artist fails to pay off the original mortgage as promised.** Same result — after the sale or when the redemption period expires, the bailiff evicts you.

✔ **At the end of the 3 to 24 months, the con artist refuses to deed the property back to you, claiming that you failed to honor the terms of your contract and forfeited your rights to the property.**

Lois's foreclosure

My journey into the world of foreclosure began not by helping others in foreclosure but by nearly losing my home to a con artist. My husband, Michael, and I had purchased our home from two very prominent public servants. Our 4,500-square-foot home rested on 6 acres and had three outbuildings. We had about $200,000 equity in the home when the trouble started.

I had health issues, my son had open-heart surgery, and my husband lost his job of 17 years — his company went out of business and left him without severance. We managed to weather those storms. We had always worked hard and paid our bills.

After Michael lost his job, he went back to school, and I started focusing on my hobby — arts and crafts. My arts-and-crafts business was thriving, so much so that Michael actually became involved. It generated our sole income. We had the best of both worlds, we worked for ourselves, and we walked across the driveway to get to work.

My father was battling cancer, so we moved my parents into our home so I could help care for him. Shortly after my father passed away, my mother had emergency surgery to remove her appendix. She developed an infection, and we nursed her back to health over the next nine months. With all the distractions, my arts-and-crafts business ultimately failed. Michael and I both tried our hands at several new jobs, but we couldn't catch up.

Instead of seeking assistance, I went into hiding. I was even too ashamed to ask our friends and the former owners of the property who entrusted us with their sanctuary for assistance, even though I was in touch with them on a weekly basis. We were the people who always helped everyone else, and now I was too ashamed to ask for help. I was embarrassed and overwhelmed.

We began receiving hundreds of letters in the mail, many from companies offering assistance. I threw them all away. Finally, after a long night of suffering I decided to call one of the companies that sounded compassionate — Fresh Start. I set up an appointment to have their reps come out to our home.

A man and woman from the company arrived. The man explained the program. He had private investors who would pay off our home and allow us to purchase it back. Our payment would remain close to what we had been paying, but we wouldn't have to worry about the missed payments and nobody would ever have to know. We just needed to sign a document — a quit-claim deed. I signed immediately, thinking the document was of little importance, and then I begged Michael to sign it. He finally signed, against his better judgment.

The next day, before noon, Nadia, the woman who'd been at our house the day before, called me asking if she could come over and meet with us again. She said that we had been scammed. She was going to make every effort to steal our paperwork back before the quit-claim deed was recorded. Nadia wanted no part of this foreclosure rescue "business" and the brothers who were pulling this scam on people. She managed to steal back our paperwork.

Later, Nadia explained the foreclosure process to me and let me know that she wanted to help people in foreclosure. She asked whether I would be willing to become a processor — sending out faxes asking for verifications of employment and income, pretty standard things. Eventually, Nadia teamed up with Ralph, who had the resources in place to assist people in foreclosure. The rest, as they say, is history. Ralph offered me a position in his foreclosure division, and we've been assisting distressed homeowners ever since.

With the alternative financing scam, the con artist usually tries to delay the process for as long as possible, so he can collect as much "rent" as possible. If you receive default papers or notices that the sheriff's sale is coming, the con artist tells you that everything has been taken care of and that the system just hasn't caught up with the payoff yet — or some story like that. You believe him and continue to pay your monthly rent. He probably even comes over to pick it up — what a nice fellow.

After the redemption expires or the mortgage goes to sale, you lose. Even if the scammer actually redeems the property, it's redeemed into his name, not yours, and you no longer own your home. If he doesn't redeem the house, what he's doing is just collecting as many rent payments as he can before the jig is up and you get evicted.

A few years ago, we uncovered a group that was preying on homeowners by collecting rents. Now, you may wonder why a con artist would risk committing this crime for a measly $600 to $1,000 a month, but this group had scammed over 100 families and was raking in a total of about $100,000 a month. Not a bad payday for driving around collecting rent checks or having them sent to a P.O. box.

If an "investor" approaches you with an alternative financing arrangement, she is usually going to ask you to sign a contract or lease stipulating the terms of the agreement. Have *your* attorney review the paperwork and explain it before you sign anything. (And this can't be just any attorney: Choose an attorney who specializes in real estate and understands foreclosure.) Con artists who are looking to steal your home with a contract often pack the contract with stipulations that make it almost impossible to comply with — they're just looking for a way to declare that you defaulted on the contract, so they can have you evicted. Evicting a tenant is a lot easier than evicting a homeowner. The con artist then can benefit in two ways — from the monthly rent she collected and from the proceeds from the sale of your home.

The alternative financing scam is usually used when the homeowners have fallen behind on tax payments on a property they own free and clear, or when the balance on the mortgage is way below the market value of the house — in other words, when the homeowners have a lot of equity in the property.

After the scammers have sucked you dry of all your equity and any savings you may have had, you have little recourse:

- ✓ **Little or no money to fight a lengthy courtroom battle.**

- ✓ **No place to live while you're trying to resolve the problem.** (You're likely evicted before you have time to stop it.)

- ✓ **Trouble locating the con artist.** Most of them work out of their cars and never meet you anywhere other than your home, a coffee shop, or some other public place. The con artist may give you a phone number, but he probably changed that number long before you figured out what was going on.

Calling an attorney after you've been evicted is often too late, but it's worth a try. The earlier you involve an attorney (preferably before you sign anything), the better chance you have of avoiding the scam altogether.

Spotting the Signs of an Overbid Scam

Even if someone else buys your home at a foreclosure sale, you may have a rightful claim to some of the proceeds from that sale, assuming the winning bid was an *overbid* — more than enough to pay off all the liens on the property. If, for example, you owe $100,000 on a $200,000 property and the high bid comes in at $150,000, that $50,000 is rightfully yours. After all, you worked hard to build that equity and should be entitled to any surplus paid at the auction.

Overbid money goes to the lien holders first. If you owed $100,000 on the first mortgage, $20,000 on a second mortgage, and $10,000 on a home equity line of credit, then you would be entitled to only $20,000 of the overbid money. The other $30,000 would be used to satisfy the other two liens.

Getting the overbid money is fairly easy. In Michigan, where we operate, you go down to the county sheriff's civil division office, show them your driver's license or photo ID, and sign a recovery form proving that you collected the overbid. They copy your ID and the signed form and issue you a check while you wait, tell you to come back in a couple days after the check has been issued, or mail it to you.

Some individuals or companies attempt to profit from overbids by selling a service to assist homeowners in claiming the overbid money. All the overbid service does is have the paperwork sent to them along with a contract that enables the service to collect the money on your behalf. They then have the check issued to them, take their cut, and send you the difference. That's hardly worth a third to a half of the overbid proceeds.

Overbid scams can take any of several forms. Here are the two most common:

✔ **The con artist convinces you to sign over the overbid money to her; in exchange, she promises that the money is going to be used to obtain a new mortgage or alternative financing to solve the problem.** The con artist then collects the money and disappears. This rendition of the scam usually occurs when the homeowners have a substantial amount of equity in the home. The end result is that the home is still in foreclosure and the homeowners lose all the equity they were entitled to — equity they could have used to put this nightmare behind them.

✔ **The second form that the overbid scam takes on is more morally than legally troubling: Some con artists charge 30 percent to 50 percent of the overbid proceeds to assist homeowners in recovering the overbid money.** That can be 30 percent to 50 percent of a good chunk of change for a couple hours of work. This just isn't right. We know of some people who perform this same service for 10 percent to 15 percent, which is more reasonable. After all, they do alert the homeowners to the existence of the overbid money and facilitate its recovery, so they deserve to earn something for providing the service, but 30 percent to 50 percent is price gouging.

After the sale, call the sheriff's office or your county's register of deeds and find out the winning bid. If the bid amount was higher than the total amount you owe on the property, obtain instructions on how to claim the overbid money yourself. Don't trust someone else to obtain it for you — you may never see a dime of it, or you may only see a small fraction of what you're entitled to. In the case of a nonjudicial sale of a trust deed, the trustee conducts the sale and is responsible for ensuring that the surplus is paid out to the rightful recipients.

Recognizing Property Tax Scams

Falling behind on your property tax payments is bad enough. Add an opportunist or a con artist to the mix, and you're about to be living in the house of pain. As soon as someone has a tax lien against your home or a tax deed, that person has a certain amount of leverage to either kick you out of your home or apply enough pressure to make you want to leave. With a little sleight of hand, in the form of a deed, the person can even steal your home right out from under you before you know what's going on.

In the following sections, we explain the basics of tax liens and deeds and reveal how a typical property tax scam goes down. Arming yourself with this knowledge is the best defense against this particular scam.

The most powerful lien on your home is a property tax lien. The government always gets its cut before it allows any other lien holders to get theirs. By paying your property taxes, you prevent opportunistic investors from obtaining a legitimate tax lien or deed. However, if you're destined to lose the home anyway, you may want to stop paying your property taxes (see Chapter 13). Save the money, instead, for when you have to move out. Whoever buys your home in foreclosure gets stuck with the bill.

The overbid rescue

We once became involved with an elderly woman who was facing foreclosure. She owed less than $80,000 on her home, which, if it were in tip-top condition, could have sold for about $210,000. At the sheriff sale, the winning bid came it at about $163,000, leaving an overbid of about $83,000.

We contacted the woman to offer our assistance and help her make an informed decision on how to proceed. We realized that the overbid amount was going to draw scammers from miles around. After speaking with her, we quickly realized that she needed our assistance. She had no money and a huge overbid, making her the perfect candidate for an overbid scam. We asked to meet with her and her adult daughter, who could assist her in making good decisions. The daughter explained that her mom was going through a bit of a rough patch and that the best thing for her would be to move and sell the house.

We made an appointment to meet the woman and her daughter over at the house, to assess the situation and see what would be needed to sell quickly (within the redemption period) and move on with money in their pockets. The other thing we explained to the daughter was that an overbid was being held for her mother down at the county courthouse. She didn't know what an overbid was, so we told her we would explain it all when we came over. The house was in need of repair, and as is the case with many foreclosures, the mother simply didn't have the money to put into the house to bring it up to market value. We estimated the value to be around $150,000 to $160,000 in its current condition. They were a little disappointed, but the daughter knew that our estimate was accurate.

We explained that not all was lost. They could still walk away with over $80,000 without even lifting a finger. Well, they would have to lift a *finger,* but that was about the extent of what would be required. We explained what an overbid is and that, because her house sold for more than the balance on the first and only mortgage, she was entitled to receive the excess amount. They were delighted and asked how to do this, how long it would take, how much it would cost, and so on. We said that it was really quite easy and we would be happy to show them how to collect their money, for no fee at all.

We asked what they were doing the rest of the afternoon and neither of them had any plans. They followed us out to the county courthouse, where we showed them exactly where to go and who to speak with. They left with $83,000 more in their pocket than when they arrived.

This is a story that ended well, but if we hadn't contacted them and if they had responded to the cash recovery company whose contract and assignment information was sitting on their kitchen counter when we met with them, they would have received up to $40,000 less than what we were able to get them — $40,000 less than they were rightfully entitled to.

If you lose your home in a foreclosure sale, don't assume that you've lost all equity in it. Call the sheriff or trustee who handled the sale and find out about the overbid rules. Are overbids allowed? Was there an overbid on your property? How do you go about collecting the overbid money? Don't believe someone who tells you that claiming your overbid money is difficult or is a huge hassle. You can collect the very same amount without having to pay anyone. It's sure worth the time and trouble it takes to make a couple phone calls.

Following the tax lien/tax deed shuffle

Each state may handle delinquent tax collections a little differently, but they basically fall into one of the following two categories:

- ✓ **Tax deed states:** In a tax deed state, if you fall far behind on your property taxes, the state transfers the title to the treasurer's name and then attempts to sell the tax deed at a public auction to recoup the amount of back taxes. When an investor buys the tax deed, the investor has the right to seek to have you evicted from the premises. You could potentially lose your home for owing a few thousand dollars in back taxes.

- ✓ **Tax lien states:** In a tax lien state, the state places a tax lien on the property and then tries to sell it at a public auction to recoup the back taxes. Although the high bidder does not receive an actual deed to the property, he does receive a lien with a substantial interest rate. If you fail to redeem the tax lien, the holder of it can eventually foreclose on your home and have you evicted. However, the process typically requires more time than it does in a tax deed state.

The counties and states are very careful to make sure that you have plenty of notice before losing your home to a tax deed or tax lien holder. In most cases, you can expect to receive notices on bright-colored paper with an ominous message, such as "YOU WILL LOSE YOUR HOUSE." They really want the notice to grab your attention.

In most jurisdictions, you have some time to redeem the tax lien by paying the buyer the amount she paid at auction plus interest (which can be pretty steep). If you find yourself in a situation in which an investor has purchased a tax lien or deed to your property, consult an attorney who specializes in foreclosure to determine your redemption rights, if any. In tax-deed states, you may have no redemption rights; when an investor buys the tax deed at auction, start packing.

Unveiling the property tax scam

The property tax scam is a variation on the theme that runs through most foreclosure scams. The only difference is that, instead of using unpaid mortgages as its fuel, it uses delinquent taxes.

When homeowners fall behind on their property tax payments, their homes find their way onto a delinquent tax list, which the scammers use to identify their targets. They approach the homeowners and offer to bail them out with a high-interest loan to cover the taxes. This, in itself, is not necessarily a bad thing (depending on the interest rate, of course). What the scammers do, however, is slip a deed in with the mortgage papers (see "Using sleight of hand with the bait and switch," earlier in this chapter). In the muddle of signing a stack of documents, you end up signing a deed, relinquishing your rights to the property.

When the scammer has a deed, she can then move forward in a few different directions — taking out a mortgage on the property, leasing the property to the rightful owners, or listing it for sale. The usual MO is to take out another mortgage on the property, collect payments from the rightful homeowners for as long as possible, and default on the new mortgage (which the scammer took out under someone else's name). The scammer walks away with tens of thousands of dollars, while the homeowner is stuck holding the bag. The homeowner then has two choices: Refinance the mortgage that he never took out or lose his home in foreclosure. Scammers sometimes take a portion of the new mortgage and actually pay off the back taxes in order to cover their tracks a little better, but not always.

Avoiding Predatory Lenders at All Costs

Freddie Mac sponsors a program called Don't Borrow Trouble (www.dont borrowtrouble.com). It's billed as an "Anti-Predatory Lending Site." So, what exactly is predatory lending? It consists of highly aggressive mortgage brokers, loan officers, and lenders who try their best to convince people to take out high-risk loans — loans that the borrowers cannot pay off or are likely to have trouble paying off.

In most cases, predatory lenders do not actually hold the mortgage themselves. As soon as possible, they sell it to another company or to investors, and wash their hands of any problems that may occur down the road. After all, after they sell the mortgage, they aren't at any risk of losing money. These lenders don't necessarily operate like boiler room stock brokers, but the devastation they leave behind can be just as real.

The loans are often in the form of sub-prime mortgages, something that has gotten a lot of press recently, starting with the mortgage meltdown in 2007. A *sub-prime mortgage* is a loan offered to people who either cannot qualify for a traditional mortgage or are teetering on the brink of not qualifying. These loans typically carry high loan origination fees and high interest rates. In many cases, the loans are adjustable rate mortgages (ARMs), which we like to call "always rising mortgages." An ARM comes with a low-interest teaser rate, which is scheduled to rise months or years later. When the interest rate jumps, what were once affordable payments are now ridiculously high, driving the hapless homeowner into foreclosure. What began as the American dream quickly becomes a nightmare. We strongly discourage you from taking out an ARM under any conditions.

Property tax scam: A case study

A few years ago, we worked with a couple who had fallen victim to a property tax scam. They had lived in the same house for many years and raised their family there. They had paid off the mortgage and owned their home free and clear. The husband was a war veteran and had some complications from his years of service. His wife was always right by his side. They needed very little income to live on and were happy to be exactly where they were in life.

They ran into problems, however, when the property taxes in their area started to rise. When they moved into the area, it was a modest neighborhood, but in their later years, it had grown in popularity, property values rose, and property taxes increased accordingly. They were now unable to make their property tax payments and had fallen a couple years behind. When we met them, they owed about $10,000.

They looked into taking out a mortgage to cover the cost of the delinquent taxes, but no one would give them a mortgage to cover such a small amount. We don't know if the scammers were aware of this, but they zeroed in on the couple and befriended them. The scammers went so far as to come over for Sunday meals, bring their children over, and make this couple surrogate grandparents — this was the lowest of the low.

The scammers convinced the homeowners to take out a loan with them to cover the back taxes and save their house. The loan was needed immediately, because of the looming deadline. The couple signed the mortgage papers and unknowingly also signed a quit claim deed to their home. The taxes were paid, and the homeowners were comfortable making the affordable payments.

What the couple didn't know was that the scammers were using their quit claim deed to secure a mortgage on the couple's home in the name of a *straw borrower* (a person who takes out a loan in name only but does not receive the proceeds from the loan). The scammers took out a loan for over $100,000 on the couple's home. What's worse, the scammers made a couple payments on the loan to try to avoid any red flags for a first couple months, but they eventually stopped making the mortgage payments and allowed the home to slip into foreclosure. The scammers, of course, were nowhere to be found at this point.

The couple was now facing foreclosure on a home that they had owned free and clear. Fortunately, we were able to help them save their home, but not before they were forced to take out a mortgage to cover what was owed on the house plus penalties and fees. The free-and-clear house now is encumbered by an almost $130,000 mortgage. Various charity groups have heard the story, and it has even made the national news. To their credit, our servicemen and -women look after their own, and a veterans group stepped up significantly to help the couple out. You can read more about the story at www.dailytribune.com/stories/072707/loc_edwards001.shtml. For more stories about real estate and mortgage fraud, visit our FlippingFrenzy.com blog.

In the following sections, we show you how to spot the signs of a predatory lender and brush up on your borrower's bill of rights, so you can avoid becoming the next victim of a mortgage meltdown.

Spotting predatory lenders

Like most con artists, predatory lenders are good at pretending that they're your friends. Unlike other lenders who are going to reject your loan application and prevent you from purchasing the home of your dreams, the predatory lender is willing to do anything and everything in his power to make your dreams come true, whether or not you can afford to pay for those dreams:

- **Fudge the numbers.** Predatory lenders may be willing to increase reported savings and income on your loan application to improve your chances of being approved for a loan.

- **Offer a silent second mortgage.** If the loan requires a down payment, the lender may be willing to provide you with another loan to cover the cost of the down payment and not report it on the loan application for the first mortgage.

- **Refinance the mortgage for more than the property is worth.** This creates a negative-equity situation that is highly risky. If you cannot make the payments, you will almost certainly lose your home, because you have no equity to save you.

- **Encourage you to borrow more than you can afford.** Don't let anyone tell you how much of a monthly payment you can afford. Do your own math. If you feel as though you're going to have trouble making the monthly payments, then don't take out the loan. It's not all about the house — it's about quality of life. Don't work yourself to death and sacrifice your family for a house.

- **Offer you a low-interest introductory rate.** An ARM often ends up costing you an arm and a leg. Don't let a loan officer lure you into a risky loan with a low rate that is destined to rise astronomically in a few months or a year or two down the road.

Knowing your borrower's bill of rights

The concept of a "borrower's bill of rights" seems almost comical to us, not because we believe that borrowers should not have rights, but because what used to be plain old common sense now requires legislation to define. Our parents and grandparents never needed a borrower's bill of rights, because they didn't borrow more than they could afford to pay back, and because no bank in its right mind would place borrowers in high-risk loans.

Be that as it may, Michigan and other state legislatures include a borrower's bill of rights as part of their consumer protection policies. In Michigan, for example, whenever someone applies for a loan, the lender is supposed to

Predatory lending: A case study

Many people believe that homeowners have to take responsibility for their own financial health and well-being. Although that is true to a certain extent, lenders should also act responsibly. Unfortunately, greed drives many lenders to encourage homeowners to borrow much more than they can afford to pay and to take out risky, high-cost loans — loans with high fees, hidden fees, and high interest rates.

As more and more mortgage companies develop and roll out new qualification programs, more and more people who perhaps only months ago were unqualified for mortgage loans suddenly become qualified. A renter, who for years has been saving his money for a down payment in order to qualify for a mortgage, suddenly no longer needs that down payment, or at least not a 20 percent down payment. The renter hears of a program that's advertised whereby he can qualify for a mortgage. He contacts the mortgage company and applies. The mortgage company informs him that he not only qualifies, but qualifies under a new program that allows him to purchase much more house than he ever thought possible. The lender plays up the positives of the program and explains that he qualifies for a sub-prime interest rate, but the rate may adjust up every six months if

interest rates go up. If he's lucky, interest rates will sink and his payments will decrease.

All the borrower hears is that he qualifies for a $250,000 loan at 4.75 percent. What he doesn't hear is that the rate is scheduled to rise by 3 percent a year later, plus any percentage increase in the prime interest rate. In some cases, these loans don't even have a cap on how high the rate can rise.

Sure, the borrower should have read all the fine print and done the math to figure out for himself exactly how this loan would apply to his particular situation, but he was probably thinking that the lender would never actually approve a loan that was that risky. Unfortunately, this assumption is wrong. The loan officer isn't the one taking the risk. If the loan officer's money were at stake, the person would never have approved the loan. All the loan officer wants to do is get the loan approved, collect her fee or commission, and move on to the next victim.

If you have a lender who doesn't take the time to explain the process and all the pros and cons of what you're getting into, be careful. Work with someone who takes the time to explain the process and the paperwork and assists you in doing the math and comparing the numbers.

supply the applicant with a copy of the ten borrower's rights. Following is a summary of these rights:

- The borrower has the right to shop for the best loan and to comparison-shop.
- The borrower has the right to know the total cost of his loan, including interest rate and points.
- The borrower has the right to a good-faith estimate of charges.
- The borrower has the right to know of any nonrefundable charges, in the event that he decides not to actually place the loan with that lender.

- The borrower has the right to an explanation from the mortgage broker on what the broker is going to do for the borrower.

- The borrower has the right to know how much the broker is getting paid, including how much the borrower is paying and how much the lender is paying for the broker to place the loan.

- The borrower has the right to ask questions about terms and fees that he doesn't understand.

- The borrower has the right to a credit decision that isn't based on race, gender, and so on.

- The borrower has the right to know why his loan application was rejected (assuming it is rejected).

- The borrower has the right to receive the U.S. Department of Housing and Urban Development (HUD) settlement costs booklet *Buying Your Home*.

Some other items on the borrower's bill of rights include the right not to be subject to deceptive marketing tactics, the right to obtain credit counseling, the right to have favorable information reported to credit bureaus, the right not to be subject to bait-and-switch lowball rates, the right to adequate customer service before and after the closing, and the right not to have any surprises at the closing table.

When you apply for a loan, ask your mortgage broker what to expect. Often, when you apply, you don't know who your lender is going to be. Your mortgage broker packages your loan application and may send it off to several lenders for approval. Be proactive in protecting yourself. If you don't understand something, ask questions. If you're dissatisfied with the answer, ask someone else to explain it to you. Whatever you do, don't allow yourself to be set up for failure because you didn't evaluate the whole situation. According to the Truth In Lending Act, lenders are required by law to fully inform you of the costs and terms of your loan.

Protecting Yourself: Do's and Don'ts

With all the scams out there and the infinite number of variations on these scams, remaining on the lookout for everything that can possibly go wrong is nearly impossible. However, by following a few standard practices, you can avoid the most common and serious cons.

In the following sections, we explain the do's and don'ts and try to steer you clear of trouble.

Do take your time

Patience is a virtue, but it can also be a great defense against con artists. One strategy that con artists often employ is to rush you through the decision-making process. They may present you with only one or two options, even though you have a half-dozen options you could consider, and then try to make you believe that you have to make a decision immediately.

Give yourself more time by taking the initiative early in the process. The foreclosure clock is certainly ticking, so you don't have all the time in the world, but the sooner you begin exploring your options, the more time you have to make better decisions.

Do document everything

Document everything related to your foreclosure, especially any communication you have with your lender (see Chapter 3). Don't forget to document everything else as well, including conversations you have with people who show up to "help" you. If someone shows up at your house, write down the make and model of his car and even his license plate number, if possible. Have a list of questions prepared before he arrives and jot down the person's answers to those questions.

Consider setting a small tape recorder in the center of the table where you hold your meeting. Explain to the person that you would like to record the conversation for future reference. This may not be enough to send all con artists packing, but we would wager that most of them would refuse to be recorded, in which case, you can politely ask them to leave. We have a policy of taping conversations with our foreclosure clients — for their protection as well as ours.

Do read paperwork thoroughly

You've participated in at least one closing (when you purchased your current home), so you know the routine — a closing agent passes around a stack of papers, briefly describes each document, and instructs you to sign on the dotted line.

If you're like most people, you don't read a single word of those documents. It's too much of a hassle, and you trust the person who's passing the papers around. Besides, if you really did read those documents, the closing would take half the day, and everyone in the room would want to kill you about two hours into it.

Those are poor excuses for not reading and understanding documents before you sign them. If you're concerned about the time, request the documents a day or two prior to the time you're required to sign them, and then read the documents and make a list of questions before your meeting. If you're required to sign several copies of the same documents, compare them side-by-side to make sure that all copies are identical. This protects you in the event that someone slips a deed into one of the copies.

If you're going to seek legal representation, involve your attorney *before* you sign any documents. Waiting until after you sign the documents may be too late.

Don't sign anything you don't understand

You don't have to understand all the intricacies of the legalese, but you do need to know what each paragraph or clause means and how it can impact you both legally and financially. Ask yourself the following questions about every paragraph or clause:

- ✔ What does it mean?
- ✔ How does this stand to benefit or harm you?
- ✔ What triggers the clause to take effect?

Say, for example, that you don't understand what a "joint and several liability for co-signers–successors" clause does. The clause talks about persons who sign the note as being different from those who sign the mortgage, "individual liability," and "joint and several liability." You've read it, and it still makes absolutely no sense. What do you do? Ask — and keep asking until you get it.

Don't sign something obligating yourself to its terms without knowing what duties and liabilities you're responsible for. You don't need to feel embarrassed, and certainly don't let anyone make you feel as though you're being an imposition. The people asking you to sign the documents may not be representing you, but they should take the time to explain the documents they require you sign.

Don't sign over power of attorney without a full understanding

Power of attorney (POA) is a document that gives someone else the right to make decisions or act on your behalf . . . not that there's anything wrong with that. In some cases, POA is very helpful; for example, when a parent is too ill

---

So what is joint and several liability?

Joint and several liability, by the way, means that the bank can try to collect from both signers of the note, or only one of them — it's their choice. It's sort of a "one for all and all for one" thing; the bank can sue all parties "jointly" or individual parties "severally."

It's a pretty standard clause and doesn't affect the deal much at all, unless of course you're a parent acting as a co-signer for one of your offspring on his first home loan. In such a case,

you may want to rethink the joint and several liability, because your personal assets may be in jeopardy if junior defaults on the loan.

That's the meaning of *joint and several liability* explained in a nut shell, and if we can explain it, anyone asking you to sign a document should be able to explain other terms mentioned in their documents in much the same way. Don't trust anyone who can't or simply brushes it off as "unimportant."

---

to attend to his own legal matters or pay his own bills. In the wrong hands, however, a POA can give the recipient the power to do some real damage.

POAs generally come in two flavors: an unlimited, durable POA, and a limited (or specific) POA. In the following sections, we explain both types.

In almost all cases, we recommend that you not sign over power of attorney to a business or individual who's assisting you. All that person will be doing is signing paperwork on your behalf, and this is paperwork that you should read and understand yourself before signing. You may want to give POA to a trusted family member if you can't be somewhere to sign the papers, but you should read the documents yourself beforehand and, if at all possible, sign them yourself.

Unlimited, durable power of attorney

An unlimited, durable power of attorney assigns the grantee unlimited power to make decisions and take action on your behalf. The grantee can execute deeds, mortgages, bills of sale, and so on. The term *durable* means that the grantee holds this power and will continue to hold it even in the event that the grantor becomes incapacitated. This is the broadest grant of power and authority, allowing the grantee to do just about anything. Figure 9-1 shows a sample unlimited, durable power of attorney document.

The opening clause in the POA specifically states that the grantee is supposed to act in a "fiduciary capacity." This basically means that the person is supposed to treat your money better than she treats her own money. Conveniently, con artists take this to mean that they can treat themselves to your money.

Power of Attorney

Powers of Agent. I grant to Agent full power and authority to deal with my estate, property, and affairs as fully as I might or could do if personally present. All powers shall be exercised in a fiduciary capacity in my best interests and for my welfare. The following specifically enumerated powers are intended to amplify, rather than to limit or restrict, the general power of attorney granted here:

a. to buy, sell, mortgage, or otherwise deal in any way in any real or personal property, or any interest in the property, on whatever terms Agent shall think proper, including the power to buy United States Treasury Bonds that may be redeemed at par for the payment of federal estate tax;

b. to collect, hold, maintain, improve, invest, lease, or otherwise manage all of my real or personal property or any interest in the property;

c. to transact every kind of business of any kind;

d. to deposit and withdraw (by checks or withdrawal slips) in or from any banking institution, any funds, negotiable paper, or moneys that may come into Agent's hands as Agent or that I now or later may have on deposit or be entitled to;

e. to exercise any incidents of ownership I may possess with respect to policies of insurance except policies insuring the life of Agent;

f. to make application to any governmental agency for any benefit or government obligation to which I may be entitled;

g. to engage in any administrative or legal proceedings or in any litigation in connection with the premises;

h. to act as my Agent or proxy in respect to any stocks, bonds, shares, or other investments, rights, or interests I may now or later hold, including the power to redeem, transfer, or convert United States Savings Bonds;

i. to engage and dismiss agents, counsel, and employees, and to appoint and remove at pleasure any substitute for Agent, in respect to all or any of the matters or things mentioned in this document and on whatever terms Agent shall think fit;

j. to prepare, execute, and file income and other tax returns, and other governmental reports and documents;

k. to transfer any interest I may have in property, real or personal, to the trustees of any trust created by me for my benefit, specifically including the power to assign, endorse, and transfer any stocks, bonds, options, or other securities of any nature at any time standing in my name and to execute any documents to effectuate the foregoing;

l. to have access to my safety deposit box or boxes.

Restrictions on Agent's powers

Notwithstanding the foregoing, Agent

a. cannot execute a will, a codicil, or any will substitute on my behalf, or change the beneficiary on any life insurance policy that I own;

b. cannot make gifts on my behalf.

Durability. This durable power of attorney shall not be affected by my disability except as provided by statute.

Figure 9-1:
An unlimited, durable power of attorney gives the grantee the power to do just about anything on your behalf.

Limited power of attorney

A limited (or specific) POA typically restricts the person's power to a specific transaction. This allows the grantee to handle the transaction as if the grantor were doing it herself, but it doesn't give the grantee the power to do anything else except what is specifically listed.

Limited POA is often used in real estate transactions for a particular parcel of land, as shown in Figure 9-2. It may grant POA to the spouse, for example, who can sign on behalf of the couple. After the transaction is completed, the power is usually revoked or expires within a relatively short period of time.

Figure 9-2:
Limited power of attorney significantly restricts the grantee's powers.

Power of Attorney

I, **[name of person granting power of attorney]** of **[address]** appoint **[name of attorney]** of **[address]** as my true and lawful attorney (Attorney) for me in my own name, place, and stead, giving and granting to my Attorney full power and authority to perform all rights and things requisite and necessary to complete any negotiations and agreements pursuant to a purchase agreement entered into by me dated [date of purchase agreement], for the sale of the real property located in **[village/city/township]**, **[county]**, described as

[insert legal description, tax identification number, and address]

(Premises) and to convey all of my right, title, and interest in the Premises.

Part III

Digging Your Way out of the Foreclosure Pit

The 5th Wave   By Rich Tennant

MORTGAGE LOAN OFFICER

"In lieu of foreclosure, I thought we could work something out. How about reducing my payments by 50%, and I'll promise to live in only half of the house?"

In this part . . .

When you're facing foreclosure, you may feel as though you've fallen into a pit that gets deeper and deeper the harder you try to climb out of it. Keep in mind, however, that you have several options at your disposal — several tools that you can use to climb out of that pit and perhaps even save your home.

In this part, we explore the many foreclosure options and lead you through the process of how to take full advantage of them. You discover how to haggle with your lender before the foreclosure sale, refinance your way out of foreclosure, get out from under your house by selling it or giving it away, buy yourself some additional time by filing for bankruptcy, do nothing (and see where that gets you), and recover after the foreclosure is behind you.

Chapter 10

Beating the Foreclosure Rap with Bankruptcy

In This Chapter

▶ Brushing up on bankruptcy basics

▶ Checking out the different chapters of bankruptcy

▶ Restructuring your debt under Chapter 13 bankruptcy

▶ Protecting your equity and assets under Chapter 7 bankruptcy

▶ Finding out what Chapter 20 bankruptcy is all about

*P*eople we talk with often have a skewed view of what bankruptcy is all about. They envision getting up to their eyeballs in debt and then filing for bankruptcy to make all that debt magically disappear. They seem to think that a bankruptcy angel is waiting in the wings to deliver them from the evil bill collectors. Other people have the mistaken notion that bankruptcy is a fail-safe way to save their home. Maybe they'll lose everything else, but at least they get to keep their home and won't have to make any more payments.

Although bankruptcy isn't quite the magic pill many people assume it to be, it may be one of your best options. If you've fallen behind in your mortgage and you're now able to afford payments, filing Chapter 13 bankruptcy could actually be the most cost-effective way to solve your problem. Attorney fees should be in the $3,000 range, but you could keep your house and eliminate all (or a significant portion of) your unsecured debts (such as credit card debts) as well.

Bankruptcy would also stop the foreclosure long enough for you (in a Chapter 13 bankruptcy) or a trustee (in a Chapter 7 bankruptcy) to sell your property, pay off the mortgages, pay yourself your homestead exemption (more about this later), and leave a few remaining crumbs to your other creditors. Even after paying your attorney fees, you may have some cash (from your homestead exemption), no debts, and a credit record that's fairly clean.

In this chapter, we bring you up to speed on bankruptcy basics, lead you through the process of choosing which chapter of bankruptcy is best for your situation, and reveal the steps to take to file for bankruptcy.

Now for our shameless disclaimer: We are not attorneys, nor do we pretend to be. Filing for bankruptcy and dealing with the courts and with bankruptcy trustees is a very complicated process that requires the skills of a highly qualified bankruptcy attorney. We strongly urge you to seek competent legal assistance (see Chapter 4). Our intent in this chapter is to introduce you to the bankruptcy option and provide some basic guidance to prepare you to team up more effectively with your attorney.

Grasping the Purpose of Bankruptcy

As the old saying goes, "You can't get blood out of a turnip." You also can't collect money from people who are unable to pay their bills. That's why we have bankruptcy and bankruptcy court.

When John and Jane Doe can't repay their debts, bankruptcy provides a more civilized way of dealing with the problem than sending Guido over to the couple's house to rough them up. With your attorney's assistance, you can size up your debts and assets and present a solution to pay off as much debt as possible, either by liquidating assets or paying off the debts over time. These solutions typically involve one or more of the following:

- Forgiving all or some of the debt
- Selling off some or all of the debtor's assets to pay all or a portion of the debt
- Setting up payment plans to pay off any remaining debt

The purpose of bankruptcy is to give people who experience serious financial setbacks a second chance. People generally want to repay their debts, but certain life-changing events can prevent that from happening. Instead of throwing people who experience financial setbacks into debtor's prison, the government has set up courts that allow individuals to put their financial crises behind them and get on with their lives.

Although bankruptcy laws are complicated, bankruptcy generally falls into one of two categories:

- **Bankruptcy to reorganize:** You can claim bankruptcy to reorganize your debt (and possibly have some portion of the debt forgiven) so you can repay some or all of the debt.

✔ **Bankruptcy to liquidate:** You can choose a liquidation in which a trustee can *liquidate* (sell off) nonexempt assets and use the proceeds to repay as much of the debt as possible, with any remaining balances being wiped out.

Gaining temporary relief from an automatic stay

As soon as you file a bankruptcy petition, the petition triggers an *automatic stay.* It's like pressing the Pause button on your DVD player. It stops the bill collectors and the repo men in their tracks and gives you some time to catch your breath and pursue other options. Technically speaking, the stay prevents all your creditors from:

✔ Hounding you to pay

✔ Repossessing your property

✔ Attempting to enforce a lien against your property

✔ Initiating or continuing any judicial proceedings against you

Foreclosure is subject to the automatic stay because it is a judicial proceeding against you, an attempt to enforce a lien against your property, or an attempt to repossess your property. Filing a bankruptcy petition stops the foreclosure in its tracks.

Being prepared to have the stay lifted

Just because you can file a bankruptcy petition and obtain an automatic stay does not mean that your creditor is without rights. Upon being notified of the automatic stay, a creditor, particularly a foreclosing bank, may immediately head to court in an attempt to have the stay lifted (known as *relief from the stay*) for any of the following reasons:

✔ **Lack of adequate protection:** The property is losing value and if the foreclosure is delayed any longer, the creditor's stake in the property is at risk.

✔ **Lack of equity in the property:** In other words, even if the debtor sold the property, he wouldn't get any money out of it to assist him in repaying his debts.

✔ **You filed a prior bankruptcy that was dismissed within the year preceding your present bankruptcy.** You can't just keep filing for bankruptcy. If you have a partner, however, your partner may be able to file separately from you. Consult your bankruptcy attorney to determine the best option.

✔ **Single-asset real estate bankruptcy:** This situation applies to real estate that generates substantial income for the debtor and is really beyond the scope of the book, so pretend you never heard about it.

Okay, so that sounded like a lot of legal mumbo jumbo, so what does all of this really mean? It means that the bank may be granted relief from the stay and may be able to proceed with the foreclosure, regardless of the fact that you filed for bankruptcy. However, if you have equity in your home and a realistic plan for catching up on back payments or selling the home to satisfy the debt, the court is probably going to reject any request from your lender to have the stay lifted.

In 2005, Congress passed the Bankruptcy Abuse Prevention and Consumer Protection Act (BAPCPA), which is basically a series of amendments to the federal bankruptcy laws that make it more difficult for a person to dodge his debt through bankruptcy. Two of the more relevant amendments affecting the automatic stay include the following:

✔ **The debtor may be denied protection via the automatic stay if the debtor filed for bankruptcy with an attempt or as part of a scheme to "delay, hinder, and defraud creditors."** This amendment is designed to prevent debtors from selling or transferring ownership of their property before filing for bankruptcy, in an attempt to avoid the creditor's lien without the creditor's consent or the court's approval.

✔ **The debtor may be denied protection via the automatic stay if the debtor attempts to "hinder or delay" the process by filing multiple bankruptcy petitions in succession.** You can't delay the foreclosure forever by simply filing for bankruptcy every time the stay is lifted.

These changes in the bankruptcy code were enacted in an attempt to prevent debtors from abusing the bankruptcy system. The court does not deny a debtor relief if the debtor is genuinely seeking the protection of the bankruptcy courts, but you should consult with a bankruptcy attorney before you file a bankruptcy petition, so that your relief from creditors is not trumped by the creditors' relief from your automatic stay.

Flipping to the Chapter That Works Best for You

Bankruptcy court is a federal court governed by a complex set of statutes known as the *Bankruptcy Code,* established by the U.S. Congress. This all boils down to the fact that the average citizen can't make heads or tails of it. If you want to try, we recommend that you check out a book that's devoted to this topic: *Personal Bankruptcy Laws For Dummies,* 2nd Edition, penned by James P. Caher and John M. Caher (Wiley). In addition to bringing you up to speed on the complexities of the Bankruptcy Code, this book lays out your options and provides valuable advice on how to choose and work with a bankruptcy attorney.

As explained in *Bankruptcy Laws For Dummies,* 2nd Edition, you can file for different *chapters* of bankruptcy — seven in all (six plus another one that's a combo deal):

- **Chapter 7:** Liquidation for individuals and businesses.
- **Chapter 9:** Municipal bankruptcy, which you can safely ignore for now.
- **Chapter 11:** Reorganization of debt, primarily by businesses but sometimes useful for individuals who have plenty of assets.
- **Chapter 12:** Restructuring of debt for family farmers and fishermen, which we do not cover in this book.
- **Chapter 13:** Restructuring of debt with a payment plan for individuals who have a steady income.
- **Chapter 15:** Ancillary and international bankruptcy, which we also choose to ignore, because these are such special cases.
- **Chapter 20:** This is the combo deal — a combination of Chapter 7 and Chapter 13.

In the following sections, we describe the two most common types of bankruptcy — Chapter 7 and Chapter 13 bankruptcy in greater detail, to assist you in choosing the type of bankruptcy that's right for your situation.

Liquidating with Chapter 7 bankruptcy

In Chapter 7 bankruptcy, you cash out your chips, quickly wipe out most or all of your debts, and then walk away from the table, either empty-handed or with a little cash in your pockets. In 90 percent of Chapter 7 bankruptcies, debtors get to keep all their property, because it is protected by exemptions.

All creditors are not created equal

Not all creditors have the same rights and powers to shake you down for repayment. Creditors typically fall into one of the following three categories:

- **Secured:** A secured creditor is one that issues loans that are protected by collateral. Your car loan, for example, is secured by the car; if you don't make your payments, the creditor can legally repossess your car. Likewise, your mortgage loan is secured by your home, as explained in Chapter 5.

- **Unsecured:** An unsecured creditor is one that issues loans that are *not* protected by collateral. Unsecured creditors, such as credit card companies, stand to lose the most in bankruptcy, which is one of the reasons they charge so much interest.

- **Priority:** Priority creditors are a special class that fits between the secured and unsecured creditors. These folks may consist of taxing authorities and recipients of child support. They generally have priority over unsecured creditors.

Although this information may seem unimportant at first glance, it is very important in determining who has the right to collect from you and who doesn't. Your bankruptcy attorney can assist you in using this information to draw up a strategy for paying off the creditors whom you are required to pay.

Understanding the process

The process begins when the United States Trustee appoints a trustee. The trustee collects your *nonexempt assets* (any possessions that you have to turn over to the courts, by law). The trustee then liquidates the assets and distributes the proceeds to your creditors. At the end of the process, you generally owe nothing. Better yet, you get to keep a good deal of your stuff, including a chunk of the equity in your home that's protected by the homestead exemption and virtually all of your retirement savings. This can represent hundreds of thousands of dollars in some cases.

Exempt assets vary from state to state. Your attorney can explain exactly what is and is not exempt in your state.

The trustee determines how much the asset (your home, for example) is probably worth, subtracts the statutory exemption amount, subtracts any liens that cannot be voided by the bankruptcy (such as a mortgage), and figures out how much cash would be left over, if any. If selling the asset would generate cash after *administration costs* (closing costs, sales costs, paying the trustee, and so on), then the trustee is likely to sell the asset and use the proceeds to pay something to creditors. The trustee also pays you any exempt amounts due to you under the law.

If the trustee determines that the asset isn't worth selling, she may abandon the asset, meaning you keep it, subject to any secured liens against it, such as a mortgage on a house or a loan in which the car has been put up as collateral.

After the court discharges the Chapter 7 and lifts the stay, these creditors can then pursue state court actions to recover the asset if you default on the loan.

If you try to sell your home while the bankruptcy is in progress, any purchase agreements you receive are subject to the trustee's approval. You can't simply sell your home and keep the money.

Determining whether Chapter 7 bankruptcy is right for you

Your attorney can assist you in assessing your situation and choosing the best option, but here are a few conditions that may make you a perfect candidate for Chapter 7 bankruptcy:

- ✔ **You do not have a steady stream of income.** If you do have a steady flow of income, you may be required to reorganize your debt under Chapter 13.

- ✔ **You can accept the fact that you aren't going to be repaying your debt.** Most people feel personally responsible for repaying their debts, and cannot live with the fact that under Chapter 7 bankruptcy, most creditors will get nothing.

- ✔ **You don't care about keeping your home.** In fact, you would prefer selling it, cashing out any exempt equity you may have in it, and getting on with your life.

- ✔ **You have few or no valuable assets.** If you have plenty of valuable assets, you would probably do better by selling them yourself.

A trustee can determine, after examining your financial records, that you have a *no-asset case* (that is, the value of your nonexempt assets is not worth pursuing). In such a case, you get to keep all your assets. According to some estimates, 90 percent of all Chapter 7 bankruptcies end up as no-asset cases.

Reorganizing your debt under Chapter 13 bankruptcy

In Chapter 13 bankruptcy (often referred to as *reorganization bankruptcy*), you get to keep your stuff. The only problem is that you have to keep making payments on the loans you used to purchase that stuff.

Understanding the process

To take advantage of Chapter 13 bankruptcy, you have to submit to the court complete financial records, showing your income, assets, and monthly expenses along with a repayment plan. Your repayment plan must demonstrate how you're going to make full or partial payments to your creditors over the course of a three- to five-year repayment period.

Assuming the court approves your plan, you're required to make the regularly scheduled payments. If you hold up your end of the bargain, the matter is resolved at the conclusion of the repayment period. If you fail to make payments, the court may dismiss the bankruptcy, and your creditors can, once again, attempt to collect on the debts. What typically happens is the debtor makes up the missed payments over time and continues to make payments as required by the mortgage.

Spend some time with your bankruptcy attorney to review all your financial information and make sure the information is accurate and complete. Your bankruptcy plan needs to be realistic and doable, so be honest.

Determining whether Chapter 13 bankruptcy is right for you

Is Chapter 13 bankruptcy the way to go? Here are a few conditions that may make you a perfect candidate for Chapter 13 bankruptcy:

- ✔ **You have a steady source of income.** You won't even qualify for Chapter 13 unless you have a steady source of income that's sufficient to cover your current living expenses, plus make some sort of monthly payments on your outstanding debt.

- ✔ **You want to keep your stuff.** If you have a strong emotional connection to your home and other assets and you're committed to retaining possession of them, then Chapter 13 may be the best option. It may also be a good option if you have plenty of valuable assets and stand to lose a lot of money by having a trustee liquidate them.

- ✔ **You feel obligated to repay some portion of your debt.** Chapter 13 bankruptcy is often appealing to people who feel responsible for repaying their debt and don't simply want to have that debt erased under Chapter 7.

- ✔ **You want to keep making payments on your debt.** Although the court may not require you to repay the debt in full, you can expect to be making at least partial payments. If you want to do this, Chapter 13 may be the best option. If you can't, or would prefer not to, pay off these debts, Chapter 7 may be the better choice.

Combining your options under Chapter 20

Some bankruptcy attorneys employ the so-called "Chapter 20" bankruptcy by filing Chapter 7 bankruptcy to discharge a portion of the debt, and then filing Chapter 13 bankruptcy to reorganize any debt that Chapter 7 bankruptcy did not erase. This allows the debtor to avoid repaying a good chunk of debt, and then prevents remaining creditors from enforcing their rights to collect the full amount of secured loans, such as mortgages.

A Chapter 13 case study

Chapter 13 bankruptcy allows you to catch up on missed or late payments and keep your home and all the equity in it. To demonstrate exactly why Chapter 13 bankruptcy may be preferable when you have plenty of equity in your home, consider the following case:

✔ The debtor has a house that is valued at $150,000.

✔ The existing mortgage is $100,000 (which means the debtor has $50,000 in equity).

✔ The debtor resides in a state where only $30,000 of a home's equity is exempt.

✔ The bank is foreclosing on the mortgage.

The debtor has $50,000 in equity in his house. If the debtor were to file Chapter 7 bankruptcy, the homestead exemption would allow him to keep $30,000 of the $50,000 in equity. The trustee could then take the remaining $20,000 in equity to repay debt to the creditors. The trustee would liquidate the house, pay the bank the $100,000 balance owed on the mortgage, pay the debtor his $30,000 homestead exemption, pay herself for her efforts, and distribute the rest to creditors based on priority.

By filing for Chapter 13 bankruptcy, the scenario would change considerably. The property is not sold, so the bank is forced to allow repayment as defined in the bankruptcy plan. The debtor keeps all $50,000 in equity, as long as he completes the repayment plan successfully. But any repayment plan must address this $20,000 in nonexempt equity. To be approved by the court, any Chapter 13 plan must provide that, over the course of the plan, creditors must receive as much as they would have received if the debtor had filed Chapter 7 instead of Chapter 13. This is known as the *best interest of creditors test*. If a debtor had, hypothetically speaking, filed Chapter 7, the trustee would sell the property, pay off the mortgage as well as a real estate sales commission of about $9,000, leaving about $11,000 for creditors. So, to gain court approval, any Chapter 13 plan would need to provide for payment of $11,000 plus the total of any missed mortgage payments.

For example, say the debtor is three months behind on a $3,000 monthly payment — that's $9,000 total (in addition to owing a considerable amount of money on other debts). In Chapter 13, the bankruptcy court may allow the debtor to catch up on the back payments with regular payments to the trustee, after which time, the monthly payment would go back to being $3,000. Think of it as a forbearance agreement that's handled through the courts where most of your other debts can be eliminated.

The BAPCPA of 2005 attempts to curb bankruptcy abuse, including this clever strategy. The BAPCPA prevents you from obtaining discharge under Chapter 13 if you already received a discharge under Chapter 7, Chapter 11, or Chapter 12 in the past four years. However, you won't need a second discharge of debt under Chapter 13, because you'll be paying any debts remaining after Chapter 7 in full. Another restriction makes you ineligible for a Chapter 13 discharge if you already received relief in another Chapter 13 case in the past two years.

Obtaining a discharge is a big deal. In Chapter 13, if you hold up your end of the agreement, you receive a discharge, which allows you to continue making your regular payments as you did before filing for bankruptcy. If you don't receive a discharge, then the creditors are free to pursue additional remedies available to them under the law. If you don't receive a discharge under Chapter 7, you lose any nonexempt property and still have to repay any outstanding debts.

Playing the Bankruptcy Card

If you're convinced that bankruptcy is the best option for you, then contact a qualified bankruptcy attorney who can file the necessary paperwork on your behalf and keep you informed about what you're required to do to uphold your end of the bargain. If you're disorganized or undisciplined, don't expect to breeze through bankruptcy. You're obligated by the court to provide periodic information and timely payments. This is another reason to make sure the attorney who represents you is very thorough and experienced.

In the following sections, we describe the paperwork you need to file and then go on to explain the general requirements for living up to the bankruptcy judgment.

Gathering financial records

Prior to meeting with your bankruptcy attorney, gather important financial records, including the following:

- Outstanding bills
- Recent bank statements
- Paycheck stubs for the past six months
- Documents showing any other income you received over the past six months, including bonuses
- A copy of your mortgage
- A copy of your car loans
- Information about any other debts you may have
- A complete list of assets — anything of value
- A copy of your most recent federal income tax return
- Anything else your attorney tells you to bring in

When filing for bankruptcy, provide complete and accurate information. If the court learns of any assets, income, or debts that you failed to report, it could dismiss your petition or even find you guilty of perjury, resulting in fines and possible jail time. Don't try to hide information.

Meeting with your attorney

Your attorney is likely to discuss your secured and unsecured debts and exempt and nonexempt assets with you, to determine which assets the creditors are entitled to collect on in the bankruptcy.

Ask your attorney which debts the bankruptcy is going to erase and which ones you're still responsible for paying after bankruptcy. Some debts are especially difficult to dodge, including unpaid taxes, student loans, and child support. Be well aware of the financial position bankruptcy is going to leave you in before filing, so you can decide for yourself whether filing the petition is worth it.

A good bankruptcy attorney should explore with you all your options, not just bankruptcy.

Filing a certificate of credit briefing

The BAPCPA of 2005 requires a debtor to file a *certificate of credit briefing* or a *certificate of exigent circumstances* prior to filing a bankruptcy petition:

- ✔ **Certificate of credit briefing:** Within 180 days prior to filing a bankruptcy petition, you must obtain a credit briefing from a certified credit counseling agency, which is supposed to assist you in making an informed choice on filing for bankruptcy. You can find a list of government-approved credit counseling agencies at www.usdoj.gov/ust/eo/bapcpa/ccde/cc_approved.htm. You can usually obtain your credit briefing over the phone or via the Internet.

- ✔ **Certificate of exigent circumstances:** If you're unable to obtain a credit briefing prior to filing a bankruptcy petition, you must file a certificate of exigent circumstances explaining why. The word *exigent* means "critical" or demanding immediate attention — a circumstance that is probably demanding all your time and energy. Courts disagree on what qualifies as an *exigent circumstance.* For example, most would say that if you have to file bankruptcy to stop a foreclosure sale and you try but are unable to obtain counseling before bankruptcy, you could satisfy the requirement by getting counseling with 30 days after filing. Note that there are two kinds of waivers for obtaining credit counseling: temporary (due to exigent circumstances) and permanent (due to mental or physical disability or military service).

If you and your attorney decide that bankruptcy is the way to go, obtain credit counseling right away. Your attorney should be able to direct you to a reputable counselor who can provide low-hassle credit counseling.

You can usually obtain credit counseling over the phone or on the Internet within a couple of days, so courts are reluctant to grant waivers. Also, very few courts will grant a waiver if you did not at least try to get counseling prior to filing for bankruptcy. Don't take the chance. Just do it.

If you try for an exemption and don't get one, the court will dismiss your case. If you then file a second case within a year, the automatic stay will last for only 30 days, unless you can persuade the court to extend it.

A few courts have ruled that credit counseling on the same day that the bankruptcy is filed is no good. So, waiting at least one day to file after receiving counseling is probably safer.

Passing the means test

The *means test* is the bankruptcy court's way of determining whether you qualify for Chapter 7 bankruptcy or must file for Chapter 13 bankruptcy. The latest provisions in the Bankruptcy Code are designed to prevent abuse of the system. Congress didn't want people to walk away scot-free if they could afford to pay a portion of their bills. The means test is supposed to determine whether you can afford to pay off some of your debts and, therefore, should be in Chapter 13 rather than Chapter 7.

People who earn less than the median income for their states do not have to take the means test. Those earning more than the median income must take the means test, but most people will be able to pass it and qualify for bankruptcy. Aside from the means test, a court still could rule that someone is ineligible for Chapter 7 if her budget showed that she had significant income left over after paying all expenses.

The means test is truly mind-boggling. Fortunately, bankruptcy attorneys have computer programs to perform the calculations. All you have to do is provide your bankruptcy attorney with the amount of your income and the amounts due on your debts.

Filing your bankruptcy petition

Filing the bankruptcy petition is almost anticlimactic at this point. Your attorney is going to fill out the paperwork based on the financial information you provided and file it in court.

Your job is to verify all the information contained in the bankruptcy petition (prior to the filing) and sign copies of the petition in numerous places. After you've signed the petition, your attorney can file it with the bankruptcy court that oversees your jurisdiction.

The court then sends a notice of commencement to each creditor listed on the petition. This lets the creditors know that you've filed for bankruptcy and that the automatic stay is in effect.

As soon as your attorney files your bankruptcy petition, obtain the case number and the date on which the petition was filed. If a creditor calls you to collect on a debt, simply let the creditor know that you've filed for bankruptcy and provide the creditor with the case number and date. The court may take a while to send out the notice of commencement, so this strategy keeps the creditors off your back until they receive official notice.

Fulfilling the post-petition, pre-discharge debtor education requirement

Congress does not want you to repeat the same actions that landed you in court in the first place, so according to the BAPCPA of 2005, prior to issuing a discharge of debt at the end of the bankruptcy, the court requires you to obtain debtor education. In other words, you have to take a course on how to budget your money and steer clear of future financial pitfalls.

The program is not that difficult and can equip you with the skills you need going forward. Whether these programs are effective, we can't say — but you are required to take such a program in order to receive your discharge.

Shielding Your Equity Under Chapter 7

When you liquidate assets under Chapter 7 bankruptcy and "cash out your chips," as explained earlier in this chapter, you stand to lose a lot of your stuff and any equity you have built up in it. Your goal, with the assistance of a competent bankruptcy attorney, is to shield as much of that equity to keep the prying fingers of the trustee away from it.

We're not advising you to lie or withhold information on your bankruptcy petition, but we do advise you to make the most of the bankruptcy code. Compare it to the process of filing taxes. A good tax accountant can show you how to shelter your investments and make the most of tax deductions and exemptions that you're entitled to under the law. In the same way, a good bankruptcy attorney can assist you in taking advantage of asset exemptions and making sure that expenses in liquidating your assets (such as commissions paid to a real estate agent) are accounted for.

In the following sections, we reveal how your equity may be protected in Chapter 7 bankruptcy and how you may be able to legally protect equity by having it classified as exempt.

Calculating your equity in the house

When dealing with equity, start by calculating the current equity. The formula is pretty simple. Take the current value of the property, subtract what you owe on it, and the resulting dollar figure represents equity. Here's an example:

Market value	$200,000
First mortgage on the house (balance)	–$110,000
Second mortgage on the house (balance)	–$25,000
Lien for back taxes	–$3,500
Construction lien (new windows)	–$5,000
Equity	**$56,500**

If you or the bankruptcy trustee were to sell the house, you would (theoretically, at least) have $56,500 to pay off the rest of your creditors. Of course, this doesn't account for the cost of selling the house, such as an agent's commission.

In the following sections, we show you how various other factors can affect the amount of theoretical equity you have to work with, and how much of this equity you get to keep.

Scaling back your equity on paper

When you calculate the amount of equity you have in your home, you may think that you stand to lose a lot by filing Chapter 7 bankruptcy, but the actual outcome may not be so bleak. The bankruptcy trustee is going to do some calculations to reduce the amount of that equity that creditors are entitled to.

In the following sections, we reveal the two most common ways a trustee reduces the amount of equity on paper to give you a fresh start with more cash in your pocket.

Deducting the estimated liquidation costs

When you look at theoretical equity, the dollar figure may come across as quite substantial, at first. But when viewed through the kaleidoscope of bankruptcy, it takes on a different light. For example, the bankruptcy trustee subtracts some of the costs of liquidating that asset:

- ✔ **Subtract the federal asset exemption or the state exemption, which is usually larger.** Using the federal exemption, for example, the trustee would subtract $20,200, leaving $36,300 of equity available. (See the "Subtracting your homestead exemption" section for additional details.)

- ✔ **Subtract any discount you may have to offer to sell the home in a hurry.** Because the house must be sold in a hurry, in what is commonly called a fire sale, the trustee may estimate that the house is going to sell for 5 percent below its true market value. For a $200,000 house, that means selling the house for $10,000 less. The trustee is now down to $26,300 equity in the property.

- ✔ **Subtract the real estate agent's commission.** To sell the house, the trustee must hire a real estate broker, who charges a 6 percent commission or $11,400. Now the trustee is down to having $14,900 in equity.

- ✔ **Subtract the trustee's payment.** The trustee doesn't work for free, of course. She earns a percentage of what's left (up to 25 percent on the first $5,000 and a lower percentage as the amount remaining grows). In our example, in which $14,900 remains, the trustee would earn about 10 percent or $1,490, leaving $13,410 in equity.

This scenario makes it clear why there isn't really any equity even when it appears, at first glance, that a piece of property has a lot of equity in it. By the time you take away all the administrative costs, very little is left to distribute, and the trustee is likely to declare it a no-asset case.

Subtracting your homestead exemption

The federal homestead exemption for nonexempt assets in bankruptcy, as of this writing, is $20,200 (adjusted for inflation and other factors). This means that according to the federal government, you can keep up to $20,200 of the equity in your home. Your state may be more or less generous (for example, Texas and Florida have no limit on homestead exemptions, while Washington, D.C., and New Jersey have no homestead exemption).

Clamping down on homestead exemption abuse

Prior to the passage of the BAPCPA of 2005, the homestead exemption was very vulnerable to abuse. In the past, people who were deep in debt in a state that had an unfavorable homestead exemption could sell all their assets and purchase a huge house in a state with a favorable homestead exemption, such as Florida, live there for 180 days, and then file for bankruptcy and claim a homestead exemption on the entire amount of equity in the home.

To prevent people from taking advantage of states with more favorable homestead exemptions, the BAPCPA of 2005 changed the rules. The BAPCPA now requires a 730-day continuous domicile prior to filing bankruptcy in order to choose a state homestead exemption over the federal exemption. If that requirement isn't met, then the court looks to the state where you were domiciled for the majority of the 180-day period preceding that 2-year period.

This change prevents debtors from planning their bankruptcy to strategically cheat creditors, but it probably won't affect the average person filing for bankruptcy.

Consult your attorney to decide which homestead exemption (state or federal) is best for you.

The homestead exemption tops out at $125,000 regardless of the state in which you reside in either of the following cases:

- ✔ **The court determines that you've been convicted of a felony, demonstrating that the filing of the case was an abuse of the provision of the Bankruptcy Code.**

- ✔ **You owe a debt arising from a violation of federal or state securities laws, fiduciary fraud, racketeering, or crimes or intentional torts that caused serious bodily injury or death in the preceding five years.** This limitation is inapplicable if the homestead property is "reasonably necessary for the support of the debtor and any dependent of the debtor."

- ✔ **You acquired your homestead within 1,215 days of filing bankruptcy.**

Because each state has its own requirements and exemption, deal with a competent bankruptcy attorney who can assist you in maximizing your homestead allowance.

Protecting your personal property assets

Your home is probably your most valuable asset, particularly if you have loads of equity in it. However, you probably have some personal property that has some value, as well. Can the trustee sell off this other stuff to pay creditors? Well, that depends.

Federal Bankruptcy Code and jurisdictions place limits on what can be sold off to satisfy debt. After all, giving borrowers a "fresh start" in bankruptcy doesn't mean leaving them penniless with no possessions. If you need a car and certain other possessions to do your job, for example, you may be able to keep them or at least pay the trustee a certain amount to retain possession of them. In addition, you'll probably also get to keep property that has some emotional value, such as your wedding ring.

In a vast majority of cases, the trustee determines which exemptions you qualify for, based on your assets and where you lived over the past two and a half years. A bankruptcy attorney who knows how to use exemptions strategically can assist you in protecting your assets and making your case qualify as a no-asset case. For additional tips on maximizing your exemptions, check out *Personal Bankruptcy Laws For Dummies,* 2nd Edition, by James P. Caher and John M. Caher (Wiley).

Chapter 11

Haggling with Your Lender in Pre-Foreclosure

Contrary to urban myth, your bank doesn't want to take your home away from you, especially if you owe more on it than it's worth. The bank would prefer to collect monthly payments from you over the life of the loan, which in all probability is pretty much the rest of your life. After all, why would the bank want to bother with your $100,000 home if it can earn $239,508 off of you when you make your monthly payments (assuming a 30-year $100,000 mortgage at 7 percent interest)? If the bank were to foreclose, it would miss out on the opportunity to collect its $139,508 profit.

Even worse, the bank would have to take on the expense of foreclosing, repairing, and renovating the property to make it marketable, and then paying a real estate agent to sell it. Your bank could be facing the possibility of losing thousands or tens of thousands of dollars. And one thing banks don't like to do is lose money.

The bank knows that the best solution for everyone is to help you regain your financial footing. And if your bank believes it can accomplish this goal by cutting you a little slack, it's going to be willing to make a deal. This chapter reveals the options that most lenders are willing to consider and shows you the steps to take in order to implement the desired solution.

The sooner you contact your lender, the more responsive the lender is going to be and the more time you have to resolve any conflicts before your house goes on the auction block. We can't guarantee that your bank is going to be willing to make a deal, but your chances are much better if you contact the bank early and cooperate.

Due to the mortgage meltdown that began in 2007, the federal government, through the Federal Housing Authority (FHA), is encouraging lenders to work more closely with homeowners facing foreclosure to develop solutions. You may even have the option of refinancing a high-interest subprime loan into a federally insured FHA loan with a lower interest rate, but you won't know unless you discuss your options with your bank.

Contacting Your Lender ASAP

If you're a card-carrying member of the National Procrastinators Society, we encourage you to cancel your membership — at least until you've resolved your foreclosure issue. As time passes, options fade away:

- ✔ **You can't negotiate a forbearance after the bank forecloses.**

- ✔ **A bank won't accept a deed in lieu of foreclosure after it initiates foreclosure.** However, the bank may be willing to exchange cash for keys if it can get you to move out earlier, after the foreclosure sale.

- ✔ **You won't have enough time to sell the house yourself, if that's something you want to do.**

- ✔ **You may run out of time to obtain a loan to reinstate the mortgage.**

- ✔ **After the redemption period expires, assuming your area has a redemption period, you lose the home, no questions asked.**

Another reason to act quickly is because as soon as your bank passes your case along to an attorney, it adds the attorney fees to the amount you need to pay to reinstate the loan.

When you call your bank for the first time, ask to speak to someone in the bank's loss-mitigation department. If the bank does not have a loss mitigation department, it should at least know what you're talking about and be able to refer you to someone on staff who handles loss mitigation. In some cases, the bank may outsource this job to its creditor attorney or foreclosure attorney, who has someone on staff specializing in loss mitigation. You may need to make several calls to find a person who can actually assist you. In the following section, we offer some guidance on how to work effectively with a loss mitigator.

Get to work immediately, gathering the paperwork you need and getting organized for meeting the loss mitigator and anyone else who can assist you. Some people don't come prepared. You know the type — they were the ones who never took notes in class and asked to borrow yours, and as adults they come to meetings without a pen and paper, assuming they'll be able to remember everything that's important. We know from experience that this approach doesn't work. Document everything. Journal the journey. Documentation really pays off in the end.

Be careful when working with your lender. Some lenders have been known to lead people on, making them think that a solution is in the works when it really isn't. Eventually, the homeowners run out of time to do anything and lose their home. If your lender or lender's representative suggests a solution, make sure you get something in writing. If the person is unwilling to provide you with written confirmation, seek other steps, such as consulting an attorney.

Practicing the Three C's of Working with a Loss Mitigator

Most banks that handle mortgage loans have a *loss mitigator* (a person dedicated to assisting borrowers to avoid foreclosure and making sure the bank loses as little money as possible from bad loans). The loss mitigator is the person you want to deal with, because the person can assist you in the following ways:

- Analyze your options.
- Convince the bank that negotiating with you is in the bank's best interest.
- Negotiate a forbearance, reinstatement, or short sale.
- Assist you in selling the house (if you choose to do so) by researching information pertaining to the house, including the title and market value; referring you to a real estate broker who can sell the property quickly for the best price possible; and overseeing the closing if one can be arranged.

Having a local attorney or loss mitigator to deal with can work in your favor. The person is likely to be aware of market conditions in your area. She can easily assess the condition of the property and comparable property values and advise the bank on how easy or difficult it will be to sell the home if the bank moves forward with the foreclosure. The attorney or loss mitigator can relay all this information to the bank and, in turn, may be given the authority to work with you directly to resolve this issue without the full foreclosure. By communicating with the loss mitigator and showing a good-faith effort to resolve this problem, you may get more cooperation than if you avoid everyone and stonewall everything.

No matter how cold and calculating a loss mitigator may appear to be, the person is a human being who appreciates being treated with respect and courtesy. If the loss mitigator has three bad loans to deal with, and you're the only person acting civilly, you increase your chances of being the one person the loss mitigator assists. *Remember:* Even if the loss mitigator gets huffy-puffy with you and threatens to blow your house down, remain respectful — unlike most of the people he deals with.

To deal effectively with a loss mitigator, practice the three C's as discussed in the following sections:

- ✔ Communication
- ✔ Composure
- ✔ Credibility

Notice that the person you're talking to at the bank is taking notes. You should be doing the same.

Communication

The range of solutions the loss mitigator can offer you is limited only by what the bank wants. The more urgent it is for the bank to dump the property and keep the bad loan off the books, the more authority it may give to the loss mitigator to resolve any issue prior to foreclosure. This is where your ability to communicate effectively plays an important role:

- ✔ **If you decide to sell the home and move, explain how much time you would need to do that.**

- ✔ **Describe the condition of the property.**

- ✔ **Have a real estate broker give you an estimate of value of the property and a price that you would need to list it at in order to sell it within a very short period of time.** Those two numbers you'll find are often very different. A house worth $150,000 may need to be priced at $135,000 in order to elicit a quick sale.

✔ **Describe the extent of any damages to the property (necessary repairs) and proof of the damages.** If the house is in very good condition and doesn't need any work, consider taking pictures to give to the loss mitigator as proof of its condition. Pictures are great tools for telling the story.

✔ **Get estimates for repairs and renovations that would need to be done in order to bring the property up to market standards.**

Work with the loss mitigator in any way you can, but remember that he doesn't work for *you* — he represents the bank. A solution is usually available that works for everyone involved, but don't let the loss mitigator take the lead and dictate the solution based solely on the information he's gathered. Gather your own information, so you aren't at the mercy of what other people tell you.

Composure

In a way, foreclosure is like playing poker. Each player — you and the bank — holds his cards and is trying to survive this particular deal. Unfortunately for you, the bank has an ace up its sleeve — it can choose to foreclose at any time. You may be holding some powerful cards, too, depending on your situation. If you have nothing more to lose than the house, and the market is lousy, for example, you can always walk away and leave the bank to pick up the pieces (see Chapter 13).

However, and it's a big *however,* if you want more than to salvage your pride, acting with a sense of composure is in your best interest. Prove that you can make logical decisions not tied to any emotions. Act as though you want to arrive at a solution that works in everyone's best interest. No one wants to work with an irrational, irate human being. Play the middle. Act calm and collected.

Just imagine what the loss mitigator may think: "If this person is going to be a pain in the shorts, even when I'm willing to make concessions, I may as well have everything my way." The bank holds most of the cards, and it can always pull the plug on negotiations. By retaining your composure, you give yourself a better chance that the loss mitigator won't pull the plug and will negotiate a better deal for you.

Don't judge a person based solely on how nicely she treats you. A person can treat you well and still fail to help you. On the other hand, someone who seems like an ice woman could be very helpful. Niceness doesn't correlate to helpfulness or competence.

Any arrangement you agree to should be in writing, signed by an authorized agent of the bank — even if the loss mitigator treats you like her best friend.

Credibility

People in foreclosure often bend the truth, thinking that their white lies will save them. This approach doesn't work. The people at the bank have heard all the stories. What they want is the truth, and they'll be more willing to work with you if you're straight with them.

Following are some tips on how to build your credibility:

- **Come clean.** If someone asks you why you're in foreclosure, tell the truth. If you've lived beyond your means, say so. The more you disclose about any foibles that led to foreclosure, the more credible you become. Admit mistakes instead of trying to hide them.

- **Be honest.** Don't say it's because of medical bills if you had a history of not paying your bills before the medical bills were an issue. The loss mitigator is likely to pull up records and check your story. If it doesn't pan out, you instantly lose credibility.

- **Act serious.** People are losing money here, so act as though you care and have a sincere interest in righting a wrong. Show up well dressed and well groomed for meetings, and treat everyone you meet with respect. Be proactive and not reactive.

- **Do what you say you're going to do.** If you can't afford to pay $200 extra per month to catch up on your payments, don't promise it. Promise only what you can reasonably do, and then do it. If you can only pay $100 extra, it's better to say that than to agree to $200 and default on it. If you tell the loss mitigator that you're going to sell your new car to make your mortgage payments, do it.

- **Present accurate facts and figures.** Whenever you present the loss mitigator with facts, make sure those facts check out. If you say your house is worth $150,000, and an independent broker confirms that figure, you earn instant credibility. If the broker says the house is worth $200,000, you're sunk. Remember that repeating the truth is easier than repeating lies. Stick with the true story — that's the one you'll never forget.

People generally start out believing you until you do something that causes them not to believe you. When you destroy your credibility or compromise the trust between you and another person, rebuilding it is very difficult. If you don't do what you're supposed to, you may not get a next time.

That's incredible!

Whenever we meet with a homeowner facing foreclosure, we always ask him to share his story and tell us how he arrived at this juncture in his life. Usually, the person can point to a single event that marks, for him at least, the moment that foreclosure happened.

The next thing we do is pull the client's credit report, so we teach him how he can dispute anything on the report that may not be his and get a clearer idea of what his long-term financial history has been.

When someone tells us that the death of his elderly mother caused the problem, but his credit report shows a history of late and missed payments while his mother was still alive and

kicking, we become more than a little skeptical of other information he offers. For us, and for most banks, attorneys, and loss mitigators, honesty is a major factor in building and maintaining credibility.

We would rather hear from the homeowner that he made some bad decisions or bought a house mistakenly thinking he could afford it than that the death of a loved one is his alibi. The death may have been the final nail in the coffin (pardon the pun), but in most cases it isn't the cause of the problem. Overspending, poor money management, gambling, laziness, and overusing credit cards are the more likely, long-term causes.

Reinstating Your Mortgage, Like Nothing Ever Happened

Reinstating your mortgage consists of paying a lump sum to cover all missed payments and any additional interest, fees, and penalties you've incurred as a result of the missed payments. After you reinstate your mortgage, it's as if nothing ever happened — except for the fact that you may have another loan to pay off, if you had to borrow money to reinstate.

Reinstating a mortgage requires money upfront. If you don't have the money and can't get it, the decision has been made for you — reinstating is out of the question. If you can get the money, then reinstating may be the best option.

In the following sections, we reveal various ways to get your mitts on the much-needed cash, offer suggestions on how to convince your bank to allow you to reinstate your mortgage, and show you when it's probably a lousy idea to reinstate.

Digging up the cash required to reinstate

Reinstating your mortgage sounds like a great idea until you try to figure out how you're going to come up with the money. Here's a short list of possible sources for cash:

- Friends
- Relatives
- Bank loan
- Private lender
- Loan against your retirement nest egg
- Loan from your boss
- Assets — sell your stuff
- Friday night's Texas Hold'em tournament

Sell something! If you never sold that vintage car you drove on your first date and you're storing it in your barn, find out how much it's worth and sell it. If it's worth $50,000 and you could sell it quickly for $31,000, do it! After all, where will you store this beauty when they take the house away from you?

If someone you know can gift you the money, and you can cover your monthly mortgage payments from here on out, reinstating may be an ideal option. If that's not the case, however, you need to consider the ramifications of refinancing, particularly how you're going to afford to make payments on another loan when you can't afford to make your mortgage payments. (We address this concern in Chapter 6.)

Borrowing against the equity in your home

Grab a calculator and figure out how much equity you have built up in your home. To do this, simply subtract the total amount you currently owe on the home from a reasonable price that you're sure you could sell the home for today. If you end up with a positive number that's more than a few thousand dollars, then borrowing against the equity of your home to reinstate the mortgage may make sense and be a realistic option. If your home is sold in foreclosure, you stand to lose any equity you have in it, so borrowing to protect that equity may be a wise decision — the more equity you have, the wiser the decision.

You may also be able to use the equity in your home to convince friends or family members to float you a loan. Let them know that if you can't catch up on your payments, you can always sell the home and pay them back, assuming, of course, that this is true. Show them the value of the home minus what you owe on it. You can even offer them a second mortgage to secure the loan. This may provide them with the comfort and confidence they need to assist you.

Even if you can't afford the monthly mortgage payments after reinstating the loan, this option is worth considering. You can reinstate to buy yourself some time, protect your equity, and immediately place your home on the market to sell it. Selling it yourself and cashing out the equity is always preferable to having the bank or an investor purchase and sell it, taking the equity for themselves. Reinstate and then put the house up for sale, fire-sale it, or sell to an investor or family member. The way in which you decide to sell it makes no difference. What you *don't* want to do is walk away from large sums of equity. Reinstating allows you to sell the home and walk away with some cash to start anew.

Reinstating early, before the official foreclosure proceedings begin, may also enable you to sell your home for more money than if let the home slide into foreclosure. Good agents know when a house is in foreclosure and will advise their buyers to structure an offer that reflects your desperation to sell quickly. By reinstating, you can hide the fact that money is tight and you need to sell quickly. You can play hard to get. Keep in mind that you do need to sell, and if the market is slow, you should be a little more flexible in negotiating the sale price.

Getting a little help from your friends (and relatives)

Friends and relatives are often willing and perhaps even eager to assist loved ones in need, assuming, of course, that the loved ones are working hard to improve their own situation. Mom, Dad, Grandma, and Grandpa can remember back to when they were young, struggling to make a better life for themselves and their children. What they can't relate to is someone spending more than she can afford, living for material possessions, and not being willing to work extra hours or an extra job to put food on the table. In other words, friends and relatives are usually willing to help those who help themselves.

We discourage those who are motivationally challenged from seeking assistance from friends and relatives. You must be determined enough to live independently from your family that the assistance they provide you will be assistance well spent.

Getting a little help from your friends and relatives doesn't have to be limited solely to financial assistance. Sure, if you have a rich uncle who doesn't mind giving you a wad of cash, or your parents have sufficient savings to float you a loan, pursue those options. Friends and relatives, however, can assist you in other ways as well, such as the following:

✔ They can watch your children a few times a week, so you can moonlight to boost the household income until you can get caught up and back on your feet.

✔ They can drive you back and forth to work — if you don't work too far away.

Cutting a deal with Grandma

We once dealt with a young couple who had one child and another on the way. Because the wife could no longer work, they fell behind on all their bills. When Grandma heard of the situation, she decided it was time to step in and offer some assistance. She gave them some money to catch up on delinquent payments and pay some of the more pressing bills. This freed up the couple's weekly and monthly cash flow.

The couple was grateful and wanted to find some way of paying back Grandma. She wouldn't hear of it. She didn't want repayment in the form of money. She did, however, specify several conditions for the gift:

✔ The husband needed to work extra hours or find a second job.

✔ The great-grandchildren were to be brought by for a visit at least once a week.

✔ When the couple's children or grandchildren fell on similar hardships, they would return the favor.

Grandma told a brief story of how she and her late husband were once given a boost from her father under the same terms. She said she was getting a little worried, because until they came along and needed help, she was concerned that she was going to die before she was able to fulfill the third part of the promise she made to her father. We all chuckled a little.

Last we heard, everyone was doing fine. The husband found another job, and even took night classes at the local community college so that, one day, he could work just one job and be able to provide for his family. Grandma saw the children every Sunday afternoon, and what could have been a very stressful situation turned into a real success story. We haven't heard anything for the last couple years — and when we don't hear back from clients, that's usually a good thing.

✔ They can cook a meal for your family once or twice a week — casserole, anyone?

✔ They can clean your house, so you can work overtime or take on a second job.

✔ They can fix your car, if you have a mechanic in the family.

Few people are willing to continue to support deadbeats who don't work toward improving their current situation. Eventually, the benevolence wears out and the house of cards caves in on itself.

Rebounding from a financial speed bump

Temporary financial setbacks can lead to foreclosure, but as long as the setback is temporary, you can usually rebound by reinstating the mortgage. Temporary setbacks include one-time occurrences, such as a death in the family (with unexpected funeral expenses), an auto accident that required time off work, or a major expense that drained the family resources. If you could just get caught up on the missed payments, you could now afford the monthly mortgage payments.

Whether you have equity built up in the home doesn't matter in this scenario. If you can afford the home, you like the home, you want to stay, and you have a fair to good interest rate, reinstatement may be the best choice for you. Make up the missed payments (borrow it if you have to), resume your payments, and you should be well on your way to a rosy financial future. Think nothing of the foreclosure again, other than to be thankful that you were able to stave it off and completely rehabilitate yourself.

Recovering from a major, life-changing event

A major, life-changing event, such as the death of a major breadwinner or a divorce, can hit you in the wallet as well as in the heart, but some people are able to make the adjustments necessary to keep their homes. If you find yourself in a similar situation, first decide whether staying in the home makes sense. Here are some indications that staying in your home is better than moving:

✔ You have a great interest rate.

✔ You have equity in the home.

✔ You live in a great neighborhood.

✔ The neighborhood has excellent schools for your kids.

When staying put makes sense

We once interviewed a woman who was facing foreclosure and unsure of her options. During the interview, we discovered that she was recently divorced. Her husband had run off with another woman and left the state. She had two children and was now the sole breadwinner.

Fortunately, she had a good job that was just a few miles from home. Her mother lived down the street and often watched the children when she had the opportunity to pick up some overtime. Her children were in good schools, and the teachers and principal knew the family, was well aware of the situation, and watched out for the kids.

In this case, the family had the support they desperately needed. It made sense for her to do all that she could to save her home and remain in the neighborhood. The other option was far less appealing, both financially and emotionally. In this case, uprooting the children would have caused even more chaos after suffering the loss of their father.

When you're assessing your options, think ahead and consider the ramifications of possible decisions. Selling the house to get out from under it may seem like the perfect solution, but you have to live somewhere and pay rent or make a house payment. If you decide to move, is that going to put you and your family in a better position?

- You live close to all the services you use.

- Moving would require a change of jobs, and you're not sure that you'd be able to secure employment with comparable pay and benefits.

- If you were to sell and move right now, you would probably find yourself paying as much or more for a new place to live.

- Moving would probably mean living in an area where everything would be much less convenient.

Most people loathe the thought of moving, but don't base your decision on the fact that you're opposed to making a change. Base your decision on what would be best for you and your family at this point in time. Don't simply stay put if remaining in the home is going to ultimately lead to foreclosure a few weeks or months from now. In such cases, you may be better off saving the money you would spend to reinstate, and looking for the best way to move on.

Convincing your bank to reinstate your mortgage

Your bank is probably not exactly eager to offer the option of reinstating the mortgage. You've already missed payments or paid late, so your credibility is already in question. At this point, you have to reveal your plan and prove to the bank that, after reinstating, you can resume payments. Present the bank with a plan that includes the following:

- **Where you're going to get the money to reinstate the mortgage:** This may include plans to sell assets, borrow from friends or relatives, empty your piggybank, or find a second job.

- **If you're borrowing the money to reinstate the loan, how you're going to pay back that loan:** The bank wants to know that you're not going to get into a pinch with that other loan.

- **A realistic amount you can pay per month to catch up on your payments:** Don't pump up the numbers to try to make yourself look good. Promise only what you can deliver.

- **Your plan for resuming payments:** Did you experience a temporary setback that is no longer an issue? Are you working extra hours or another job?

- **The date on which the bank will receive payment:** Make sure you keep your word and pay the bank when you say you will.

If you can't afford to catch up on *missed* payments right now, but you can afford to resume making your monthly mortgage payments, your bank may be willing to add the amount due to the principal balance, so you'll pay it off at the end of the term. This may add a few months to your mortgage and cost a little more, but it may be enough to get you through the current crisis.

If your bank agrees to reinstate the mortgage, obtain a letter via fax or mail stating the conditions of reinstatement, so you can be sure to fulfill all the conditions by the specified date. This letter also gives you written proof of the agreement, so your bank can't deny it later. Keep careful records to show that you've honored your end of the agreement.

Knowing when not to reinstate

As you may have guessed, some homeowners facing foreclosure shouldn't even consider reinstating their mortgages. If any of the following apply to you, you're an unlikely candidate for reinstatement:

- ✔ Your current interest rate is astronomical, so you'd be better off refinancing to a lower rate.
- ✔ You'll never be able to afford the house.
- ✔ The house needs a lot of work, and you have no money to cover repair and renovation expenses.
- ✔ You're unemployed, and prospects don't look good for future local employment.
- ✔ You have little or no equity in the house to justify the outlay of money needed to protect it.
- ✔ You're in a house that's way too large for your current situation, and downsizing makes sense.
- ✔ You have little, if any, incentive for staying in your neighborhood.

This is not an exhaustive list, but you get the point. If you can't afford to stay in the home long-term and you have little or no equity to protect, why bother? You won't be righting the ship, but rather stuffing bubble gum in a cannonball hole. You're going to sink — the only question is, how much of your current life, assets, and well-being are you going to allow to be dragged down with the ship? Take some time to analyze your situation and use your head instead of your heart. ***Remember:*** A house is just a house; your home is wherever you and your loved ones choose to live.

Working Out a New Payment Plan with a Forbearance Agreement

Forbearance is sort of like reinstating the mortgage, except for the fact that instead of paying all the money due all at once, you're allowed to make up missed payments and fees over time. For example, say you normally pay $1,000 per month and you're behind by two payments. You now owe $2,200 in back payments plus penalties and interest. Instead of having to pay $2,200 all at once, the bank may agree to spread the payments out over the next eight months. Instead of paying $1,000 per month, you're required to pay $1,275 per month until you've paid off the $2,200 you owe.

Knowing what to expect

Banks that are willing to agree to a forbearance typically have the equivalent of a no-haggle policy. They write up the agreement, and it's often a take-it-or-leave-it proposition. You may have some input, but don't get your hopes up.

The good news is that you don't have to sign a forbearance agreement. If you have better options, you can choose to pursue those — or you can simply walk away if the forbearance is just going to delay the inevitable for a month or two. Never sign anything that's going to set you up for failure sometime down the road.

Convincing your bank to agree to forbearance

If forbearance seems like an option you may want to explore, ask the bank if it would consider it. In most cases, the bank requires that you provide detailed financial information before it agrees to a forbearance. Because of your missed payments, you're a higher risk, and the bank wants to know how you're going to make larger monthly payments now when you were unable to make smaller monthly payments in the past. Be prepared to present the following:

- ✔ Bank statements
- ✔ Pay stubs or employment records
- ✔ Monthly income information

- ✔ Recent credit report (The bank should be able to look this up, but it never hurts to have a copy with you.)

- ✔ Budget information, including all your monthly expenses

- ✔ Current housing market situation (slow, steady, or hot)

- ✔ A statement and any proof you have related to the physical condition of your home

The condition of your home can work for you or against you. If the property is in excellent condition, you have lots of equity in it, and the market is sizzling hot, the bank probably realizes that it can make money off the foreclosure and is likely to make you jump through hoops to prove that you're forbearance-worthy. If the property is dilapidated, the market is stagnant, and you have little or no equity in the home, the bank probably doesn't want the house and is willing to take the risk that you can pull yourself out of foreclosure. Then again, if the bank sees that you don't care for the property, it may assume that you're not trustworthy and deny the forbearance option.

If you really want the forbearance agreement, point out all the reasons it would be good for the bank. Explain that the market is slow, you have little equity in the house, the house is in poor condition, and you're committed to making good on the loan. Let the bank know that you did your homework and know what the bank is facing if it forecloses.

Whatever you do, don't throw good money after bad. If forbearance is simply going to cost you money and delay the inevitable loss of your home, then seek other options. As Kenny Rogers sings in *The Gambler,* "You've got to know when to hold 'em, know when to fold 'em, know when to walk away, know when to run. . . ."

Scrutinizing the forbearance agreement

A forbearance agreement is likely to be as lengthy as, and perhaps even more convoluted than, the mortgage you signed when you purchased your home. All the language, however, boils down to this: If you pay what the bank says by the day it says, you get to stay. In other words, if you don't honor the conditions stipulated in the agreement, you face foreclosure — and you're not likely to get a second chance.

Read the entire agreement carefully. If you don't understand a particular clause, ask the bank's representative to explain it to you. You don't need detailed explanations of each and every clause, but by the time you finish reading the document, you should be able to answer the following questions:

✔ How long is it going to take to satisfy the terms of the agreement and be placed back on your regular monthly payment schedule and amount?

✔ Is your interest rate going to increase? If so, by what percentage? Will the increase be erased when you satisfy the terms of the agreement?

✔ Is the bank adding a bunch of junk fees to the amount you'll owe? If it is, can you live with this?

✔ Are you going to have additional payments tacked on at the end of the mortgage, or will you have to pay longer on your mortgage?

✔ What happens if you're late with a payment or, heaven forbid, you miss one?

✔ How much more, if at all, is your payment above what it was before?

Don't make promises that you can't realistically keep. If you sincerely want to save your home and are in a financial position in which you can honor the terms of the forbearance agreement, then by all means, go ahead and sign on the dotted line. If you exaggerate the numbers and puff up your income or hide some expenses, you may set yourself up for failure. Even worse, if you fail to live up to the terms of the agreement, your bank is going to be much less willing to give you a second chance. *Remember:* The key is honesty.

Convincing Your Lender to Accept Less Than What You Owe with a Short Sale

Banks hate to lose money, but what they hate even more is losing *more* money, and that's the idea behind a short sale. With a *short sale,* the bank agrees to accept less than full payment of the loan balance, knowing that if it does not accept, it's likely to lose even more money in foreclosure. Depending on the mortgage amount, a bank loses an average of $25,000 to $1 million during a typical foreclosure.

One possible drawback related to a short sale is that if the bank forgives a certain portion of your debt, the tax collector may demand a chunk of that forgiven debt in the form of a capital gains tax. Consult a certified public accountant (CPA) or, better yet, a tax attorney to determine the possible ramifications of a short sale as they apply to your situation.

A short sale may be a good option for you, if your situation meets the following conditions:

Short-sale boom

From 2005 to the publishing of this book, Michigan was experiencing a serious correction in its housing market. That state had just come off some of the greatest growth rates in its real estate market, perhaps in its entire history. As with most good things, this housing boom had to come to an end, and when it did, man, did it ever. The foreclosure rates skyrocketed, unemployment shot through the roof, and the real estate market went into a tailspin.

People found themselves with mortgages on homes that, because of the market downturn, were 100 percent to 150 percent of the true market value of their homes. Banks and mortgage companies found themselves facing an age-old question: "To foreclose or not to foreclose?" Homeowners found themselves facing adjustable-rate mortgage (ARM) adjustments that put them into double-digit interest rates. Banks were unwilling to loan the money to refinance because they weren't sure whether the loan that was fully secured today may be under-secured tomorrow.

The more forward-thinking banks began to consider short sales as a very real option to limit their loses. Banks were taking less than what was owed so that homeowners could close on their homes and sell, instead of the banks having to foreclose and sell later at substantially greater losses.

✔ You have little, no, or negative equity in the home.

✔ You want to resolve the situation, because just walking away doesn't seem ethical to you.

✔ You can pretty much break even by selling the home, if the bank agrees to the short sale.

✔ The housing market is stagnant or in decline, making it tough for the bank to resell the property.

When it makes sense (as with the example in the "Short-sale boom" sidebar), the bank may write off a portion of its loan, chalk it up to poor market conditions, and move on. Make sure it moves on, though — get a release or something on paper that says the bank is not going to hold you liable for the *deficiency* (the reduction in the loan amount).

Talking to the right people

The first person you talk to at the bank is probably not the person who is ultimately going to assist you in resolving your foreclosure issue. Banks, like most companies and corporations, are structured to insulate the decision-makers from the malcontents. You're going to have to patiently work your way through several layers of gatekeepers and tiers of incompetence before you reach someone who can actually get something done. Here are some tips to expedite the process:

- ✔ **Write down the name, phone number, and extension of everyone you talk to.**

- ✔ **Jot down notes, to keep a record of what you discussed and what each of you agreed to.**

- ✔ **Follow up with a phone call or a visit.** You want everyone you contact to get to know you personally, so you gain advocates at all levels. Having key bank employees vouching for you to the powers that be is priceless.

- ✔ **When you ultimately meet the person who has the authority to sign off on the short sale you're proposing, deal with the person as directly as you can and try to deal exclusively with that person, if possible.** Provide her with the information she asks for and help her understand the situation the bank and you are facing.

Be particularly careful when speaking with the person who can ultimately assist you. If you go on the attack, you may never get past the gatekeepers again. He probably won't return your calls, and instead of dealing with you, he may decide that foreclosing is the easier option. Likewise, don't waste the his time. Prepare well for the meeting, present your situation as clearly and succinctly as possible, do what you say you're going to do, and avoid the temptation to call him ten times a day for a status report.

Knowing what to say

Don't expect the bank to offer you the option of a short sale. The bank's representatives may not be aware that the option is in the bank's best interest, so you may need to educate them. State the facts, plain and simple. If, for example, you've been very close to falling behind on your mortgage payments for the past three months and know that you can't afford the home, call the bank and inform its representatives of the following:

- ✔ You're afraid that you're going to be falling behind on your payments because of _____.

- ✔ You want to place your home on the market but you're afraid that if you sell in the current market, you'll be taking a loss unless you can get a short sale.

- ✔ You've already contacted a broker, who has done a market analysis and valued your house at $150,000, for example. The problem is that you owe $147,000. By the time you're able to pay the commission, transfer tax, closing costs, and so on, you won't be able to get the bank the full $147,000.

✔ You and your broker are going to do everything to maximize the sales price.

✔ You won't be pocketing any money — you just have to get out from under the monthly mortgage payments.

✔ You don't want to have to have a foreclosure on your record, and fore-closing wouldn't do the bank any good, because by the time it sold the home, it would probably get even less for it.

The bank is highly unlikely to say "yes" right away, but ask its representatives to think about it and get back with you. Tell them that, in the meantime, you're going to list the home. Try hard to get an offer, and when you do, present the offer and show the representatives the amount of money the bank can expect if the buyers end up closing on the transaction. An offer, provided it is a legit-imate one, is the best way to show the bank that what you're saying is true and that you're not just trying to skip out of paying.

Explain that you know this isn't ideal, and that if you could have it any other way you would, but your hands are tied. You can't make the house worth more than it is, and you don't have the money needed to bring it up to the top retail value. The bank can send a representative out to take a look, and it can even suggest that you use a certain broker, but you just can't see how you can make it work so that the bank comes out satisfied in full.

Most banks are not going to agree to a short sale if it means that you get to walk away with thousands of dollars in your pocket. Your bank may allow a commission to be paid to a broker, but it's unlikely to allow *you* to profit from the short sale. However, if you've consulted with a bankruptcy attorney and have some proof that bankruptcy is going to cost the bank a lot more money, you may be able to work out a short sale that puts some cash in your pocket. If the bank seems unresponsive to your offer, simply let its representatives know that you're going to have to file for bankruptcy, because you don't know what else to do; that usually catches the bank's attention.

Knowing how to say it

How willing the bank is going to be to negotiate a short sale, or any other deal for that matter, depends as much on your attitude as on the facts of the case. If you approach the bank's representatives with an attitude that they owe you something, or with a chip on your shoulder that's the size of a rail-road tie, these representatives are going to be less than fully cooperative — and understandably so.

Who needs this?

Part of our business consists of assisting homeowners who are facing foreclosure. When we hear about homeowners in pre-foreclosure or see a foreclosure notice, we send the homeowners a letter introducing ourselves and what we do. When the homeowners respond, we meet with them at their home or in our office to answer any questions they have and analyze their options.

In one case, a couple responding to a letter that Paul had sent, arrived at the office with what we would consider to be not the optimum attitude. Paul tells the story:

"I set up the appointment and the couple met me at my office. I was very familiar with where they lived — in fact, it was not very far from where *I* lived. I met the couple in the lobby and showed them to a conference room. In the short time it took to make that trip, I could already sense the tension. That's nothing new — people in foreclosure are usually suspect of everything and everyone — but I knew, or at least I *thought* I knew, that I could diffuse that tension as soon as we sat down and started talking.

"I asked the couple to tell me a little of what had caused them to slip into foreclosure. The wife did all the talking, giving short answers and coming across rather coarsely. After just a few minutes she came right out and said, 'Okay, what's the story? How can you help us? How much is it going to cost me? There better be a good-faith estimate.'

"I was more than a little taken back. Here I was trying to help them solve their problem and she was jumping down my throat. I immediately knew that there was no diffusing this tension, ever. I politely told them that she was right — I didn't think I would be able to help them after all. I calmly thanked them for coming and hoped it had not seemed like a waste of their time.

"In order for me to help them, I needed to know that we could work together on a solution. I was totally turned off by the attitude I observed. I knew that we would be clashing on everything, and it was better for both of us to save the hassle. What she forgot was that I was not the one in foreclosure. When they left my office, my problems left with them, while they still had their problem and were no closer to a solution than when they arrived."

This is an extreme example, but we use it to illustrate the point that, when you deal with the bank or anyone else who can assist you in your time of need, *you* are the person who needs to work out a solution. You need to be able to act calmly and cordially with these other parties; they don't have to be nice to you. Don't be a pushover — stand up for yourself when needed — but don't be a rabid grizzly bear looking to tear the head off the next person you meet.

When you speak, admit to the difficult situation you've found yourself in and explain that you're seeking a solution that is acceptable to everyone involved. This problem needs a reasonable solution. Explain how you would like to see the issue resolved, and advocate for yourself and your family's needs without getting angry or nasty about it. Don't be a pushover, but don't think that the bank owes you something or is trying to fleece you.

Feelings of frustration are understandable, but if you think you can strong-arm or shout your way to a deal, you're mistaken. You may need to be firm at times, but be ready to concede when the concessions seem fair and reasonable. When showing the need for a short sale, gather the information and be as accurate as the data will allow you to be. You gain a big advantage if you can confidently and clearly explain to the bank's representatives that the bank stands to lose $15,000 more if they don't agree to a short sale.

Tread lightly, especially at first, know the facts, and know what you want. You have a better change of arriving at the point where you want to be if you have a road map for getting there.

Trading Your Deed for a Clean Bill of Health

Offering a deed in lieu of foreclosure is like handing your home over to the bank and saying, "I can't pay you, so take the house." Of course, this isn't always an option and may not be the best option for you. When is a deed in lieu of foreclosure something you should consider? In the following situations:

- ✔ When you have little, no, or negative equity in the home.
- ✔ When the bank will accept a deed in lieu of foreclosure.
- ✔ When you won't have to pay tax on the amount of debt that is going to be forgiven (see "Convincing Your Lender to Accept Less Than What You Owe with a Short Sale," earlier in this chapter).
- ✔ When the bank won't try to pursue a *deficiency judgment*. In other words, if the home isn't worth a sufficient amount to pay the balance of the mortgage in full, the bank won't file a claim for the rest of the money.

A deed in lieu may not be an option if additional lien holders have a claim to the property. In such a case, you may want to contact the junior lien holders and let them know that the senior lien holder is planning to foreclose. The junior lien holder may decide to buy out the first lien position and then offer you a deed in lieu of foreclosure or some other solution. The more the junior lien holders stand to lose when the senior lien holder forecloses, the more motivated they'll be to work with you.

Not all banks accept a deed in lieu of foreclosure, either because they don't know about them or because your mortgage contains a *covenant to pay* (your personal promise to pay the debt in full). If your mortgage contains a covenant to pay, your mortgage is said to be *recourse debt.* If the bank fore-closes on the house and can't sell it for the amount you owe on it, the bank can hold you liable for the deficiency and go after your other assets. In other words, the bank would be unlikely to accept a deed in lieu of foreclosure and forgive your debt, because through foreclosure and other legal actions, it may be able to wring more money out of you. Of course, if you have no money and nothing of value that the bank can take, the bank may accept the deed in lieu of foreclosure just to gain closure.

Find out whether your state allows for deficiency judgments. If it does, then check your mortgage to determine if it includes a covenant to pay (see Chapter 4). If your state allows deficiency judgments, your mortgage contains a covenant to pay, and you owe more on the home than what it's worth, the bank can go after anything of value that you own to satisfy the debt.

If your mortgage doesn't include the covenant to pay, but rather pledges only the collateral as security, then it is *non-recourse debt,* and the bank can only look to the value of the property to recoup its money. In this case, the bank may be more willing to accept the deed in lieu of foreclosure, if only to save on attorney fees and expedite the process of gaining possession of the property.

Whether a deficiency judgment is allowed may also depend on the method used to foreclose. Nonjudicial foreclosure, for example, may disallow a defi-ciency judgment, whereas judicial foreclosure may allow it. Many jurisdic-tions allow deficiency judgments if the homeowners have a redemption period, but disallow deficiency judgments when homeowners have no redemption rights.

One of the drawbacks of offering a deed in lieu of foreclosure is that you don't get the benefit of any redemption period, and you don't get any equity out of the house. You pack up and move with only your possessions and your credit score intact.

Remember: Many great people have gotten into real estate as a result of their experience in foreclosure. In all challenges are opportunities.

Chapter 12

Borrowing Your Way out of Foreclosure

*Y*ou're in this foreclosure mess because you can't make payments on the money you borrowed, so it may seem a little insane at this point to think about borrowing even more money, but borrowing your way out of foreclosure may be your best option. This is especially true if you experienced a temporary financial setback, such as a job loss, and have a new job with sufficient income to make loan payments. You can consolidate your debt by refinancing your mortgage, take out a home equity loan or line of credit to cover other expenses, borrow from a private lender to reinstate your mortgage, or even borrow from friends or relatives.

In this chapter, we lead you through the process of exploring various borrowing options, finding low-cost loans, and using the equity in your home to reestablish your financial footing.

Contact a qualified and trustworthy loan officer or mortgage broker to assist you in exploring your refinance options (see Chapter 4). Your loan officer or mortgage broker can also tell you fairly quickly whether you would qualify for a loan. A credit counselor may also be able to assist you in consolidating your debt and working out deals with creditors (see Chapter 8).

Exploring Your Options

Borrowing your way out of foreclosure can mean different things to different people. One person may need a few thousand dollars to reinstate the mortgage. Another person may have gotten stuck with a high-interest mortgage loan and needs to refinance with a lower-interest loan. Another person may owe $25,000 or more on high-interest credit cards and need to refinance to consolidate debt.

In Chapter 6, we lead you through the process of getting a handle on your current financial situation. Once you have an accurate financial portrait, you can begin to explore various options for borrowing money to determine which option would be best for you. Following is a list of the most common options:

- **Refinancing for a lower interest rate:** You got roped into a high-interest mortgage, or some shady loan officer sold you an adjustable-rate mortgage with a low introductory interest rate that has recently adjusted up. Your current mortgage has no significant prepayment penalty, and you qualify for a mortgage loan with a lower interest rate. By refinancing, you could afford the lower monthly payments.

- **Refinancing to consolidate debt:** You owe several thousand dollars on high-interest credit cards and other loans (such as a car loan) and have a substantial amount of equity in your home. By refinancing, you would have one affordable monthly payment that is less than your current total payments, plus the interest you would be paying would be tax-deductible. (Before encumbering your home to pay unsecured debts, be sure to check out your bankruptcy options, as explained in Chapter 10 of this book.)

- **Taking out a home equity loan or line of credit:** Your current mortgage is at an interest rate that is substantially lower than any rate you could get right now, you have equity in your home, and you need to borrow some money short-term to get through a temporary financial setback. Home equity loans or lines of credit may come with higher interest rates than a standard mortgage loan, but if you need the money for a short amount of time, these types of loans can be less costly in the long run.

    A home equity loan is for a fixed lump sum. A home equity line of credit lets you borrow up to a certain amount as needed. You pay interest only on the amount you borrow. For example, if you set up a $50,000 home equity line of credit and use only $10,000 of it, you pay interest only on the $10,000.

- **Borrowing from friends and relatives:** You cannot qualify for a loan from a bank, and you have friends or relatives who are in a position and willing to provide financial assistance. In Chapter 6, we talk about hitting up your friends and relatives for gifts or loans. This is often the best source of cash, although you need to handle it properly, so any loans or gifts do not compromise your relationships.

- ✓ **Borrowing from a private lender:** You cannot qualify for a loan from a bank, your friends and relatives cannot provide financial assistance, and you can pay the loan off relatively soon. Private lenders may be willing to loan you the money, but expect higher interest rates and shorter terms. Many loans from private lenders require a balloon payment — you pay a certain amount every month for so many months, at the end of which time, you must pay the balance of the loan.

- ✓ **Working a deal with a real estate investor:** You ran out of time and now an investor owns or will soon own your home, but now you can actually afford the house. In addition, you have no other liens on the property that can reattach themselves if you buy the property back from the investor, and the investor is willing to sell you the home on contract or via a lease-option agreement. (See Chapter 7 for details about buying your home back with a land contract or lease-option agreement. Chapter 4 discusses the actual contracts and agreements in greater detail.)

If a temporary loss of income or a large one-time expense triggered your foreclosure, and you have tens of thousands of dollars of equity built up in your house, you may be able to borrow your way out of foreclosure, pay off high-interest credit card debt, and essentially start from scratch without losing your home or your dignity. Just make sure that, after you bail yourself out of trouble, you don't rack up a huge balance on your credit cards again and end up in worse shape months later, having already increased your mortgage balance to pay off your previous credit card debt.

Calculating How Much Moolah You Need

We can't possibly give you a single formula for calculating how much money you need in order to get out of and stay out of this foreclosure jam. Some people need only a few thousand dollars to reinstate the mortgage, while others may need hundreds of thousands of dollars to refinance the old mortgage and cash out enough equity to pay off high-interest debt. How much you need is going to depend a great deal on the option you choose (see the preceding section, "Exploring Your Options").

If you choose to refinance, plan on doing it once. Homeowners often fail to cash out enough equity the first time and end up refinancing over and over again. The financing fees completely strip the equity out of their homes. Predatory lenders have been known to practice this ploy to line their own pockets, so don't get sucked into it. If you're going to refinance, cash out as little as possible but enough to get and keep yourself out of trouble, assuming, of course, that you qualify to borrow that much. Make a list of all the high-interest debt and other bills you want to pay off with the cashed-out equity:

- ✓ **Current mortgage:** The biggest debt you probably have to pay off with the proceeds from the refinance is your current mortgage. How much money would you need to pay off the balance?

- ✓ **Credit card balances:** Interest on credit card balances is typically astronomical. How they get away with charging that much interest and not being dragged into court for usury is beyond us. Make the most of your refinancing by paying off that high-interest debt. Just make sure you don't rack up a huge balance after refinancing, as too many people do.

- ✓ **Car loan:** If you have a low-interest car loan, you have no reason to use the equity in your home to pay it off. But if the monthly payments are high, paying off the car loan with the refinance proceeds can benefit you in two ways: It spreads the payments out over 30 years (or whatever term you choose and qualify for), and it makes the interest you're paying tax-deductible.

- ✓ **Medical expenses:** Many people end up in foreclosure over unexpected medical expenses. If you have sufficient equity in your home, you can use it to pay off those medical expenses and then, essentially, pay them off over the next 30 years.

- ✓ **Loan fees:** Most lenders charge fees to process a loan, as explained in the next section, "Calculating the Cost of Refinancing." Although you're allowed to pay these fees upfront, you probably have no cash to do so, so plan on paying for them out of the proceeds from the refinance.

- ✓ **Taxes:** If you owe any property tax or state or federal income tax, consider including what you owe in your refinance amount.

Add up all the debts you want to pay off by cashing out the equity in your home. If the amount is greater than your current mortgage balance plus the equity in your home, then remove some of the debts, starting with those that have the lowest interest rates. In other words, you want to pay off the high-interest debt first. Try to get as close to a fresh start as possible.

Know your limits. Under no circumstances should you agree to monthly payments that you can't afford or that you're likely to struggle to make if you hit a bump in your financial road. As Freddie Mac says on its anti-predatory-lending Web site (www.dontborrowtrouble.com), "Don't borrow trouble."

Calculating the Cost of Refinancing

Rich people may be able to refinance for free or find low-cost refinancing options, because they're low-risk borrowers. The rest of us usually get socked with some sort of fees, including loan origination fees, points, processing fees, notary fees, attorney fees, wire transfer fees, and so on. These fees should always be included on the good-faith estimate that the lender provides you prior to closing. The cost of refinancing also includes the increased amount of interest you end up paying over the life of the loan. (See "Calculating interest over the life of the loan," later in this chapter, for details on how to account for all these costs.)

If you have enough equity in your home, these costs can be paid for out of the proceeds from the refinance. However, you should be aware of the costs, so you can make a well-informed decision as to whether refinancing is worth it. If refinancing is ultimately going to cost you $50,000 over the life of the loan, for example, you may want to reconsider your options. Perhaps selling your home and buying something more affordable would be more prudent.

In the following sections, we show you how to do the math and calculate the total cost of refinancing. When you have the numbers, the decision is up to you.

If someone shows up at your door offering some creative financing solution to rescue you from foreclosure, proceed with caution. Many of the people who claim to want to help you are simply out to help themselves to whatever equity you have in your home. (See Chapter 9 for tips on how to steer clear of quick-fix scams and schemes.)

Tabulating loan fees . . . including those notorious hidden fees

If you're refinancing through a traditional lender, we can almost guarantee that you're getting your loan through a mortgage broker or a loan officer who works for a mortgage broker. This person usually earns money in two ways: receiving a commission from the bank that ultimately lends the money, and charging you a loan origination fee. In addition, other services related to the processing of the loan are going to charge fees.

You don't have to worry about the commission, because you don't pay that, but you do need to be aware of all the fees. Here's a short list of fees that we pulled from a relatively recent good-faith estimate on the refinance of a $100,000 mortgage:

Loan origination fee	$750
Loan discount (points)	$1,000
Appraisal	$325
Processing fee	$375
Underwriting fee	$175
Administration fee	$375
Flood certification	$21.50
Closing or escrow fee	$215
Document preparation fee	$50
Notary fees	$60

Title insurance	$280
Title search	$175
Recording fees	$60
State tax/stamps	$8
Total	**$3,869.50**

The total is an example of what you can expect to pay at closing, either out of pocket or from the proceeds of the refinance (the equity you cash out).

When shopping for mortgages (see the "Bargain-Hunting for Low-Cost Loans" section, later in this chapter), be sure to obtain a good-faith estimate, in writing, from each lender. This estimate can be very valuable when comparing the cost of loans. What the lenders *won't* tell you is that many of these fees are negotiable, and the cost of processing a loan is not as steep as some lenders make it out to be.

Calculating interest over the life of the loan

A 30-year, $200,000 mortgage at 7 percent interest is going to cost you over $479,000 when all is said and done, assuming you live in the home for 30 years. How much interest are you scheduled to pay on your current mortgage? How much interest can you expect to pay on your new mortgage?

The formula for calculating this is pretty straightforward:

Interest = (Monthly Payment × Term × 12) – Loan Amount

For a 30-year, $200,000 mortgage at 7 percent interest, the monthly payment is $1,330.60, so the formula would go like this:

($1,330.60 × 30 × 12) – $200,000 = $279,016 in interest alone!

These numbers are only for comparison purposes. Very few people end up staying in their homes for 30 years. Most people sell by the fifth year. The actual life of the loan is however long you own the home and pay on the mortgage. Unfortunately, because of the way banks calculate mortgage payments, you end up paying way more in interest during those early years compared to what you pay in interest during the last five years.

Calculating the total cost of the loan

Now that you know the total fees that the lender charges for the loan and the amount of interest you can expect to pay over the life of the loan, calculating the total cost of the loan is fairly easy:

Fees + Interest = Total Cost of Loan

Using this formula, calculate the cost of your current mortgage and your new mortgage. Depending on the interest rates and fees, you may actually save money by refinancing. If, however, the new loan is going to cost significantly more over the life of the loan, you may want to reconsider.

Two schools of thought may influence your decision of whether refinancing is worth it. Some people focus solely on the monthly payment. If they can refinance and consolidate their debt so they have one affordable monthly payment that's less than the total payments they're now making on their home, car, and credit cards, they consider refinancing a great option. Other people look at the total cost of the loan over the life of the loan, and if refinancing is going to cost them significantly more over the course of 30 years, they want no part of it. The choice is up to you. We just want you to have all the facts and figures you need to make a well-informed decision.

If you have plenty of equity built up in your property and would like to live off that equity for several years while planning to sell your home, consider a reverse mortgage. For more information, check out *Reverse Mortgages For Dummies* by Sarah Glendon Lyons and John E. Lucas (Wiley). Some reverse mortgages have age restrictions (you have to be older than a certain age), so this may not be an option for you.

Boosting the Equity in Your Home

Equity is the cash you stuff in your pockets after you sell your home and pay off all the liens against it. If your home is worth $300,000 and you owe $180,000 on the first mortgage and $30,000 on the second mortgage, then you have $90,000 equity in the home.

Equity usually increases about as fast as an oak tree grows. It takes forever, and you usually can't do much to speed it up, although some factors can contribute to increasing the equity:

✔ **Rising market values:** As the value of your property rises, you earn equity without having to lift a finger.

✔ **Paying down the principal:** Every time you make a payment on most mortgages (except interest-only mortgages), you pay down the principal and owe a little less on your home. You can accelerate the increase in equity by paying extra toward the principal. Some homeowners pay a little extra every month, while others make an extra payment per year or choose a mortgage with a shorter term — say 15 years instead of 30.

✔ **Fixing up the place:** Maintaining your property and keeping it up to market standards with the right renovations can increase the value of your property, which boosts your equity.

You can't do much to raise market values, and because you don't have extra money for paying down the principal, those first two options are pretty much off the table. You may, however, be able to fix up the place without spending a bunch of money. This is called investing *sweat equity* in your home. By investing sweat equity, your home may appraise higher, allowing you to borrow more money. In the following sections, we reveal some low-cost ways to improve the appearance and value of your home.

Don't borrow a bunch of money for home renovations so you can boost the value of your home before selling it. In most cases, you won't be able to recoup your costs. Consult your real estate agent before shelling out a bunch of money on home improvements.

Pruning and primping for curb appeal

Curb appeal is the number-one priority. By making your home look good on the outside, you announce to the world that the property is well-maintained inside and out. Here are some cost-effective ways to improve your home's curb appeal:

✔ Trim tree limbs and shrubs.

✔ Mow and edge the lawn.

✔ Remove dead or dying shrubs or flowers.

✔ Apply a fresh layer of mulch in any flower beds.

✔ Remove clutter and eyesores.

✔ Fill driveway and walkway cracks.

✔ Repair windows and screens.

✔ Paint the front door and trim.

✔ Paint the garage to match the house.

✔ Clean the gutters and repair any damaged sections.

✔ Make sure all the exterior lights work. Replace the light bulbs, if necessary.

De-cluttering the premises

Living in a house is like getting old: You look at yourself in a mirror and wonder where all that extra stuff came from. When you own a home, you naturally acquire more and more stuff until you can barely wade through the halls. Removing the clutter can make the entire house look bigger and cared for. Fortunately, removing the clutter costs you nothing but time and effort, and it can earn you a few bucks, too. Here are some suggestions:

✔ **Sell it, store it, give it away, or dump it.** Sell anything of value on eBay (www.ebay.com) or have a garage sale. Store anything you never use but still want to keep. Give away stuff you don't use and can't sell — you can donate it to a church or to an organization like Goodwill. Dump whatever's left.

✔ **Clear out the attic and garage.**

✔ **Clear the counters.** Remove nonessential items, including electric can openers, blenders, toasters, flour tins, cookie jars, and knife racks. Hide the rags and sponges and ditch the dish drainer. Make your counters look like the workspace of a famous chef.

✔ **Tidy up your closets.** Closets quickly become as cluttered as those overhead storage compartments on airplanes. If you can't entirely clear them out, empty out as much as possible and organize the rest.

Scrubbing your house from top to bottom

If an appraiser steps into the bathroom and nearly passes out, we can almost guarantee that the appraisal is going to suffer for it. By scrubbing your house from top to bottom, you freshen up the joint, make it smell a little nicer, and show that you take pride in maintaining your home. Here are some suggestions:

✔ Dust everything.

✔ Scrub down all the counters, sinks, toilets, showers, and baths.

✔ Sweep and mop the floors.

✔ Knock down the cobwebs from the ceilings and walls.

✔ Vacuum the carpets.

✔ Wash the windows.

Imagine yourself hosting a party. You want to make the place look and smell nice for your guests. Think spring cleaning, not just weekly cleaning.

Performing a few affordable renovations

Most people facing foreclosure don't have the money to gut the kitchen and install all-new cabinets and countertops, and that may not be a good idea even if you did have the money. You can, however, perform a few affordable renovations to make the house look as good as it possibly can:

- ✔ Patch any holes in the walls.

- ✔ Apply a fresh coat of paint to all rooms using flat, neutral colors and semigloss white for the trim.

- ✔ If the carpet is worn or damaged in a high-profile room, have it replaced. You may be able to pick up some cheap carpet that's been discontinued at your local building-supply store.

When the appraiser shows up, be sure to point out any repairs or renovations you've done since purchasing the home. A new furnace or air-conditioning system, new windows, kitchen or bathroom remodels, a new deck, and other improvements can make a difference.

Bargain-Hunting for Low-Cost Loans

People who are in the market for a loan usually feel as though they are at the mercy of banks and other lenders. But the process of borrowing money is very consumer-oriented — you shop for a loan that provides you with the money you need at the lowest cost possible. Think of it as *buying* a loan.

When shopping for a loan, your goal is to find the loan that will cost you the least amount of money for the *term* (duration) of the loan, with monthly payments that you can afford. The monthly-payment part is fairly easy to figure out, because lenders have to tell you what your monthly payments are going to be upfront. Determining how much the loan will cost you over the term of the loan, however, is a little trickier.

In the following sections, we offer some guidance on how to shop around for great deals on loans and how to compare different loans from different lenders.

For additional advice on searching for low-cost mortgages, check out *Mortgages For Dummies,* 2nd Edition, by Eric Tyson, MBA, and Ray Brown (Wiley).

Asking your current lender for a deal

Why would your current lender consider lending you more money when you can't even pay your current mortgage? Well, if you have sufficient equity in your home and are facing foreclosure due to some temporary setback, it could be a win-win situation for you and the bank. The bank doesn't have the hassle and expense of foreclosing and can collect even more interest from you, and you don't have to run around looking for another lender to borrow money from.

Your lender may be willing to float you a home equity loan or line of credit (see the "Exploring Your Options" section, earlier in this chapter) or assist you in securing a loan in one of the following two ways:

- **Mortgage modification:** Your lender may be willing to change the terms of your original mortgage to make the payments more affordable and assist you in catching up on payments. For example, if you need $10,000 to catch up, the bank may be able to add that amount back into the principal. Or, the bank may simply add time on to the end of the mortgage, so instead of having 25 years to pay on the mortgage, you're now back to having a 30-year mortgage. Your bank may also be willing to lower the interest rate.

- **Partial claim:** If you purchased mortgage insurance, your bank may be able to assist you in securing a one-time, interest-free loan from the mortgage insurance company to bring your account current. You may not have to pay off the loan for several years.

Assuming you're making a good-faith effort to repay your mortgage and are in a position to start making payments again, your lender is likely to be willing to work out a solution with you. (For additional details on working with your current lender, check out Chapter 11.)

Paying points . . . or not

Even financial gurus disagree on whether to pay points. Some advise never paying points, while others recommend doing the math and comparing the numbers. We side with the second group.

Points are interest you pay upfront. A point is 1 percent of the principal, so it's $1,000 for every $100,000 you borrow. Some lenders charge points in exchange for a lower interest rate. The lender may require that you pay 1 or 2 points to drop the interest rate by a half of a percentage point, for example.

Compare two loans: Both are 30-year mortgages for $100,000; the first is at 5.5 percent interest with 1 point, and the second is at 6.5 percent interest with no points. Which is better? Well, that depends. With the first loan, you pay

$1,000 upfront, but your monthly payment is $550.06. With the second loan, you pay nothing upfront, but your monthly payment is $617.42 — $67.32 more than the first loan.

If you plan on living in the home for less than 15 months, the second loan (no points) is a better deal. For example, if you sell the home in six months, you're only paying $403.92 more in payments, whereas you would be paying an additional $1,000 in points with the first loan. If you plan on having the mortgage for more than 15 months, then the first mortgage (with points) is a better deal.

To calculate whether you can save money by paying points, do the following:

1. **Subtract the monthly payment you would be paying on the loan *with* points from the monthly payment you would be paying on the loan *without* points.**

   This shows you how much you would save per month by paying points.

2. **Multiply the amount from Step 1 by the number of months you plan to live in the home and pay on this mortgage.**

   This shows you your entire savings over the life of the loan.

3. **Subtract the total cost of the points from the amount in Step 2.**

   Ask your loan officer the total cost of the points.

   If the answer is a negative number, you're probably better off not paying points. If the answer is pretty close to zero or is a positive number, paying points is probably a good idea.

If you qualify for a 6 percent interest rate without having to pay any points, ask the loan officer what rate you could get if you were willing to pay ½ point or 1 point. Then do the math, based on how long you plan on living in the home and paying on the mortgage. If you plan on paying on the mortgage long enough to eventually save enough to pay for the cost of the points, you're probably better off paying the points. If you think interest rates are going to drop soon and you may want to refinance at a lower interest rate within a year, however, paying points may not be such a good idea.

Choosing between fixed-rate and adjustable-rate mortgages

One of the main questions you have to answer when shopping for loans is whether you want a fixed-rate or adjustable-rate mortgage (ARM). When given the choice, consider it carefully, because an ARM could end up costing you an arm and a leg, which is even more painful than the pun.

In the following sections, we describe these two most common types of mortgage loans and offer guidance on how to decide which is best for you.

Holding steady with fixed-rate mortgages

A fixed-rate mortgage is a loan with an interest rate that remains unchanged throughout the life of the loan. If you take out a 30-year loan at 6 percent today, you still pay 6 percent interest 25 years down the road. Fixed-rate mortgages are most attractive under the following conditions:

- ✔ Interest rates are low.
- ✔ Your house-flipping strategy hinges on holding the property for several years.
- ✔ You expect interest rates to rise suddenly in the next few years.

For most homeowners, a fixed-rate mortgage with no prepayment penalty is the best choice. It really has no downside. If interest rates dip below what you're currently paying, you can always refinance into another fixed-rate mortgage at the lower interest rate.

Riding the waves with an adjustable-rate mortgage

Adjustable-rate mortgages (also known as ARMs) have interest rates that fluctuate. You may take out a loan for 5 percent and find yourself paying 9 percent the following year. This could mean you'll have to pay hundreds of dollars extra each month.

When shopping for adjustable-rate mortgages, examine the following factors to determine the worst-case scenario:

- ✔ **Initial interest rate:** The interest rate when you sign for the loan. This rate is usually lower than the one for a fixed-rate mortgage (see the preceding section).
- ✔ **Adjustment period:** The frequency at which the rate can go up or down. This period is typically one, three, or five years, but can be in months rather than years.
- ✔ **Index:** Adjustable-rate mortgages are tied to an index that typically rises or falls based on government lending rates. Ask which index the lender uses, how often it changes, and how it has performed in the past.
- ✔ **Margin:** The percentage above the index that the lender charges. Think of it as a markup. For example, if the index is at 3 percent and the margin is 2 percent, you pay 5 percent interest. If the index rises two percentage points to 5 percent, you pay 7 percent interest.
- ✔ **Cap:** The cap is the highest interest rate the lender charges, no matter how high the index rises. So, if the lender sets a lifetime cap at 9 percent, you never pay more than 9 percent interest. If the lender sets an adjustment-period cap of 2 percent and the adjustment period is one year, the interest

can rise a maximum of 2 percent each year. ARMs typically specify an adjustment period and a lifetime cap; for example, for an ARM with a cap of 2 and 6, the rate can jump a maximum of 2 percent per period but no higher than 6 percent over the life of the loan.

Don't bite when a bank dangles an unbelievably low-interest ARM in front of you. Lenders often use this marketing ploy to snag unwary borrowers and then hit them with huge interest-rate increases a few months down the road. By knowing the adjustment period and lifetime caps, you have a clear idea of the worst-case scenario.

Staying out of ARM's way

Adjustable-rate mortgages are great when interest rates are going down, but when interest rates start climbing, the results can be devastating. One couple we know financed the purchase of their home with an adjustable-rate mortgage, because the husband had just secured a new, better-paying job but didn't have the work history that a 30-year mortgage required in order to qualify for a low fixed-rate mortgage.

The loan officer explained that the couple could take out the adjustable-rate mortgage as a temporary solution. When the husband had held down the job for a while, they could come back and refinance into a traditional 30-year mortgage at a lower interest rate.

What the couple didn't know — and what no one really could have predicted — was that they bought their house at the peak of what was a record market high. Soon after they closed, the market began to tumble, and their home was no longer worth as much as it was when they first bought it.

When the couple tried to refinance, they were told that, because of the decline in the market,

they would need $10,000 in cash to pay down on the principal (because they had lost equity) to qualify for the traditional mortgage. The other problem was that the interest rate on their ARM was about to adjust up significantly. The husband had been on the job for the required amount of time, but at this point it didn't matter. When their mortgage adjusted, it would mean that their payment would increase by more than $325 a month!

They didn't have $10,000 sitting in their cookie jar, and they certainly couldn't afford the extra $325 a month. Fortunately for them, they were able to borrow the $10,000 from their parents and slip into a fixed-rate mortgage at an affordable monthly payment. It worked out for them, but for thousands of others in the same boat, it didn't, and banks were forced to foreclose in record numbers.

Unless you can afford to have your loan adjust, you need to seriously consider getting into a fixed-rate mortgage from the start. You may pay a slightly higher interest rate, but you also have the peace of mind of knowing that, no matter what, as long as you make your payments, your payment is going to be fixed.

Avoiding loans with prepayment penalties

When a bank loans you money for 30 years, it's counting on the fact that you're going to be paying interest to the bank for a long time. The bank doesn't want you refinancing with another bank a year or two down the road and cutting your initial bank out of the deal. To discourage you from refinancing, the bank may try to slip a prepayment penalty clause into your mortgage. If you refinance and try to pay off the loan early, you have to pay a stiff penalty — sometimes thousands of dollars.

 When shopping for mortgages, be sure to ask whether the mortgage loan has any prepayment penalties, and then read the mortgage carefully before signing it. If you have to refinance later, you don't want a prepayment penalty getting in the way.

Gauging your chances of qualifying for a loan

Banks don't lend money to just anybody. They look at your credit score, monthly income, annual income, expenses, and existing debt. They also examine the loan-to-value (LTV) ratio of your home — the relationship between how much you own on your home and its appraised value.

So, what are your chances of qualifying for a loan? The following sections point out some of the key areas of your financial portrait that banks examine to determine whether you're a low-risk loan applicant. You may not be able to improve in all areas, but improving in one or two areas may improve your chances of qualifying for the loan you need at a lower interest rate.

Credit score

To give your credit rating an air of objectivity, credit reporting agencies often assign you a credit score that ranges roughly between 300 (you never paid a bill in your life) and 900 (you borrow often, always pay your bills on time, and don't carry any huge balances on your credit cards).

Your credit score determines not only whether you qualify for a loan, but also how much you're qualified to borrow and at what interest rate. A high credit score lets you borrow more and pay less interest on it. A high score can also lower your home insurance and auto insurance rates — just another reason why the rich get richer and the poor stay poor.

Your credit report should contain your credit score. Anything above 700 or so is pretty good.

Savings

You can pretty much ignore this category. If you had any savings, you wouldn't be in foreclosure. However, if you have a substantial retirement nest egg that you're willing to put up as collateral, the bank may consider it "savings."

Debt ratio

Almost every lender will examine your debt ratio, so you should know what it is before the topic ever comes up. Simply put, your debt ratio is the ratio of how much you pay out in monthly bills compared to your gross monthly income. Generally speaking, you can estimate your debt ratio by dividing your total monthly payments (on loans and credit cards) by your total monthly income:

$$\text{Debt Ratio} = \text{Total Monthly Payments} \div \text{Total Monthly Income}$$

Your total monthly payments apply only to payments on loans, not for other expenses like groceries, gas, or clothing. They include payments on long-term debts, such as such car loan or student loan payments, alimony, child support, or a balance you carry on one or more credit cards.

According to the Federal Housing Authority (FHA), your debt ratio should not exceed 41 percent for all your existing debt plus the house payment. This is called your *back-end ratio.* Your debt ratio for the house payment alone, including property taxes and insurance (your *front-end ratio,* also known as your *housing ratio*) should not exceed 29 percent. If your total gross household income is $6,000 per month, your house payment alone should not exceed $1,740:

$$\text{Total Gross Income} \times 0.29 = \text{Maximum House Payment}$$

Loan-to-value ratio

The loan-to-value (LTV) ratio is a mathematic representation of how much you own on your home compared to its appraised value. If your home appraises for $250,000 and you owe $200,000 on it, the LTV is $200,000 ÷ $250,000, or 80 percent. Anything below 80 percent is considered great and often qualifies you to borrow more money at a lower interest rate.

Banks also use LTV ratios to justify lending money to high-risk borrowers. Even if you have a low credit score and a history of paying your bills a little late, if your LTV ratio is low, a bank may be willing to cut you some slack and approve your loan. In other words, the more equity you have in your home, the more likely the bank will approve your loan.

Be realistic and know how much you can really afford to borrow. Don't cause yourself stress and future problems by trying to stretch your finances too thin. If, after you do your calculations, it looks as though you can't afford to borrow more money, don't. Check out some of your other options instead (see Chapter 7).

Paying Down Your Debts

Assuming you secure a loan, use it wisely. We see far too many people take out a loan to recover from foreclosure and then repeat the same mistakes that put them into foreclosure in the first place. For most of these folks, that means racking up huge amounts of high-interest credit card debt.

Americans in general carry a massive amount of debt. A trustee who worked in the U.S. Department of Justice in the Bankruptcy Courts recently told us that it isn't at all uncommon for him to see individuals with $30,000, $40,000, and even $70,000 in credit card debt. When it all finally becomes too much to handle, they're forced to file for bankruptcy. Most credit cards carry an 18 percent to 24 percent interest rate. When you do the math, you're talking about a $1,400-per-month *minimum* payment (on a $70,000 balance at 24 percent interest). The payment on a 30-year $200,000 mortgage at 6 percent interest is less than $1,200, and when you make that payment, you're actually building equity in your home.

Maybe you've heard the phrase "Not all debt is bad debt," and that's fairly true. After all, entrepreneurs borrow money all the time to invest in their businesses and generate profits. However, some debt is bad, especially when you carry a high balance on a high-interest credit card.

If you have sufficient funds to pay off high-interest credit card debt, pay off the debt, stop using the cards, and then deposit what you would have been paying the credit card company each month into your savings account.

Make a list of all your debts and arrange them in order, with the highest-interest debts first. If you have any money left over from the amount you borrowed, use it to pay off those high-interest loans first. Over time, try to reduce your debt load as much as possible. That way, the next time you apply for a loan, you may be able to qualify much more easily for higher loan amounts with lower interest — and you'll be much less likely to find yourself in the foreclosure pit again.

Borrowing more money makes absolutely no sense if it's simply going to put you in the same situation months down the road. When you know what your monthly payments are going to be, ask yourself, "Can I really afford this?" If the answer is "No," then refinancing is not the best option for you. (For additional details about options and exit strategies, check out Chapter 7.)

When we encounter a homeowner who's drowning in debt, we often purchase his home, help him pay off his debt, and teach him how to reestablish his credit over a 24-month period. Our goal is to place the homeowner on the path to long-term financial health, so he can purchase an affordable home and avoid any future foreclosures.

Chapter 13

Cutting Your Losses: Unloading Your House

....

....

When you first purchased your home, you probably thought you were living the great American dream. Now, you may be feeling as though you're experiencing the great American nightmare. You feel as though you're standing in a bucket of concrete that's just been pushed overboard in the middle of the ocean. If you could just shed yourself of this burden, you could get on with your life. After all, when you were young, you managed somehow to live on a lot less money than what you've been spending over the last few years.

According to our rough estimates (based on a combined total of more than 40 years of assisting distressed homeowners), in approximately 90 percent of foreclosures, the homeowner's best option is to sell the property or deed it to an investor who's willing to pay off the remainder of the mortgage. By selling the house (with the assistance of a qualified real estate agent) rather than waiting for the legal system to take it from you, you're in a stronger position to take control of the situation, cash out any equity you've built up in the house, and salvage your credit. This chapter shows you how to cash out so you're ready to move forward. And if you have no equity in your home, this chapter shows you how to skedaddle without losing even more money.

Whenever you unload your home for less than you owe on it, be aware that your bank may be able to sue you for the difference. If the judge grants a deficiency judgment, that debt could follow you even after you unload the home. Consult a reputable and competent bankruptcy or foreclosure attorney about the possibility and ramifications of a deficiency judgment prior to selling your home for less than is required to pay off the liens against it.

Knowing When Unloading the House Makes Sense

After we meet with homeowners, they often realize that they can no longer afford their home. The payments have simply become too much of a burden, and they need to "get out from under it." This conjures up images of the Wicked Witch flattened by Dorothy's house in the *Wizard of Oz,* and for these homeowners, they probably feel a lot like that witch.

Some homeowners, however, really struggle with the decision. The roof over their heads is not just a house but a home — a place were they've had their fondest memories. The couple loves the school system, and the kids have loads of friends in the neighborhood. The family is well-established and deeply rooted in the community, and not a one of them wants to up and leave.

The decision is tough, but as a homeowner and perhaps a parent, it's up to you to make those tough decisions and establish a solid financial foundation that provides food and shelter for your family and keeps the home heated and the lights on.

In the following sections, we explore two scenarios in which dumping the house makes sense.

You have lots of equity in the house

One of the most tragic outcomes of foreclosure occurs when homeowners with plenty of equity in their homes fail to act. We've seen someone with $50,000 of equity in her home simply sit back and watch some investor purchase her homes at a foreclosure sale and rake in all that equity for himself. The homeowner not only ended up losing her home, but she lost up to $50,000 that was rightfully hers. If the homeowner had simply sold the home herself, she could have had that $50,000 to use as a down payment on a more affordable piece of property.

Before selling your home, consult a bankruptcy attorney and check out your options. If you file Chapter 7 bankruptcy, a portion of the equity in your home will be protected by the homestead exemption, which can be pretty hefty in some states. Your other debts will be wiped out as well. But if you sell the home to an investor, the proceeds will probably be taken by the Chapter 7 trustee because they no longer qualify under the homestead exemption.

If you have gobs of equity in your house and you can't or won't take other options to retain possession of it, sell the house and pocket the equity.

If you don't have at least 10 percent equity in your home, you're probably going to break even or have to bring some money to the closing table to pay the difference. Consider the following example:

> You can realistically sell your house for $100,000. The broker's commission is $6,000 (6 percent of the sale price). The state transfer tax at 0.75 percent comes to $750. The county transfer tax at 0.11 percent comes to $110. Title insurance costs another $800. Moving costs come in at somewhere around $500. Plus, you have to pay off the balance of the mortgage of $90,000.

Best-case scenario, you walk away with $1,840, and that's assuming that none of the numbers change, which is a big assumption. If you have only 5 percent equity in your home, you can expect an even worse scenario — one in which you sell your house and have to pay some extra money to get the lender off your back. (In Chapter 11, we discuss the option of negotiating a short sale with your lender to ensure that this doesn't happen.)

Selling your home for a profit is often easier said than done. If you purchased your home while the market was sizzling and have to sell during a big chill, you could find yourself owing more on the home than you can possibly sell it for. In addition, you may discover that selling your home requires much more time than you or your agent anticipated. A "quick" sale can easily turn into an eight-month adventure.

You have little, no, or negative equity in the house

If you have little, no, or negative equity in the house and little hope of being able to make the payments in the near future, getting rid of the house should probably be at the top of your list of options. With a short sale and the help of your foreclosure-experienced real estate agent, you may be able to shed the house and break even. If that's not an option, then giving the property away or simply vacating the premises may be an appealing choice. An investor may agree to take the property off your hands, as explained later in this chapter in the section "Striking a Deal with an Investor," or you can give away your home, as described in "Ditching Your House."

The magic number is 10 percent. If you have less than 10 percent equity in your home, you're probably not going to make any money and you may lose additional money by selling the home. If the home sells for less than you owe on it, for example, one of your creditors may file for a deficiency judgment, in which case you'll need to make up the difference or file for bankruptcy to have that debt erased. Consider other easier and less costly exit strategies.

Hiring a Top-Notch Real Estate Agent

When you think about hiring a real estate agent to sell your home, the thought of paying a 6 percent or 7 percent commission may send shivers down your spine. How can you possibly afford to hire a real estate agent when you can't even afford your house payment? Well, studies show that when a qualified agent properly lists and markets a home, it sells in significantly less time and for more money than if the homeowners try to sell it themselves. In fact, the additional amount of money the home sells for is often more than enough to cover the agent's commission.

The key is to find an agent who's most qualified to sell your home. In the following sections, we lead you through the process of selecting a top-notch real estate agent.

By law, your agent is prohibited from disclosing the fact that you're facing foreclosure. He has a fiduciary responsibility to the seller (that's you!) to get the best price and terms for the seller. If the real estate agent starts sharing your situation with the market, you're more likely to get low-ball offers on your home.

Finding an agent with the right stuff

All real estate agents are not created equal. You need an experienced agent, one who is well connected and is consistently on the top-producer lists. You need an agent who focuses on listing and marketing houses, and not one who just occasionally accepts listings. You want and need results, so you need an agent who can *deliver* results.

Look for the agent who has the most SOLD signs up in your neighborhood. This person is probably the top listing agent. She knows the market, is probably well connected, and has an edge over the competition.

Tracking down an agent

You can find dozens of real estate agents in your neighborhood simply by flipping through the local phone book or searching online, but how do you find the best of the best? Here are a few suggestions:

- **Register online at HurryHome.com.** HurryHome.com will pass your contact information along to several real estate agents in your area, who will then get in touch with you to set up an interview.

✔ **Ask your friends, relatives, and neighbors for recommendations.** They can tell you which agents they've had success with and which ones disappointed them.

✔ **Search online at the National Association of Realtors Web site (www.realtor.com).**

✔ **Check the classified ads in local newspapers and other publications.**

✔ **Check out the listings in local real estate magazines.**

When you find an agent you want to talk with, first track down the person's Web site and see what he has to offer. Most highly successful agents have their own Web sites. Use your favorite search engine, and type in the person's name plus the brokerage the person works for and your city or town. You can learn a lot from these Web sites and get a pretty good idea of how capable the person is at online marketing.

Real estate agent or Realtor: What's the difference?

A real estate agent is anyone who has a state license to negotiate the sale or purchase of a property and works for a real estate broker or brokerage company. A Realtor is a real estate agent who's also a member of the National Association of Realtors. The United States has more than 2 million real estate agents, but only 1.2 million of these are Realtors.

So, what's the difference? Because the qualifications for obtaining a real estate license vary from state to state, the quality of real estate agents varies much more than the quality of Realtors. The National Association of Realtors requires its members to complete additional training and testing to improve their knowledge

and abilities and encourages members to follow a strict code of ethics. The association also provides its members with additional resources and tools to assist in finding and marketing properties effectively.

Of course, this association membership doesn't mean that a particular Realtor is more qualified than a given real estate agent, but the odds are pretty good that you'll receive superior advice and service from a Realtor. To find a bona fide Realtor, look for the Realtor logo on business cards and stationery. Almost all Realtors make a point of proudly displaying this logo. You also can find a Realtor in your area by checking out www.realtor.com.

Checking credentials

Most top-producing agents are lifelong learners who invest in education. Make sure the agent you choose has the following credentials:

- ✔ **Realtor:** A Realtor is a real estate agent who is also a certified member of the National Association of Realtors. See the "Real estate agent or Realtor: What's the difference?" sidebar to determine the difference between a Realtor and an ordinary real estate agent.

- ✔ **Graduate Realtor Institute (GRI):** The GRI designation indicates that the Realtor has participated in and graduated from the Realtor Institute program and has mastered the solid base of information required to become a competent Realtor. This is the designation that most Realtors begin with.

- ✔ **Certified Residential Specialist (CRS):** Realtors who have the CRS designation have advanced training in listing and selling properties, and are proven to be top-producing agents. Only about 35,000 Realtors have earned the CRS designation.

In addition to checking the agent's credentials, look for an agent who has plenty of experience with foreclosures and short sales.

Interviewing prospective candidates

After you've identified two or three agents who you feel are highly qualified, interview them to find out more about their qualifications and how they plan to market your home. Here are some questions to kick the discussion into gear:

- ✔ **How many homes have you sold in the past 12 months?** You're looking for someone who has sold at least 20 homes in the past 12 months.

- ✔ **Do you have access to all the local Multiple Listing Services (MLSs)?** A large percentage of homes are sold through the MLS system, and some areas have more than one. For the most active marketing of your home, the agent must have access to all available MLSs in the area. (Your area may have only one.)

- ✔ **How long are homes in this neighborhood usually on the market before they sell?** In a healthy market, homes typically sell within 90 days.

- ✔ **How would you price my home?** Ask about the process the agent follows to determine the asking price, and then ask the price she would recommend. Don't simply go with the Realtor who suggests the highest asking price — this person may simply be trying to get your business by exaggerating the price.

- ✔ **How will you market my home?** Every agent should provide a listing presentation, during which he discusses various marketing media he'll use, including distributing fliers, placing classified ads, planting a FOR SALE sign on your lawn, marketing on the Internet, listing your home on the MLS, and so on. The Internet is a key tool in marketing homes; ask the agent to show you how he markets homes on the Internet.

✔ **How long are you going to list my home?** You'll sign a listing agreement that states the length of time the Realtor has to list and sell the home. After that time, you can re-sign with the Realtor or choose a different one. This time period is usually negotiable.

✔ **What's your list-price-to-sales-price ratio?** To sell your home quickly and for top dollar, you want to price it correctly from the start and have a marketing plan that attracts plenty of interested buyers. You should then be able to sell your home for close to the asking price. A seller's agent with a list-price-to-sales-price ratio near 100 percent is probably better than one with a ratio of 85 percent.

✔ **How much do you charge?** Realtors typically charge a percentage of the sales price — usually about 6 percent or 7 percent. If a buyer's agent delivers a buyer, then your Realtor will split the commission with the buyer's agent; it shouldn't cost you any more money.

✔ **Are you willing to accept a slightly reduced commission if you're able to locate the buyer as well as being the listing agent?** A listing agent typically splits the commission with a buyer's agent, but if the listing agent finds the buyer, she may be willing to discount the commission you pay, which is an added bonus for you.

✔ **If I find the buyer, how much commission do I have to pay you?** If you market your home and locate a buyer, your agent may be willing to discount the commission you pay, because she doesn't have to split it with a buyer's agent.

✔ **Whom do you represent?** You want a seller's agent who recognizes that her full and undivided loyalty is to you as seller. Faced with foreclosure, you want an agent that keeps your information and reasons for selling confidential. If the word gets out that you *need* to sell, the offers are going to reflect that.

✔ **What, if anything, should I do to improve the appearance of my house to generate more interest and offers?** Your agent should be able to tell you what you need to do to sell, not just sugarcoat everything. If you need to get rid of the tie-dyed wallpaper in your bedroom, your agent should tell you so. Don't be offended if the person makes suggestions. *Remember:* He's a professional trying to get your house sold quickly and for top dollar. The best agents know what buyers want.

✔ **Will you help me evaluate the pros and cons of any offers?** You want an agent who not only presents to you the price of the offer, but also explains the terms, the strengths and weaknesses, the likelihood of closing, the likely success of countering any offer, and the chance of receiving another offer if you don't accept this one.

- ✔ **Have you ever experienced foreclosure yourself?** An agent who's been through foreclosure generally has a clearer understanding of what you're going through than one who hasn't had the experience.

- ✔ **Do you understand the foreclosure process and can you explain it?** You want an agent who not only can sell your home but can also assist you in all stages of the foreclosure process.

- ✔ **Do you require an exclusive listing?** Many listing agents require you to list the home only with them for a certain amount of time. Find out whether the agent requires an exclusive listing, for how long, and whether you can cancel at any time. You want to be able to cancel the contract within a reasonable amount of time (say 30 days), if the agent is not producing the desired results.

- ✔ **Do you have a carry-over period?** With a carry-over period, an agent may demand a commission on a sale if, while he had the listing, he showed the house to someone who later decided to purchase the house after the listing expired.

Availability is critical. If you can't get a hold of your agent, and she never returns your calls, think about getting a new agent. Your agent should be attentive to your needs — after all, that's what you're paying the person for.

Although you should direct most of your questions toward your agent, ask yourself a few questions, as well:

- ✔ Do I feel comfortable with this agent?

- ✔ Is this agent listening to me and tuned into my situation?

- ✔ Do I trust this agent?

If you can't answer "yes" to all three questions, find another agent.

Motivating your agent to work hard for you

You probably shouldn't hire an agent who isn't already highly self-motivated, but you can ratchet the person's motivation up a notch by employing the following strategies:

- ✔ **Follow instructions.** When your agent tells you what you have to do to market your home, do it. When your agent tells you to clear out the garage, do some spring cleaning, and attend to the landscaping, do all of it. The person isn't just trying to make work for you; she's asking you to do what she knows you must do to sell your home quickly and for top dollar. When she sees how hard you're working, she'll be more willing to work hard for you.

✔ **Pitch in.** Tell everyone you know that your home is for sale. Send out e-mail messages, pass out fliers, call your friends and neighbors. You may be the one who finds a buyer. Your added efforts will further motivate your agent to ramp up her marketing efforts.

Teaming Up with Your Agent for Optimum Results

When selling your home, you have to realize that you and your real estate agent play two distinct roles. Your agent can list your home, market it, host an open house, show your home, and negotiate the price and terms with prospective buyers. That's pretty much where the agent's job ends.

The rest is up to you. As the seller, you have to:

✔ **Repair and renovate your home to bring it up to market standards.** Your real estate agent may be able to assist by referring you to painters, carpet companies, roofers, and other contractors, but scheduling work and getting it done is up to you.

✔ **Follow your real estate agent's advice.** You hired the best agent you could find, so listen to the expert when he offers advice.

✔ **Keep your home impeccably clean.** Your agent and other buyers' agents may show up with prospective buyers at a moment's notice. Not having your home ready at all times could eliminate a great opportunity. *Remember:* Any showing could be the one that sells your home.

✔ **Clear out of your home when people show up to see it.** Consider asking a couple neighbors whether you can come over when someone shows up to tour your home.

✔ **Keep quiet during negotiations.** Anything you say to prospective buyers and their agents may compromise your position at the negotiating table, making your agent's job that much more difficult.

Prepping and primping your house for sale

You may not have sufficient funds to transform your home into the Taj Mahal of the neighborhood, but you can make it look neat and clean:

✔ **De-clutter the premises.** Sell it, store it, give it away, or dump it. This covers every room in the house, including the basement, closets, and attic. It also covers the garage and the backyard. Yes, that vintage GTO you have up on blocks in the backyard has to go.

✔ **Clear off the countertops.** Clear everything that's not essential from the countertops, including the dish drainer, kitchen appliances, flour and sugar tins, washrags, toothbrush holders, and soap dishes. You want to make kitchens and bathrooms appear to have plenty of counter space.

✔ **Scrub the kitchens and bathrooms.** Kitchens and bathrooms can make or break a sale. Make sure they're squeaky clean, especially the sinks, showers, bathtubs, and toilets. In the kitchen, clean any appliances, including the refrigerator, stove, oven, microwave oven, and dishwasher. Visitors do look inside. Make sure the cabinets are clean, too.

✔ **Tidy up the other rooms in the house.** Make the beds, arrange the pillows, vacuum out the sofas and recliners.

✔ **Dust everything.** Dusting is one of the worst jobs on the planet, but if you clear the counters, shelves, and mantels, it's not quite as bad.

✔ **Vacuum the carpets and wash the floors.** Don't just do a cosmetic job. Move everything so you can clean under it.

✔ **Wash the windows inside and out.** In addition to washing the windows, make sure the window coverings — curtains, drapes, and blinds — are clean.

✔ **Attend to the landscaping.** Trim the trees and shrubs as needed, and mow and edge the lawn.

The first impression visitors should have when they walk into and through your home is the feeling you get when you first step into a hotel room suite. Nice hotel rooms always look ready to move into, but not lived in. Visitors should be able to see themselves moving right in and calling this home.

Staging your house to get top dollar

If you've ever taken a tour of a model home, you know what staging a house is all about. The builder or a professional stager furnishes the model home with tasteful décor, furniture, and carpets, making anyone who visits want to move in that same day. Tastefully decorated or staged homes create a positive emotional response that triggers the urge to buy. All other things being equal, a buyer purchases the house that feels more like home.

You can hire a professional stager to either arrange your furnishings for you or completely furnish the house from scratch for a flat rental and setup fee. To save some money, you may choose to do it yourself. Following are some tips to get you started:

✔ **Remove personal and politically incorrect décor.** Clear family portraits, religious icons, political paraphernalia, that moose head over the fireplace, and anything else that could prevent someone from envisioning himself living in the house.

✔ **Add a small table with matching chairs to the dining room.** A clear glass table is often preferable to a heavy wooden table, because it makes the kitchen seem a little roomier.

✔ **In the living room, add a couch with end tables and two or three small lamps.** Make the living room look comfortable, not cramped.

✔ **Each bedroom should have a queen-size bed and a small dresser.** Arrange the bed and dresser in a way that makes it easy to walk around the room.

✔ **Light up the house.** Open the curtains and tie them back, if possible, to let the light in. Open the mini-blinds about three-quarters of the way, so more light can penetrate but so that the house doesn't look vacant from the outside. Turn on every light in the house. (Add higher-watt bulbs to increase the light, but don't exceed the maximum wattage for the light fixture.) If you're showing the house at night, turn on every light outside the house.

✔ **Bring the outside in.** Open up the house (in warmer weather), bring in some greenery from the trees, and tastefully decorate with fresh-cut flowers. No potpourri, scented candles, or air fresheners.

✔ **Play music.** When prospective buyers are coming by to see your home, play soothing background music.

✔ **Head out before visitors arrive.** Ask your agent to call you prior to any showings, so you can leave before prospective buyers arrive. This makes buyers feel more comfortable and ensures that you won't let anything slip that could undermine the sale.

Keeping every room sparsely furnished makes the entire house seem roomier, without making it feel like an empty cave.

Setting an attractive asking price

Although location may be the biggest factor in determining the value of a property, asking price is the biggest factor in how quickly the property sells. Set the price right, and the house should sell within the first 10 to 15 showings. Set the price too high, and the house will sit on the market for months or even years. Set the price too low, and you could scare off buyers who may think the house has something wrong with it, or you may end up shortchanging yourself.

Several online services offer free home valuations. You can enter your address online, and the service tells you how much your home is worth. Although these sites can be informational and fun to visit at your leisure, the estimates that these sites offer are often wrong — either too high or too low. When you're setting a price for your home, you really need an outstanding real estate agent who has an intimate knowledge of the market.

Paul's political snafu

I almost lost a sale once through a very minor oversight that brought politics into a transaction. One of the first rules of selling real estate is to never talk about religion, politics, or education. I managed to avoid those topics, but I dropped the ball when it came to one small item that was decorating the car I was driving.

I needed a pickup truck to haul some items, so I swapped vehicles with my brother, and my brother's truck happened to have a sticker in the rear window for a particular political candidate. I drove the truck to a closing, and just before the closing, my client noticed the sticker in the back window of the truck and said, "If I'd known that you supported that guy, I would never have bought this house from you."

I was a little taken aback. I hadn't even noticed the political sticker, and I knew I had never discussed politics with this client. I wondered why he thought I was a supporter of that candidate. When I asked my client about it, he said he was referring to the sticker on my truck. I explained what had happened — that I was simply borrowing the truck to haul some items. I don't know whether he believed me, but we ended up closing on the house, so I dodged the bullet.

The moral of this story: Some people have such strong feelings regarding political figures (and a variety of other hot-button topics) that they may just walk away from a deal if your views don't match theirs. Don't talk about these subjects or display anything relating to these subjects when you're trying to sell your home . . . period.

Following are some guidelines to help you set a competitive asking price:

- ✔ **Do your research.** Carefully research both the sale prices of comparable homes that have recently sold in your area and the asking prices of homes that are currently for sale. Are housing values rising, falling, or remaining steady? Calculate the price trend into your asking price.

- ✔ **Don't be greedy.** You don't have time to test the market.

- ✔ **Set the right price the first time.** Set a realistic asking price that's in line with or slightly below recent sale prices of comparable homes in your area. Set a price that you *think* is realistic, not one that you *feel* you deserve.

- ✔ **When in doubt, order an appraisal.** An appraiser can give you a highly accurate estimate of the current value of your home. This may cost you a few hundred dollars, but the appraisal will come in handy during negotiations — especially if a prospective buyer makes a lowball offer.

Meet with several real estate agents to pick their brains for an asking price based on comparable homes in your area. Agents have access to the MLS, which gives them the sales information they need to develop accurate estimates. You don't have to actually hire an agent to get some quotes on what she thinks the property will sell for. Be careful whom you trust — some agents inflate their estimates to get your business.

Weighing offers as they roll in

Assuming you and your agent did an outstanding job marketing your home, the offers should soon be rolling in. As they do, don't be tempted to pursue only the offers with the highest prices. Consider other factors, as well:

- ✔ **Earnest money deposit (EMD):** An offer that has a high EMD usually means that the buyer is serious and less likely to back out of the deal at the last minute.

- ✔ **Early closing date:** Someone who wants to close in a hurry is more likely to be able to close before your home ends up on the auction block.

- ✔ **Very few conditional clauses:** Some offers include all sorts of conditional clauses that can be very costly. The simpler the offer, the better. If the deal hinges on whether the buyers can sell their home or obtain approval for financing, the deal may take more time than you have or it may fall through.

Your agent can assist you in evaluating offers as they come in.

If you get a good offer as soon as you place your home on the market, take it. Don't reject the offer just because you think something better may come along. That first offer may be the best or only offer you'll get. For additional tips and tricks for selling a home, check out *House Selling For Dummies,* by Eric Tyson, MBA, and Roy Brown (Wiley).

Striking a Deal with an Investor

In Michigan, where we operate, most homeowners have sufficient time to sell their home. Even if someone buys it at auction, they have another six months of redemption to sell. Homeowners in other states are not so fortunate. In some states, the bank can auction off the home with only a few weeks' notice, and the homeowners don't even have an extra day to redeem.

When you're in a hurry to sell, however, you can usually find an investor with cash on hand to purchase your property. You're not likely to get the going rate for your home, but you can close in a hurry and perhaps walk away with a little cash to find new accommodations.

Never ever deed your home to an investor in exchange for the investor's promise to pay off the mortgage. Even if you're "giving" the property to the investor and walking away with nothing, schedule a closing to make sure the transfer is legal and the bank gets paid. Otherwise, the investor may take ownership of the home and leave you with the mortgage. This is an old scam that plenty of people have fallen for.

Finding an investor to purchase your home

You probably won't have much trouble finding an investor to purchase your home. They generally find you as soon as the foreclosure notice is posted. However, make sure the person is on the level by asking real estate brokers or attorneys in your area about the investor. Reputable and disreputable investors are usually well-known, and real estate professionals in your area should be ready and willing to assist you in sorting them out, or even steer you in the direction of more reputable investors.

Beware of the *bird dog* (also known as the house whore) — the dreaded middleman who is on the constant hunt for fresh blood. Bird dogs have no money of their own. They simply cruise the area looking for distressed homes and homeowners. When they find one, they peddle the information to the highest bidder or point it out to an investor who has the cash to seal the deal. Avoid the middleman and deal directly with investors. Bird dogs have no control of how the deal eventually pans out.

Agreeing on a fair price

When you sell to an investor, it's like selling something at a garage sale — don't expect to sell at the going rate. Most investors expect to earn at least a 20 percent profit from the deal. That's 20 percent above the purchase price *plus* all the other expenses for fixing up and marketing the property.

If an investor makes an offer, ask for a sheet of paper showing how the investor came up with that offer. Examine it carefully to see whether the numbers seem reasonable before you sign on the dotted line.

Selling to an investor doesn't always mean losing the home. If you have the means and are determined to retain possession of your home, you can try to buy back your home using a contract for deed or lease-option agreement, as we explain in Chapter 7. Chapter 5 contains additional details about reading and understanding such agreements.

Ditching Your House

What would happen if you just up and left — got out of Dodge before the sheriff and his posse showed up to boot you out? Ditching your home is certainly an option — a last-ditch effort, so to speak, but an option nevertheless. And the longer the redemption period in your area, the more practical this option becomes. In the following sections, we lay out a 12-step plan for a graceful exit.

If you can resolve the issue without resorting to ditching the house, by all means, do so. However, if you lost your job, you're living on noodle soup, you can barely keep the lights on, and you know that you can do nothing to save your home from foreclosure, start drawing up your exit strategy. By leaving on your own terms, you may be able to save some startup cash for your new life.

Step 1: Slash expenses

Your goal at this point is to build up a stash of cash as quickly as possible, and one way to do that is to stop the cash from flowing out (see Chapter 8). Identify all nonessential expenses — like eating out, dry cleaning bills, entertainment expenses, lawn services, kids driving to school instead of taking the bus, you driving to work instead of carpooling, and so on — and then slash them.

Now, look at the list of necessary expenses, and for each expense on the list ask yourself, "What's going to happen if I don't pay this bill?" Take your car payment, for example. What's going to happen if you don't make that payment? Eventually, the dealership is going to send the repo man after you, but not right away. You usually have a grace period and then a couple months before they take any real action. Now, we're not telling you to stop paying on your car if you really need it, but if you have two cars and you're paying on one, you may be able to stop making payments on the new car without suffering any major loss of transportation.

Repeat this process for each and every *necessary* expense, including gas, electric, water, and sewer. If you don't pay, when is the company going to take action and shut off your service? Lay out a timeline for each item and determine the minimum amount you can pay to keep everything in place, or work out some payment agreement with the utility companies.

Many communities, and even the utility companies themselves, offer assistance programs. If you're having trouble paying your heating bill, for example, contact your gas or electric company and ask whether it has any programs in place to assist homeowners who are having trouble paying their bills. If you have a community center in your area, let them know that you need assistance; they can point you in the right direction.

Step 2: Cancel unnecessary services

Cancel your cable or satellite TV service, Internet, housekeeping, cellphones, and extra land lines.

If your cellphone or other service has a cancellation fee to break the contract, ask what happens if you simply can't make the payments anymore. Request that your provider waive the fee. Explain that you're not trying to cheat the company, but you can no longer afford the monthly bill and certainly cannot afford paying a cancellation fee. Let the company know what's going on. If that doesn't work, even after you try to convince a supervisor, pay your most recent bill, turn off the phone, set it aside, and don't use it again. Document everything, so if the phone company wants to hold you accountable, you can prove that you did everything you could to avoid a messy breakup.

Step 3: Stop making mortgage payments

Did we just say to stop making mortgage payments?! Yep, that's what we said. Many homeowners, knowing that they're destined to lose their homes, keep making payments, which makes absolutely no sense. Start saving every penny you can of those scheduled mortgage payments, so you have some savings to finance your move.

While you're at it, stop paying your property taxes. Your county isn't going to haul you into court for missed property taxes until you're behind by a couple years — long after you've moved on to greener pastures.

Step 4: List the house for sale

While you're waiting, list the house with a reputable and high-volume real estate broker (see "Hiring a Top-Notch Real Estate Agent," earlier in this chapter). If you can get out by selling the home and breaking even, hurray for you! You still come out ahead, because you saved all that money you would have been spending to keep the mortgage payments current.

Step 5: Move your savings

If you have your money at the bank that holds your mortgage, move your money to another bank or credit union, or stuff it under your mattress before you miss any payments. Most banks have the right to deduct whatever you owe them from any accounts you have with them, so don't make it easy for the bank to find your money.

Step 6: Get a job

Even if you can't find a six-figure job in your field of expertise, take some job, any job. Earning $10 to $12 per hour brings in about $350 per 40-hour week, after taxes. If you and your spouse can each bring in that much money, you're talking $700 per week or $2,800 per month. Depending on how long it takes the bank to sell your property and how long the redemption period is, you could be looking at creating quite a nest egg even after covering your basic living expenses.

Now, that would be impossible to accomplish if you were paying your mortgage and all the other expenses, but you're in survival mode here, essentially paying for groceries and enough gas or electricity to cook and keep the house above 68°F.

Just because you take a job for $10 to $12 an hour doesn't mean you can stop looking for more lucrative employment. Keep sending out those résumés and making phone calls. If jobs in your field have moved out of state, you may need to make a bigger move than you initially planned.

If you have teenagers living at home, consider putting them to work, too. You'd be surprised at how many homes we've visited only to find a teenager lying on the couch, doing nothing! Get the kids up and out earning their keep. At the very least, make sure they're taking on some additional household chores while you take on a second job. It's time to stop the entitlement mentality. Everyone in the family needs to lend a helping hand.

Step 7: Start packing

While you're maintaining your existence in preparation for moving day, start sifting through your personal belongings. Figure out what you need and want to take with you, and what you can sell, give away, or leave behind. Start to box up your belongings, so you're well prepared to move over the weekend just before your time in your home comes to an end.

The less you take with you, the easier it is to move and downsize later. Sell it, give it, store it, or dump it.

If that job three states away comes through and you have to move earlier than planned, you don't want to have to sort through 12 years of accumulated stuff over the next few days. In addition, if one spouse moves before the other, you don't want the spouse left behind to get stuck with all the packing.

Step 8: Have a garage sale

As soon as you have a handle on what you want to keep and what you want to get rid of, have a garage sale and price everything to sell. If someone offers you $8 for that $20 vase, take it. The goal is to get as much money as you can, without having a bunch of stuff left over that you have to give away to Goodwill or move with you. Take whatever cash you can get and be done with it.

Closer to moving day, try to sell some of the pricier appliances, including the refrigerator, stove, any window air-conditioning units, microwave ovens, and so on. Stop short of tearing out the kitchen cabinets and sink, but sell anything that isn't really part of the house that you don't want to take with you.

Step 9: Find suitable accommodations

Four to six weeks before your scheduled moving date, find, or at least start looking for, a place to live. The reason we advise you to wait is because you should be in a better position later to afford something. In addition, if the market is in a slump, prices may be more affordable a month or two later. Don't wait too long, however; you could end up having to settle for whatever is available at the time.

If you're moving out of state, take a couple days to scout out the area and find something, or contact a real estate broker in the destination area and have him locate a rental for you. Give him very detailed information about what you're looking for, including price range, location, and features. Let him know when you'll be moving into town and that you want to have a place lined up in advance. Be prepared to pay a deposit.

Step 10: Stop paying the utilities . . . maybe

If you're moving somewhere close and you're going to have to go through the same utility company to get your gas, electric, and water in your name, then you can't afford to stop paying the utilities. If you're moving across the country, however, and certain utilities (like water) are not going to follow you, stop paying for them.

We're not saying that you should abuse the service or run up huge bills only to skip town, leaving someone else to hold the bag. Well, maybe we are, sort of, but when you're about to lose everything, you're in survival mode, so survive the best you can. Let that investor who buys your house at auction pay the water bill.

Step 11: Get some more time and maybe some money

Attend the eviction hearing and ask the judge whether you can have 30 days to vacate the premises. The judge may only grant you ten days, but that's still more than what you would have had otherwise. Ask the bank's attorney if the bank would be willing to trade "cash for keys." Suggest that you can be out by a certain date, and would be able to leave the house broom clean and turn in the keys to the attorney's office for $500 to $1,000.

Why would any bank pay you to turn in the keys? Because evictions can be expensive, and the bank knows that if you part on good terms, you're less likely to trash the place. If the bank thinks it's going to have to pay $1,800 to a court officer to perform an eviction (believing the house full of junk), the bank may be willing to give you $800 to clear it out for them and turn in the keys. It won't always work, but if it does, you're another $800 to the good.

If you're getting cash for keys, you may be required to leave the house broom clean in order to get your money. That means all the junk is out of all the rooms, the garage is free from junk (or at least it's bagged up and ready to go into a dumpster), the basement floor is swept, and the house is what you would expect to find if you were to move into it. You're not dusting and waxing the floors, but you should leave the house tidy.

Step 12: Move out

You've completed all the difficult steps. Now use some of the cash-for-keys money, rent a moving truck, pack it full of whatever belongings you have left, drop the keys off at the attorney's office, and head out of town. Try to move everything at once, so you don't have to go back and relive the painful memory.

As you look back at that FOR SALE sign in the front yard, view this as a positive move forward. Tell yourself that you had to sell to pursue a great new job opportunity or to liberate yourself from the burden of the keeping-up-with-the-Joneses lifestyle. Say whatever you want, but move on and start fresh. If you did everything we told you to do, you should have a few grand in your pocket and a new lease on life.

Chapter 14

Fiddling While Rome Burns: The Do-Nothing Approach

In This Chapter

▶ Knowing what's in store if you don't act now

▶ Steering clear of ugly confrontations

▶ Squirreling away some money in the meantime

▶ Doing nothing the smart way

*W*hen facing foreclosure, you always have the option of doing nothing. Just sit back and let the wheels of justice (or injustice, if you see it that way) roll right over you. After all, what's the worst that the system can do to you? They certainly can't get any *more* money out of you, can they? Can they burn your family at the stake? Throw all of you in debtor's prison? Tar and feather you? Of course not. Fortunately, those days are over.

If you have little equity in the house, don't have children, and don't care what your neighbors, friends, family, and colleagues think, then doing nothing is certainly an option. Otherwise, we strongly recommend against it. In this chapter, we reveal the pros and cons of doing nothing, and show you how to do nothing in the most productive way possible.

Grasping the Consequences of Inaction

You're on vacation flying to some remote destination. En route, your plane goes down. You're a little bruised, but you have no major injuries. You look around and survey the wooded area where your plane came to rest, and you can't believe this has happened to you. You're a little scared of what lies ahead in the woods — bears, mountain lions, cannibals, or something worse? You see a path, but you're not sure where it leads. You don't know where to get fresh water, and you can't tell what's edible from what's not. Instead of trying to get yourself out of this mess, you decide to do absolutely nothing, so you take a seat beneath the nearest tree and wait for the rescuers to arrive.

Two months later, a hiker stumbles upon the wreckage from the plane and notices your emaciated corpse propped up against the tree. He's a little puzzled, because you don't seem to have any major injuries from the crash, the plane's radio is still working, there's plenty of fresh water in the stream 100 yards from you, and the nearest town is only about a quarter-mile away. Yet, you look as though you died from dehydration or starvation or a combination of the two. It appears as if you did absolutely nothing. And the craziest thing is that you were sitting against an apple tree that was probably covered with fruit when you sat down below it — if you had only looked up.

In foreclosure, doing nothing is probably not going to result in you and your family starving to death or facing dehydration, but it can result in a host of other negative consequences that you should be aware of. In the following sections, we explore the likely consequences you face if you choose to do nothing.

Becoming a puppet on someone else's strings

When you receive a foreclosure notice, you may begin to feel powerless. You can't pay your bills, the bank is foreclosing, and unless a Brink's truck arrives and dumps bags of cash on your front porch, you're probably going to lose your home. Your fate is sealed, right? So why bother?

To some extent, your fate *may* be sealed, but it's even *more* sealed if you don't take action. By sitting back, you put all the power in the hands of the bank. You're no longer working according to your schedule — now you have to adhere to the foreclosure schedule. If you fail to respond to notices you receive in the mail or answer phone calls, the bank can only assume that you won't pay and don't want to work out a solution. After all, the bank can't possibly work with you if you refuse to communicate.

At this point, you're thrown into the foreclosure mill to be ground up with all the other kernels into a foreclosure mash. The bank tries to speed up the process to reclaim its collateral as quickly as possible to limit its loss or avoid a loss altogether. The foreclosure wheels start turning, and you can expect the following events to occur:

- ✔ The reinstatement period expires, and you lose the option to reinstate the mortgage.
- ✔ Someone purchases the property at auction or the bank "bids it in" at the auction, entering the winning bid by default.

- ✔ The redemption period (if any) expires, and you lose the option to buy back your home.
- ✔ The eviction date arrives, and you and your possessions are kicked out on the street.

If other creditors hold liens against your property, they may also get involved, because the foreclosure sale will wipe out their interest in the property. When the senior lien holder moves to foreclose, junior lien holders may try to foreclose first, send someone to the sale to bid the price high enough to cover their mortgage amount, or purchase the first position to protect their position. In other words, even though you may choose to do nothing, your situation may change based on what other players choose to do.

If you don't take action, someone else will, and the person taking action has control. Don't be someone else's puppet, letting him pull the strings. Don't be a pawn in the foreclosure game. Take action, and you take control. You may not be able to save your home, but by taking action, you almost always conserve more resources and have more control over how the situation ultimately unfolds.

Circling the wagons

We once dealt with a couple who were facing foreclosure due to the wife's mismanagement of the family finances. The wife never told the husband that she hadn't made the payments, and the house was put up for auction. We purchased the property and contacted the wife to let her know what was going on.

We told her that she and her husband needed to come to the office to find out more about their options. She put it off until the last week of the redemption period, which was rather unfortunate, because this was the beginning of hunting season, and the husband wasn't going to miss it. They never showed up for the scheduled meeting. Instead, they retained an attorney who sued us. Their claim was that we had promised they could stay in the home. They lost the case and then hired another attorney. They took the

half-do-nothing approach, in which one spouse knows about it and does nothing and the other is entirely clueless.

Instead of hiring an attorney late in the game to try to bail them out, the couple should have worked together from the very start to resolve their problems and catch up on the missed payments and fees. Whenever we sit down with a couple caught up in the blame game, we tell them to imagine themselves crossing the country in a wagon train in the wild, wild west. Fully armed bandits are lined up on a ridge, ready to attack. What do you do — take off on your own or circle the wagons? What's your best way to survive — alone or together?

The answer is obvious: Working together you have a better chance of surviving and digging your way out of your current predicament.

Losing your home for sure

We can't possibly guarantee that any of the solutions we reveal in this book are going to enable you to save your home, but we *can* guarantee that if you do nothing, you'll lose your home. The bank will foreclose, sell your home at auction, and evict you, if necessary. Your problem is not going to simply disappear.

In fact, the situation can get even worse. The bank could end up repossessing your home, selling it for less than you owe the bank, and then obtaining a deficiency judgment requiring you to make up the difference.

Giving away your hard-earned equity

Equity is like money in the bank. If you had tens of thousands of dollars in a bank account, you wouldn't simply let someone else cash out that money due to a few minor technicalities. Some homeowners, however, do exactly that when they fail to take action during a foreclosure. A person may owe $150,000 on a home that's worth $200,000 and simply let someone purchase the property at auction for $150,000. The buyer can then sell the property for $200,000 and become the beneficiary of all that equity — equity that rightfully belongs to the original owner.

Due to time constraints, you may not be able to cash out 100 percent of the equity in your home, but you can usually sell to an investor or put your home on the market for a reduced price to cash out a portion of that equity.

You worked for the equity in your home. You took out a loan, purchased the home, paid down the principal, and maintained the home when housing values were on the rise. Maybe you even performed some home improvements to increase the value of the property. Don't let the bank or an investor waltz in and take all that equity you worked for. (We offer some additional tips on selling your home to get out from under it in Chapter 13.)

Facing the ugliness of a forced eviction

A forced eviction is not a pretty sight. It's not as if professional movers arrive to carefully pack your belongings and load them into a moving van. A court officer and perhaps a few burly assistants show up to forcibly remove you, your family, and everything you own from the home and set it out on the street. They don't try to damage the goods, but they're on a tight schedule, so certain items can get pretty banged up.

Milking every drop of equity out of your home

When we meet with homeowners facing foreclosure, we usually have to give them a brief lesson on equity and show them various ways they can use the equity in their homes to their advantage. Not too long ago, we met a homeowner who could have taught the course himself.

We actually purchased the man's home at a foreclosure auction. The property was located in a very fast-growing and popular hot spot. The house was no prize-winning piece of property — it needed quite a bit of work to bring it up to market standards — but the location was right, and the structure of the home was sound.

Whenever we purchase a house in foreclosure, we always try to contact the homeowners so they know their options and don't fall victim to some scammer. We explain to them that our company purchased their home in foreclosure, and then we take the time to explain their options. A suitable solution is not always possible, and many times the homeowners choose to ignore us, as they've ignored everyone else all along.

But this gentleman didn't ignore us. When we contacted him, he invited us over and explained the situation to us. He was planning on moving as soon as possible. He had a brother down south who had work for him, and that's where he was heading. He had purchased the property before the area was popular, and he had raised all his children here. He had a lot of sweat equity in the property, because he had performed all the updates himself.

He let us know that he was experienced in using the equity in his home strategically. Throughout his life, he cashed out equity to finance other ventures, and when he lost his job, he used the equity to live on. Just before losing his job, he took out another mortgage on the property. He was hoping to pick up enough work to make the payments, but that never panned out. He was able to make the payments for some time by taking on side jobs, but eventually that dried up and he was now in foreclosure.

He was certain the house still had a little equity left in it, but because of his current financial situation, lack of steady income, and poor credit, he couldn't possibly qualify for another loan. He walked us around the house, showed us the problems, and explained to us that if he could pull $5,000 out, he'd be gone in a week. He told us that he had a job waiting but that it could wait another six months while he lived in the house for free during his redemption period, and he'd really rather just walk away and use the $5,000 to move and get a fresh start down south. He offered us a deal — if we were to give him $5,000, he would be gone in seven days.

That certainly sounded like a fair proposition. We knew the house needed a lot of work, but we were also aware that if he stuck around in the home for six months without paying rent, we would be the big losers. We had a rehab crew that could come in and do the required work in a hurry, and we wanted to get them in as soon as possible, so we agreed. We gave him half the money upfront and the other half as he was pulling out of the driveway with his trailer loaded and heading south.

He was able to put the foreclosure behind him and move forward with an extra $5,000 in his pocket, and we were able to take possession, renovate the property, and place it on the market in a fraction of the time it would have taken us if we'd had to wait out the entire redemption period.

We sometimes think about this guy and how he was savvy enough to milk every ounce of equity out of his home and use it to his advantage. He knew that $5,000 was the most anyone would give him because of the condition of the house and the updates that were needed to sell it for top dollar, but he also knew that we didn't want him living in the home for six months without paying us a dime. We don't know if he was successful down south or not, but we sure wouldn't call you a liar if you told us he was.

After everything is out of the home, they lock it up and leave. They don't cover your stuff with a tarp to keep it out of the rain or stand guard to keep greedy neighbors from walking off with your property. If you don't cart your property off the premises in a certain amount of time (usually 24 to 48 hours), the city has someone haul it off to the local garbage dump, and that's the end of the story.

If you think foreclosure is embarrassing, try a forced eviction on for size. Even if your neighbors don't walk off with your belongings, you can count on them watching the activities out their windows or coming over for a curbside seat. We strongly encourage you, especially if you have children, to move out at least a day or two before eviction day rolls around. Nobody can evict you if you're not there.

Witnessing evictions: Two case studies

Losing a home can be emotionally devastating, but a forced eviction is even worse. We've witnessed plenty of evictions, but the following two stand out in our minds.

Case Study 1

The first case involves a woman who was forcibly evicted from a fine home in a very nice neighborhood. We don't know the woman's situation or why she wound up in foreclosure. All we know is that when eviction time arrived, it was quite a theatrical production.

This woman was, by far, one of the most difficult people in the world to deal with. She refused to acknowledge that she was in foreclosure and refused to believe that anyone would actually put her belongings out on the street. Well, they did — and, boy, was it something.

This was a rather large house, and she hadn't moved anything — not her bed, not her living room furniture, not one pot or pan . . . nothing. When the court officer finally scheduled the eviction, he posted the usual notice stating that if she didn't vacate within 24 hours, he would be there to see her put out. She didn't vacate. In fact, while the court officer was there overseeing all her belongings being carried out to the

street, she came home in her gold Lexus, pushed the button on her garage door opener, pulled into the garage, and clicked the button again to close the door, all as if nothing was going on.

The officer met her inside and explained that if she refused to peacefully vacate, he would have to forcibly remove her, change the locks, and disconnect the remote garage entry. At that, she walked back out to the garage, got into her car, opened the garage door, and drove off. We never saw her again.

The entire neighborhood had gathered around the house to watch the show. It was really a scene. People were in lawn chairs in their front yards and on their front porches watching the whole thing unfold. We think we even saw someone trying to sell beer and hot dogs.

According to one of the neighbors, the woman came back later that night, picked out a couple things from the enormous pile of belongings, and left. She didn't come back again. After a couple days, the city had her remaining belongings loaded into a dumpster. The neighbors had pretty well picked though the stuff and taken whatever they found to be valuable by then. The rest is probably rotting in a landfill as we speak.

Case Study 2

We've even witnessed an eviction that occurred some time after we purchased the home and the owner moved out. Sound strange? It was.

We actually purchased the property at a fore-closure auction. The redemption expired and the homeowner moved out, and our crew was inside performing some renovations. As they were working, the homeowner showed up and let her-self into the home. One of the crew called our office asking what to do. We told the crew to leave the house and wait out front until we could get there. On our way, we called the police.

When we arrived, the foreman was standing out front. He said that he had sent the rest of the crew to lunch, but the woman never came out of the house. The police arrived and went inside to look around. After some time, they came out and said nobody was in the house; they could only guess that she had left out the back. We encouraged the police to look a little harder, because we were convinced that she was still in the house hiding somewhere. We also thought that she needed some psychiatric care. After all,

who comes back into a house two weeks after the redemption expires and after they have moved out and goes in while it's under construc-tion with the belief that she still lives there?

While we were talking with the officers on the driveway in front of the house, out came the woman covered from head to toe in what looked like drywall dust. When the officer asked her where she came from, she explained that, when she saw the police cars, she went into the garage and hid under a pile of broken up drywall and debris from the demolition. She had heard the officer walk through the garage looking for her and could hear us talking outside and thought she should probably come out.

We cleared up the situation and were able to contact one of her family members to come and pick her up. We hope she got the help she needed.

The moral of these stories: Losing your home can be very stressful. Don't make it even more stressful by forcing the hand of the law to evict you from the premises. It's never worth it.

Dragging your credit and your name through the mud

No doubt about it, foreclosure damages your credit, but you can minimize the damage by taking action:

- ✔ You can reinstate the mortgage.
- ✔ You can negotiate a forbearance.
- ✔ You can negotiate a short sale.
- ✔ You can sell your home and repay your debts.

In other words, taking action to resolve any disagreements between you and your bank goes a long way toward reducing the fallout. And you have to take action to make that happen. Nobody is going to do it for you.

If you choose the path of inaction, you can expect both your credit rating and your reputation to suffer:

- **A foreclosure is recorded in the public-record section of your credit report and remains there for five to seven years.** This could make it very difficult for you to obtain a loan in the near future.

- **The more you allow the foreclosure to become a public spectacle by not taking action to resolve the crisis early on, the more it's going to damage your reputation.** People will always remember you as the person on the block who had to be forcibly evicted.

We're not trying to make you feel bad about foreclosure or send the message that experiencing a foreclosure makes you a bad person. We're simply trying to scare you a little bit into taking action early on. As we stress throughout this book, only *you* can take action to improve the outcome, and the earlier you act, the better the outcome.

Reaping the Minor Benefits of Inaction

Doing nothing does carry some minor benefits. If you look back at our hypothetical airplane crash in the "Grasping the Consequences of Inaction" section, earlier in this chapter, you can make the case that, if you're the one who died of hunger and thirst, you experienced some minor benefits. At least you didn't get a blister trying to walk out of the woods, and you probably lost some weight. Other than that, you'd probably have done a lot better if you'd have been a little more proactive.

Be that as it may, you may experience some minor benefits by taking a more passive approach. Maybe you won't get so upset and stressed out. Perhaps you'll argue less with the bill collectors and attorneys. And, you may be able to save up a little money as the wheels of justice slowly move forward.

In the following sections, we introduce the two main benefits you can expect by taking a passive approach.

Avoiding direct confrontation

Some people are born to be passive-aggressive. When authority figures demand something, those with a passive-aggressive personality simply say okay and then do nothing. Foreclosure notices, phone calls, attorneys, police, you name it — nothing bothers the person who takes a passive-aggressive approach. She simply drives everyone around her nuts.

If you owe more on your home than what it's worth, you don't care about losing it, and nobody else in your family cares about losing the home, then employing a strategy of passive resistance is certainly an option. And one of the main benefits is that you never have to confront anyone and nobody can possibly engage you in an argument. You simply agree to everything that the bank wants and then proceed to do whatever you want.

We point out the benefits of remaining passive-aggressive, but we still discourage you from taking this approach. The negative consequences are too great. You end up losing everything and making everyone around you frustrated and angry.

We know that not everyone can be assertive, but you have to be smart. If you're not someone who thrives on confrontation and you're willing to do anything to avoid it, then find someone who's better at it. If you have a spouse, your spouse may be better equipped to deal with collectors, attorneys, and loss mitigators. And if you don't have that special someone in your life, then you have to do what Paul's daughter Emma suggests: "Suck it up." Pretend you're an actor, and play the role for however long it takes to get through this period of your life. The alternative is more painful — you lose everything you worked so hard to build.

Saving money for as long as it takes

When doing nothing includes not making your monthly mortgage payments or paying other bills, you can save a considerable amount of money over the course of the foreclosure proceedings, particularly if your area has a long redemption period. In Chapter 13, we provide a 12-step plan for vacating the premises with as much money in your pocket as possible.

When you're not making your monthly mortgage payment or paying other bills, you may be tempted into thinking that you're suddenly rich and can afford to go on a spending spree. This is not the time, however, to buy that four-wheeler you always wanted. Sock away that extra cash, so when it comes time to leave, you have some cash on hand to finance your move.

Doing Nothing the Right Way

Doing nothing the right way seems like a contradiction, and, in a way, it is. If you do absolutely nothing, you can't possibly do it right or wrong. However, if you simply refuse to do anything to save your property or any equity in it, you can conserve your resources for a graceful exit. Of course, conserving resources requires careful planning and saving on your part, and this actually requires that you do *something,* however little that may be.

Doing nothing the right way boils down to a three-step process:

1. **Stop paying as many bills as possible.**
2. **Save every penny you can.**
3. **Move out before you're evicted.**

In Chapter 12, we lay out this approach in greater detail. Here, we provide you with the shorter version.

Stop paying your bills

When you're resigned to the fact that you're losing your home and you really have no equity to speak of, why throw good money after bad? Why waste time and resources on solutions that are going to leave you no better off than you are now, and possibly leave you in even worse shape? Slash expenses by not paying bills.

Here are some of the bills you can safely stop paying:

- **Monthly mortgage:** They're going to take your house anyway.

- **Property taxes:** Whoever purchases the home at auction can pay this bill for you.

- **Water bill:** The water bill is usually attached to the house, so the buyer of your property can pay this one for you, too.

- **Utility bills:** You may need to keep paying these bills to keep the lights and heat on for a while, but a month or two prior to the time you have to vacate the premises, you can stop paying these bills. The utility companies will send you notices of missed payments, but they probably won't get around to shutting things off for a couple months.

And here are some bills you can do away with by simply canceling your service:

- **Cellphone bills:** Call your cellphone company and cancel the service. People used to live with one phone per family, and it can certainly be done. If you have a lengthy service contract, let the company know that you can't pay.

- **Cable or satellite TV:** This is another unnecessary expense. Call and cancel.

- **Internet service:** Unless you need the Internet to work and generate income, cancel the service.

Pay your mortgage first and worry about paying your credit cards later. Many people who are facing foreclosure make their credit card payments first, because the credit card companies are relentless in their pursuit. As a result, their home ends up in foreclosure. After you're past the foreclosure (whatever the outcome), you can focus on making your credit card payments, if possible. Your credit card company is not going to take away your card because of the foreclosure, and you want to keep as much good credit as possible. In addition, you probably won't be able to get a new card, because you now have a foreclosure on your record.

If you live in a jurisdiction that has a lengthy redemption period, plan your move a week or two before the redemption period expires. If you move out too soon, you end up paying rent someplace else and taking on other expenses. You're better off living rent-free and saving all that money in anticipation of your move. Where else could you possibly live for free?

Start saving every penny you can

When you stop paying bills, all your income goes into your pocket. Keep it there. Save every penny possible, so you have a substantial stash of cash when the time comes to move out. If your savings account is with the bank that holds your mortgage, be sure to move that money to a different bank or credit union, or find a secure location in your home to store the money. You don't want the bank to have access to your stash — unless, of course, you trust banks more than we do.

If possible, secure a second job during this time, so you have even more money when the time comes to move. Even a part-time job can generate a substantial amount of income when you don't have to pay bills out of it. Keep in mind, however, that this is the time to save, not the time to adopt a new lifestyle — don't use the extra cash to go out to dinner, take up a new hobby, or work on your golf swing. Save the extra money you're earning.

In some cases, you may be able to convince the bank or the investor who purchases your property at auction to give you cash for keys and for leaving the premises "broom clean" (removing your belongings and sweeping up after yourself). This may allow you to move out earlier, if that's what you want to do, while obtaining some extra cash to finance your move. We estimate that it costs the bank or an investor about $100 per day in holding costs for every day you remain in the property. That's about $3,000 per month. If your jurisdiction has a long redemption period, the bank or investor can save a lot of money by tossing a couple thousand dollars your way.

Head out before the bailiff arrives

A forced eviction is not something you want to go through or put your family through (see "Facing the ugliness of a forced eviction," earlier in this chapter). Do yourself a favor — don't drag the situation out to the point of a full-blown eviction. If you have children or a spouse, you really need to make even more sure that you save them the embarrassment of an eviction.

Each jurisdiction is a little different, but in most cases, an officer of the court contacts you prior to eviction day. When you're in court or when the court officer calls to give you the deadline, comply with it. You can even schedule a time when the court officer can come over to pick up the keys. Explain that you followed the court's instructions and are planning to be out on a certain day, and the court officer can come over to pick up the keys and have the locks changed.

The court officer is not responsible for the fact that you ended up in foreclosure. The person is simply performing a task as instructed by the court. Court officers don't like evictions either, so do your best to make the officer's job a little easier. Vacate the premises before the officer needs to forcibly evict you and your family. The court officer is a person with a family just like you — he would much rather see you move voluntarily than be a part of a forced eviction.

Retain your dignity. You don't want your friends, family, and neighbors seeing your dirty laundry on the curb. Give yourself adequate time to move, and keep in mind that sometimes delays occur and can disrupt your exit plan. Give yourself some extra time.

Chapter 15

Regaining Your Financial Footing after Foreclosure

*W*hen foreclosure hits, you may feel as though your family has just been battered by a Category 5 hurricane. You may or may not have lost your home, but your finances are flattened, your credit ranking is in the cellar, and you may still be so embarrassed that you've become isolated from your friends and family — the very people whom you rely on most for emotional support.

Foreclosure can be devastating, this is true. But you can minimize the damage by how you choose to respond to it. By looking at foreclosure as a minor setback in a long, successful life, you can get over the speed bump, change the way you handle your finances, and, with a little hard work and determination, begin to rebuild a sound financial foundation and a new life. This chapter shows you how.

Dealing with the Fallout

Digging out of a financial hole is tough, but digging out of the foreclosure pit is even tougher, because now you have a bruised and battered credit rating and ego. In other words, you have a big challenge ahead of you and you're in a weakened state to meet that challenge.

One of the first steps in recovering from foreclosure is to know what to expect and then deal realistically with your new reality. In the following sections, we uncover some of the biggest changes you're likely to face and offer some suggestions on how to deal with those changes most effectively.

Keeping in touch with loved ones

Losing a house is a definite bummer, but losing family and friends is a real tragedy that we witness all too often. After a foreclosure, homeowners often condemn themselves to emotional exile, walling themselves off from friends, neighbors, and their extended family because they feel shame over what happened to them. In addition, friends, neighbors, and family members may not know what to say or how to say it, so they avoid the situation, not wanting to make it worse. Maybe they feel a little guilty for not offering some assistance, too.

People are the most valuable part of your life, so do whatever's required to bring your loved ones back into your life. Let them know that you're a foreclosure survivor — that you experienced a bad time in your life and talking about it is okay. When you begin talking about it, others may be more open to sharing their own stories of financial hardship.

Family advice

Although you should certainly seek emotional support from family members, be careful about following their advice. We had a client who was in foreclosure due to an adjustable rate mortgage (ARM) adjustment and the fact that she had no escrow account to cover property tax and insurance payments. A loan originator approved her for a loan that she should never have taken on. The value of her property was rapidly declining while her payments were rising.

Her father advised that she should make her house payments and not pay her credit card debt. Her sister advised her to make the credit card payments and forget about making the house payments. Her mother advised that she get another job and pay everything, even though the daughter was already working six days a week and raising a child on her own.

After reviewing all the details, our advice was that she maintain her credit card payments, list the condo for sale, and try to negotiate a short sale with her lender (because her property was no longer worth enough to pay off the balance of her mortgage). She could live in the condo for free during the redemption period, save as much money as possible, and leave the premises peacefully and in good condition. We also recommended that she document her story in detail for future reference.

Her sister has asked her to live with her for a year while she gets back up on her feet. If she sells the property, she'll only have a few late payments on her record. If she loses the property in foreclosure, she'll have a detailed record of what happened to help her explain the incident to future lenders. In any event, she will have maintained her credit for the future.

Every foreclosure is unique, and you may have trouble describing your experience to others, but what is *not* unique is the resilience of the human spirit. You can and will make it through this. Many very successful people around the world have failed miserably multiple times before they ever experienced success. We know that's not much consolation in your present situation, but it's very true. This situation can be a temporary setback for you, or it can become a permanent state of mind — it's really up to you. The best thing you can do is surround yourself with friends and family who understand and accept you, or at least are present to get you through the situation.

Scaling back your lifestyle

Foreclosure is like a financial earthquake that registers about 9.5 on the Richter scale, but it can produce some serious aftershocks as well. If you couldn't get a handle on your spending to spare yourself from losing your home, then now's the time to start. Later in this chapter, in the "Establishing and sticking to a budget" section, we offer some advice for creating a budget, but you can immediately start to cut back on the discretionary spending:

- **Eating out:** In today's fast-paced society, eating out has become the norm — even a necessity for some. It's also a very expensive habit. Try your best to prepare your own meals at home. And don't cheat by purchasing prepared meals and simply heating them up; that's expensive, too.

- **Vehicle expenses:** Look at how much that car you drive is costing you. Is it a gas guzzler? How much does it cost to insure? Do you have an old clunker that's always in the shop racking up huge repair bills? See if you can find another vehicle that's more reliable and cost efficient. Of course, don't sacrifice reliability by purchasing an old jalopy.

- **Entertainment expenses:** How often do you go out to the movies? How many nights a week do you hang out at the bar with your buddies or have a ladies' night out? How much are you spending, on average, per week on these outings? Try to scale back by finding your entertainment at home. Instead of going out to the movies every weekend, rent a movie for three or four bucks and buy some microwave popcorn and 2-liter bottles of soda at the grocery store. Instead of going out to the bars, rotate houses for party nights.

- **Cosmetics:** Sorry ladies, but cosmetics is another area where a lot of money can be saved. Go easy on the makeup and nail polish. Instead of having your nails done every ten days, schedule an appointment for every three weeks, or do your nails yourself. Book only one hair appointment per month instead of once a week.

- **Golf and bowling:** Golfing and bowling can be quite expensive. If you go every week, try cutting it back to once a month.

This is not an exhaustive list of discretionary spending categories. It's just something to get you started. Take a close look at your situation and the categories where you tend to overspend. Are you a clothes hound? Do you tend to go overboard on vacations? Do you like to treat family and friends to good times and lavish gifts? When you spot your weaknesses, focus in on those areas and start slashing.

To give yourself some added motivation, create your own cost-cutting chart, graph, or logbook. Write down how much you spend on average in each discretionary expense category each week, and then keep a running record of how much you saved by implementing your cost-cutting strategies. Track your progress for one month, three months, and six months, and see just how much you really did keep in you pocket, or at least freed up for the real necessities. If you don't need the extra money to cover bills, save it in a separate savings account. The amount you save could spur you to cook up more ideas on how to slash expenses.

Expecting to pay higher interest rates and fees

One of the painful ironies of life is that the people who need to borrow money at lower interest rates can't, while those who can afford to pay more interest are offered no- or low-interest credit. Banks also give their clients who have the most money more interest and lower bank fees. Go figure. That's the nature of the beast, however, and you're going to have to deal with it.

After you've suffered through a foreclosure, the situation gets even worse. Obtaining loan approval is nearly impossible, and if a company is willing to offer you credit, it's going to make you pay through the nose to get it.

You aren't in a good position to get credit, and credit would probably put you right back in the situation you were in, so our advice is to buy on credit only if you absolutely have to. If your car dies and you need a car for work, you may need to take out a car loan at 13 percent interest if you have no other options. However, trading in your old car (and getting less than what you owe on it) and taking out a high-interest loan to buy a new car probably wouldn't make much sense. Don't overextend yourself financially.

Avoiding Past Mistakes and Misfortunes

After a catastrophe, performing a postmortem is often a good idea. It enables you to identify weaknesses, figure out the series of events that led up to the catastrophe, and start on a path that steers clear of those same mistakes and misfortunes in the future. Your postmortem should address the following four questions:

✔ Did I cause my own problems due to my spending habits?

✔ Did anything outside of my control contribute to causing the problem?

✔ Did I cause my own problems by lacking discipline in making payments?

✔ What can I change in the way I handle my finances to prevent these same problems from recurring?

Even if part of the problem was out of your control, you can make adjustments to areas of your life that are within your control.

As the philosopher George Santayana once said, "Those who cannot learn from history are doomed to repeat it." If you gain wisdom from a serious loss, it can become no more than a temporary setback, but if you fail to learn anything from it, it becomes part of your lifestyle that keeps repeating.

Taking an unbiased look at your financial situation is often difficult, if not impossible. You may overlook blemishes that are readily obvious to anyone who's not intimately involved in the situation. Just look at families on those reality TV shows. Everyone watching the show can immediately tell what's wrong with the family and what the family needs to do to get back on track, but everyone in the family is entirely clueless. Consider calling in a close friend or family member for assistance — someone you know who really has a good handle on her family finances. If that's not an option, consider seeking the assistance of a credit counselor, as explained in the following section.

Avoid calling someone who is going to be judgmental and highly critical of you and your family. You need assistance — you don't need to be kicked when you're already down. If you're not good at handling finances, however, someone who is more capable can offer you very valuable assistance.

Teaming Up with a Credit Counselor

When you're sick, you see a doctor. When your car breaks down, you take it to a mechanic. When your marriage is on the rocks, you see a marriage counselor. When your roof leaks, you hire a roofer. Yet, when people can't get a handle on their finances, which plays a huge role in their success and happiness, they don't call anyone for assistance. Instead, they muddle through and usually fall into the same traps that got them in trouble in the first place.

One of the first steps you should take when you experience a financial disaster such as foreclosure is to call a professional who is trained and experienced in handling such disasters — a credit (or debt) counselor. A credit counselor can

✔ Analyze your income and expenses to see where you stand financially.

✔ Provide you with a detailed portrait of your financial situation.

✔ Explore options that match your resources, lifestyle, and goals.

✔ Explain the steps you need to take to achieve your financial goals.

✔ Work with your creditors to forgive or restructure certain existing debts.

A typical counseling session lasts about an hour. You can then expect to have follow-up sessions if needed. Your credit counselor should be able to provide you with a personalized debt management plan at the end of your counseling session.

In the following sections, we show you how to choose and work with a credit counselor to regain your financial footing.

If all a credit counselor is going to do for you is negotiate payment plans with your creditors and charge you a high fee for the service, don't bother; you can do this yourself. If you're having trouble budgeting and meeting your financial goals, and a credit counselor has a program that can assist you, this could be of great value. Some of the credit counseling programs are actually owned or supported by the credit industry.

Finding a credit counselor with the right stuff

Do an Internet search for "credit counselor," and you discover more than 3 million links, many of which are for credit counseling agencies. You can close your eyes and click a link, but you may end up with a credit counselor who's in the business just to rip off people who are already in financial trouble.

Here are some tips to assist you in tracking down a credit counselor who has the experience, expertise, and solid gold reputation you need:

✔ Ask friends, family members, and other people you know to recommend a credit counselor.

✔ If you belong to a church, ask if they have any free or affordable programs.

✔ Ask your bank to recommend a credit counselor. Banks usually know several local credit counselors who have solid reputations.

✔ If you work at a university or for the military, ask if they have any leads on qualified credit counselors.

✔ If you belong to a union at work, ask your union for referrals.

✔ Look for a local credit counseling agency — someone who agrees to meet with you in person rather than simply over the phone or online.

✔ Obtain information about the credit counseling agency and its services and fees *before* supplying any detailed information about your financial situation.

✔ Make sure the agency has an office building, a mailing address, and a legitimate phone number. Work with brick-and-mortar establishments.

✔ Obtain a referral from the National Foundation for Credit Counseling (NFCC). You can search for an NFCC credit counselor online at www. nfcc.org or call 800-388-2227.

Most credit counseling agencies bill themselves as nonprofit organizations. That does not mean that they offer free or affordable services, or that the services the agencies offer are legitimate. Some agencies charge high hidden fees or ask for voluntary contributions, which can sink you deeper in debt. Make sure you find out about all fees upfront.

When you have a list of potential candidates, check their credentials. Contact your state's attorney general, a local consumer protection agency, or the Better Business Bureau to see if the companies have had any complaints filed against them. You can also check with the NFCC, as discussed earlier in this section, to determine whether an agency is a member in good standing with the NFCC. This can help you pare down your list of candidates.

✔ **State attorneys general:** Visit the National Association of Attorneys General (NAAG) at www.naag.org, where you can find a clickable map of the United States. Point to your state to view contact information for your state's attorney general, or click your state to open the Web page for your state's attorney general.

✔ **Better Business Bureau:** Visit the Web site of the Better Business Bureau (BBB) at www.bbb.org. Here, you can search for a company and pull up a BBB report about it, or find information about local BBB offices.

Interview the remaining candidates on your list. The Federal Trade Commission (FTC) recommends that you ask the following questions:

✔ **What services do you offer?** Look for an organization that offers a range of services, including budget counseling, and savings and debt management classes. Avoid any organization that pushes a debt-management plan (DMP) as your only option before it spends a significant amount of time analyzing your financial situation.

✔ **Do you offer information?** Are educational materials available for free? Avoid organizations that charge for information.

✔ **In addition to helping me solve my immediate problem, will you help me develop a plan for avoiding problems in the future?** Choose a credit counselor who addresses both your immediate concerns and your future finances.

✔ **What are your fees? Are there setup and/or monthly fees?** Get a specific price quote in writing.

✔ **What if I can't afford to pay your fees or make contributions?** If an organization won't help you because you can't afford to pay, look elsewhere for help.

✔ **Will I have a formal written agreement or contract with you?** Don't sign anything without reading it first. Make sure all verbal promises are in writing.

✔ **Are you licensed to offer your services in my state?** Make sure any credit counselor you choose to work with is licensed to operate in your state.

✔ **What are the qualifications of your counselors?** Are they accredited or certified by an outside organization? If so, by whom? If not, how are they trained? Try to use an organization whose counselors are trained by a nonaffiliated party.

✔ **Can you assist me with secured debts, like my mortgage?** Credit counselors, especially those who work on behalf of credit card companies, specialize in unsecured debts. You want a counselor who can assist you with your secured debts as well, such as your home mortgage and car loans.

✔ **What assurance do I have that information about me (including my address, phone number, and financial information) will be kept confidential and secure?** Your credit counseling service should have a privacy policy in place and be willing to share it.

✔ **How are your employees compensated?** Are they paid more if I sign up for certain services, if I pay a fee, or if I make a contribution to your organization? If the answer is yes, consider it a red flag and go elsewhere for help.

For more information on consumer issues or to file a complaint with the FTC, visit www.ftc.gov or call 877-382-4357 (TTY 866-653-4261).

Negotiating repayment plans with creditors

Most credit counseling services offer a debt-management plan (DMP), which sort of functions as your mom. The service usually orders you to stop taking on any more credit and arranges payment plans with your creditors. You deposit a certain amount of money on a regular schedule with the agency, and the agency makes payments on your unsecured debt, including your credit cards, student loans, and medical bills.

If you don't have any unsecured debt, then you probably don't need a debt management plan, but if the bill collectors are constantly harassing you, having someone handle your bills can take some of the heat off.

Although a debt-management plan may sound like a good idea, keep in mind that you're trusting the agency to handle your money and pay your bills. Make sure the agency is legitimate, your creditors agree to work with the agency, and the agency is making the payments on schedule. If it fails to make the payments, you could be in a world of hurt — you handed the agency all your money while you continued to rack up more interest and fees.

The FTC recommends that you ask the following questions before signing up for a debt-management plan:

- **Is a DMP the only option you can give me?** Will you provide me with ongoing budgeting advice, regardless of whether I enroll in a DMP? If an organization offers only DMPs, find another credit counseling organization that also will help you create a budget and teach you money management skills.

- **How does your DMP work?** How will you make sure that all my creditors will be paid by the applicable due dates and in the correct billing cycle? If a DMP is appropriate, sign up for one that allows all your creditors to be paid before your payment due dates and within the correct billing cycle.

- **How is the amount of my payment determined?** What if the amount is more than I can afford? Don't sign up for a DMP if you can't afford the monthly payment.

- **How often can I get status reports on my accounts?** Can I get access to my accounts online or by phone? Make sure that the organization you sign up with is willing to provide regular, detailed statements about your account.

- **Can you get my creditors to lower or eliminate interest and finance charges, or waive late fees?** If yes, contact your creditors to verify this, and ask them how long you have to be on the plan before the benefits kick in.

- **What debts aren't included in the DMP?** This is important because you'll have to pay those bills on your own.

- **Do I have to make any payments to my creditors before they will accept the proposed payment plan?** Some creditors require a payment to the credit counselor before accepting you into a DMP. If a credit counselor tells you this is so, call your creditors to verify this information before you send money to the credit counseling agency.

✔ **How will enrolling in a DMP affect my credit?** Beware of any organization that tells you it can remove accurate negative information from your credit report. Legally, it can't be done. Accurate negative information may stay on your credit report for up to seven years.

✔ **Are you allowed to recommend bankruptcy if that would be my best choice?** Some agencies prohibit their credit counselors from suggesting bankruptcy even if that's your best option. Make sure the counselor has the power to present you with all your options.

✔ **Can you get my creditors to** *re-age* **my accounts — that is, to make my accounts current?** If so, how many payments will I have to make before my creditors will do so? Even if your accounts are re-aged, negative information from past delinquencies or late payments will remain on your credit report.

Before you send any payments to your credit counselor, contact your creditors and make sure they've agreed to the arrangement, and continue to make payments to your creditors until the new payment plan goes into effect. When you receive your statements from your creditors, make sure the payments are showing up. In other words, make sure your credit counselor is paying those bills as promised.

Also, consult with your accountant or a tax specialist regarding the tax implications of any cancellation of debt. Yep, the government may expect you to pay taxes on the amount of debt that your creditors write off. Talk about kicking someone when they're down! Fortunately, due to the mortgage meltdown that started in 2007, some changes may be in the works at the IRS to relieve distressed homeowners of this added tax burden.

Settling debts you can't possibly pay

Many credit counseling agencies offer to negotiate your debt. Instead of paying the full $20,000 you owe on your credit card, the agency can negotiate with the credit card company to accept a payment of, say, $8,000. Furthermore, agencies that offer debt negotiation often promise to have all record of the bad debt permanently erased from your credit history.

Sounds like a great deal, eh?

Well, it *would* be a great deal if all the promises were legitimate. First, very few creditors are going to accept a payment of less than 50 percent of the total balance owed as full payment of the debt. Second, creditors are bound by law to provide accurate data to the credit reporting agencies. And third, if the agency promises to make the payment on your behalf, watch out — it could be out to scam you out of your money and leave you even deeper in debt when additional interest and penalties are added to the balance you now owe.

If you work out a settlement with a creditor, ask for the nonpayment to be removed from your credit report, or at least noted as having been satisfied. Get it in writing before you pay the agreed-upon amount to settle the debt.

The FTC offers some great "tip-offs to rip-offs" related to companies that offer debt negotiation services. The FTC warns you to avoid companies that:

✔ Guarantee they can remove your unsecured debt.

✔ Promise that unsecured debts can be paid off with pennies on the dollar.

✔ Require substantial monthly service fees.

✔ Demand payment of a percentage of savings.

✔ Tell you to stop making payments to or communicating with your creditors.

✔ Require you to make monthly payments to them, rather than to your creditor.

✔ Claim that creditors never sue consumers for nonpayment of unsecured debt.

✔ Promise that using their system will have no negative impact on your credit report.

✔ Claim that they can remove accurate negative information from your credit report.

If a credit counselor advises you to repair your credit by changing your name, address, or Social Security number (often referred to as "getting a new nine-digit" to avoid suspicion), watch out. These Web sites often reference the Federal Trade Commission (FTC) so they will appear more credible. This could be illegal in your state and is certainly unethical in all states. Work out a solution with your creditors instead of skipping town, either literally or figuratively.

Establishing and sticking to a budget

Spending $100 on a single night out is not tough to do. An average family of four can do it with dinner and a movie. Do that once a week, and you've already gone through $400 of your monthly budget. Get a $3 cup of coffee every day on your way to work, and you just spent $60 a month to feed your caffeine fix. We won't even start on how much money goes up in smoke in a household with cigarette smokers. If you're wondering, "Where does all that money go?", then it's time to find out and start reining in your spending.

Perhaps the most valuable service a credit counseling agency can offer you is in the area of establishing and sticking to some sort of spending plan. A qualified counselor can analyze your income and expenses, make sure you set enough money aside to cover your monthly bills, and assist you in identifying the discretionary spending categories where you're having the most trouble. A

Paul's friend's wife: The budget Nazi

I have a friend whose wife is very good at keeping tabs on the family budget. She's so good that she has tabs on the 74¢ in loose change in *my* sofa. They are honest, hard-working people who made the decision that the wife would stay home with the children, while the husband would work outside the home. That means that they needed to make things work on a single income. The wife's job was to make sure it did.

One day on his way home from work, my friend stopped at the local convenience store and purchased a soda. He entered through the back door of his home, finishing the last few swallows, thinking nothing of it — until his wife spotted him. She immediately confronted him, demanding to know where he thought they were going to get the extra money to buy soda. She wanted to know if he thought that those kind of expenditures were within the family budget. According to my friend, you'd have

thought that he had walked through the door with a new set of name-brand golf clubs.

When my friend told this story at a recent get-together, we all had a good laugh, including his wife. My friend finished up the story by saying, "You laugh now, but it wasn't too funny at the time. I thought I was going to be sent to bed without dinner." His wife, in perfect form, added, "Just stay within the budget, big spender."

Now, you may think that the wife in this story was a little over the top and that she had no right to cross-examine her husband like the Spanish Inquisition, but someone in the family has to step up and hold other family members accountable if you have any hope of regaining your financial footing. All those tiny expenses that you took for granted in the past now jump to the forefront, and you need to keep close track of them. Everyone needs to be onboard with this new plan, because it's going to take some real getting used to.

credit counselor can make your family accountable for its spending when you can't hold yourself and the rest of your family accountable.

If the idea of drawing up a budget is painful to you, realize that you have several options. Tracking every penny spent is only one way to go. Here are some strategies to consider:

- ✔ **Classic budget:** Identify all your expense categories, including housing, food, automobile, entertainment, clothing, pets, medical, and vacations, and set spending caps for each category.

- ✔ **The envelope system:** This variation of the classic budget consists of designating a separate envelope for each expense. When you get your paycheck, you cash it and stick a certain amount of money into each envelope to cover expenses in each category. If you have only $300 a month for groceries, that's all you can spend on groceries.

- ✔ **Pay yourself first:** Make a commitment to save a certain amount of money each month, and use the rest to pay bills and expenses. If you have any money left over at the end of the month, use it to pay down your debt.

- **Allowances:** Give each member of the family an allowance to spend on whatever he needs or wants. The rest of the money goes to cover monthly bills and other necessary expenses.

- **Cutting up the credit cards:** If you rack up huge balances on credit cards every month, cut up your credit cards and stick with cash and checks. Sometimes, charging it can be just too easy.

For more about budgeting and debt management, check out *Managing Debt For Dummies,* by John Ventura and Mary Reed (Wiley).

Reestablishing Your Credit

When your credit is bruised, your first order of business is to build it back up. Paying your bills on time is a good first step. Make a commitment that you're never ever going to be late paying a bill, even one day late. Drop the payment in the mail a day or two earlier than normal, just to make sure the check arrives on time.

In the following sections, we recommend some strategies for reestablishing your payment history and rebuilding your credit rating.

Don't learn a bigger lesson than there is to be learned. Mark Twain once said that a cat who walks on a hot stove will never walk on a hot stove again . . . but then again, he'll never walk on a cold one either. Don't let foreclosure discourage you from buying another home, starting another business, or living life to its fullest.

Credit-score stats

Credit reporting agencies rely on one or more statistical models to determine your credit score. One of the most popular models is the Fair Isaac Company (FICO) rating system. The credit company assigns numerical values to particular pieces of data in your credit history, such as the length of your credit history and the various types of interest you're paying. Then it plugs these numbers into the statistical model, which spits out your credit score. It's basically a numbers game that weighs the data on your credit report in the following manner:

- Thirty-five percent of the score is based on payment history.

- Thirty percent is based on outstanding debt, or how much you currently owe.

- Fifteen percent is based on the length of your credit history, or how long you've been borrowing.

- Ten percent is based on recent inquiries on your report (whenever a lending institution requests a report).

- Ten percent is based on the types of credit you have, such as mortgage or credit card interest.

Borrowing your way to a better credit rating

A great way to reestablish your payment history and raise your credit score is to obtain a secured loan with your bank. Go into your bank with $1,000 in cash and ask a loan officer to give you a $1,000 loan. We can almost hear you saying, "Why do I need a $1,000 loan if I already have $1,000 in cash?" Well, because it shows the bank that it can loan you some money without taking on much risk.

Here's what you do:

1. **Deposit the $1,000 with the bank as security for the loan.**

   The bank gives you the $1,000 loan with confidence.

2. **Make your monthly payments like clockwork, showing that you can be trusted to make payments.**

   Eventually, you pay off the loan in full.

3. **Ask the bank to extend you a $2,000 loan with the $1,000 as security.**

4. **Make your payments on time and pay off the loan.**

5. **Get your security money back from the bank — the $1,000 you initially deposited.**

6. **Take out another loan for $1,000 and pay it off over time.**

   This time, the bank gives you the loan without having to secure it with a deposit. You are now on your way to reestablishing your credit history.

This can be a slow process, but it is an important one. If the bank won't work with you, you can check into getting a secured credit card, which works the same way: You post a dollar amount, and the credit card company issues a credit card with a spending limit equal to what you posted. After a series of payments, the company may be willing to extend true credit to you. Make your payments on time, and you're one step closer to fixing your credit completely. Just make sure the secured card is one that's reported to the credit reporting agencies.

Damaging credit is easier than fixing it, so mind your p's and q's, and don't be late with even one payment, not even a day late. Also, make sure that the credit card company or the bank is reporting to the credit bureaus so that you get credit for your timely payments.

Taking out a credit card or two

Some financial gurus recommend that you use a credit card to reestablish your credit. Just charge a little and then pay off the balance in full when you receive your monthly statement. That's great for people who can control their credit card addiction, but for those who can't, that's like telling someone at Overeaters Anonymous to down a couple doughnuts every morning so they won't eat so much at lunch.

If you have the discipline to manage a credit card, however, charging some purchases and then paying off the balance as soon as you receive your statement can boost your credit score.

 Set a cap on your credit card spending, and keep tabs on how much you're spending. Every time you charge a purchase, write down the amount you charged and the total you charged for the month. When you reach your cap, stick the credit card in a safe place so you won't be tempted to use it.

 Paying bills on or before the due date is best. Paying within the ten-day grace period is okay, but not stellar. Paying after the grace period but within 30 days is considered a "slow pay." Paying after the 30-day mark dings your credit rating and usually costs you a late fee.

Socking away some money

When you apply for a loan or any other type of credit, the bank looks at your overall financial health. Paying your bills on time is a good indication that your finances are healthy, but it is not the only indication. Banks also look at how solvent you are — your debt-to-income ratio and how much money you have socked away in the bank. If you have $10,000 in savings, the bank is more likely to loan you some money than if you have a six-month savings account balance that averages $25.

Every paycheck, or at least once a month, add a little money to your savings account. You don't have to deposit thousands of dollars, but make a regular deposit of at least $10 to $25 — whatever you can afford. This can really add up over the course of a year and can give you a nice little nest egg to fall back on when unexpected expenses arise.

Buying a more affordable pad

Even if you saved your home from foreclosure, you may still consider selling it after you survive the foreclosure, simply to put your family on firmer ground. If you're struggling just to make your house payments and buy a few cans of soup every week despite your best efforts to get ahead, then buying a more affordable home may be the best solution.

How does this boost your credit rating? Well, when banks are deciding whether to lend you money (see Chapter 12), they look at your debt ratio and the loan-to-value (LTV) ratio on your home. Your debt ratio is your total monthly expenses divided by your total monthly income. The LTV ratio is how much you owe on your home versus how much it's worth. By owning a more affordable home, you decrease your debt ratio and increase the LTV ratio, making you a more attractive borrower.

A smaller home should cost less to heat, cool, maintain, and insure. It should also cost less in property taxes. When shopping around for a more affordable home, check out how much the previous owners paid monthly for utilities, taxes, and insurance. You can sock away all that money you save on a monthly basis to further boost your credit score.

Keeping Tabs on Your Credit Report

Good credit is gold. Without it, you have access only to your money. With it, you can put other people's money to work for you. Whenever you apply for a loan, the lending institution performs a credit check — sort of a background check to make sure you're not up to your gills in debt, your income covers expenses, and you pay your bills on time.

If the credit check reveals that you're not creditable, the lending institution rejects your request for a loan. You don't want that to happen, because if it does, when you apply for future loans and the loan officer asks, "Have you ever been denied credit?", you have to answer, "Yes." And then it's goodbye loan.

To ensure success at obtaining loans, become proactive. Check your credit report every three months or so and correct any errors. No irregularity is too small to correct. An experienced loan officer can assist you with examining and correcting your credit report when you apply for a loan, but we encourage you to stay ahead of the game to avoid any problems that may arise when applying for loans.

Obtaining a credit report

As of September 1, 2005, the Federal Trade Commission has made it mandatory for the three major credit reporting companies to provide you with a free credit report once every 12 months. To obtain your free credit report, do one of the following:

- ✔ Submit your request online at www.annualcreditreport.com.
- ✔ Phone in your request by calling 877-322-8228.
- ✔ Download the Annual Credit Report Request Form from www.annual creditreport.com/cra/requestformfinal.pdf, fill it out, and mail it to Annual Credit Report Request Service, P.O. Box 105281, Atlanta, GA 30348-5281.

If you've already gotten a free credit report this year and want something more recent, you can order a credit report for less than $10 from any of the following three credit report agencies:

- ✔ **Equifax:** 800-685-1111 or www.equifax.com
- ✔ **Experian:** 888-397-3742 or www.experian.com
- ✔ **TransUnion:** 800-916-8800 or www.transunion.com

Obtaining a credit report from all three agencies is best, because some creditors report to only one or two of the three agencies. You can order a report (for extra) that includes data from all three agencies.

Checking for discrepancies

When you receive your credit report, inspect it carefully for the following red flags:

- ✔ Addresses of places you've never lived
- ✔ Aliases you've never used, which may indicate that someone else is using your Social Security number
- ✔ Multiple Social Security numbers, flagging the possibility that information for someone with the same name has made it into your credit report
- ✔ Wrong date of birth (DOB)
- ✔ Credit cards you don't have

- Loans you haven't taken out

- Records of unpaid bills that you either know you paid or have good reason for not paying

- Records of delinquent payments that were not delinquent or you have a good excuse for not paying on time

- Inquiries from companies with whom you've never done business (When you apply for a loan, the lender typically runs an *inquiry* on your credit report, and that shows up on the report)

An address of a place you've never lived, or records of accounts, loans, and credit cards you never had, may be a sign that somebody has stolen your identity. Yikes! Contact the credit reporting company immediately and request that a fraud alert be placed on your credit report. For tips on protecting yourself against identity theft and recovering from it, check out *Preventing Identity Theft For Dummies,* by Michael J. Arata, Jr. (Wiley).

Checking your credit score

To give your credit rating an air of objectivity, credit reporting agencies often assign you a credit score that ranges roughly between 300 (you never paid a bill in your life) and 900 (you borrow often, always pay your bills on time, and don't carry any huge balances on your credit cards).

Your credit score determines not only whether you qualify for a loan, but also how much you're qualified to borrow and at what interest rate. A high credit score lets you borrow more and pay less interest on it. A high score can also lower your home and auto insurance rates — just another reason why the rich get richer and the poor stay poor.

Your credit report should contain your credit score. If it doesn't, contact the credit reporting agency and request your score.

Part IV
The Part of Tens

The 5th Wave   By Rich Tennant

"When we bought it 5 years ago the mortgage payments seemed huge. But we got used to it. Please, pull up an orange crate and make yourself comfortable."

In this part . . .

*E*ach and every *For Dummies* book you pick up includes a Part of Tens, with at least a couple chapters packed with tips, tricks, and other bite-size tidbits that you can munch on whenever you have a few minutes to spare and need a little brain food.

In this Part of Tens, we reveal ten foreclosure delay tactics that can buy you some additional time, ten scams and scumbags that target people in foreclosure, and ten tactics to get your life back on track after foreclosure.

Chapter 16

Ten Delay Tactics

In This Chapter

▶ Buying time with reinstatement or forbearance

▶ Banking on court delays and causing a few of your own

▶ Tossing a wrench in the works with bankruptcy

▶ Taking your sweet time moving out

▶ Slowing down foreclosure with a tax lien

Surviving foreclosure to fight another day often requires that you become a master of passive resistance and what world champion heavyweight boxer Mohammed Ali referred to as the rope-a-dope maneuver. You just hang on the ropes, buy yourself some time, save your money, and then either stop the foreclosure (if you're in a position to do so) or move out with the money you managed to squirrel away while you were living in the house for free. In this chapter, we reveal the top ten foreclosure delay tactics.

Delay doesn't mean that you postpone taking action. To get more time, you have to invest some time and effort. As you're in the process of buying yourself more time, keep working on long-term solutions to either keep your home or gracefully exit it.

Calling Your Lender

Calling your lender as soon as you feel as though you're going to have trouble making your monthly mortgage payments isn't a bona fide delay tactic, but it can keep the foreclosure dogs at bay. As long as you contact your lender and stay in touch, your lender is going to feel less pressure to take immediate legal action.

In addition, as you and your lender discuss your options, you're likely to become aware of other opportunities to buy yourself even more time. Your lender will probably request additional information and documentation to assess your current financial position. This means you have time to gather documents and time to wait while your lender reviews them. As you pursue solutions that your lender suggests, you may gain even more time.

Negotiating a Forbearance

You can use a forbearance (see Chapters 7 and 10) as a permanent solution to foreclosure, but it can also work as a delay tactic. With a forbearance, the bank allows you to catch up on missed payments over the course of several months. If you owe $3,000 in back payments, for example, the bank may allow you to pay an extra $250 per month for 12 months.

If you're certain you can make those additional payments long enough to implement a long-term solution, then negotiating a forbearance could be a great way to keep the bank from moving forward with the foreclosure. You could then try to sell the home, refinance your mortgage, or explore other options discussed in Chapter 7 of this book.

A forbearance is going to cost you some money, so if you think you're eventually going to lose the home anyway and have very little, no, or negative equity in it, this is not one of the best delay tactics. You would be better off cutting your losses (see Chapter 13).

Negotiating a Mortgage Modification

Your bank wrote your current mortgage, and it can rewrite your mortgage any time it wants, assuming you agree to the new terms. The bank can roll your missed payments into the mortgage amount, lower the interest rate, and even add several years to the end of the mortgage to make your monthly payments more affordable. The bank may even be willing, under extenuating circumstances, to forgive a portion of the missed payments. A mortgage modification can function as either a long-term solution or a delay tactic that gives you more time to find a suitable solution.

Reinstating your mortgage or negotiating a forbearance or mortgage modification requires that you contact your lender. If your lender passed your loan to a servicing company, the loan servicer may not have the power to modify the mortgage, but the servicer can refer you to someone who can assist you. (For additional details on how to haggle with your lender, check out Chapter 11.)

Filing a Demand to Delay the Sheriff's Sale

In some jurisdictions, you can file a demand to delay the sheriff's sale. This can give you up to 6 or 12 months of extra time, assuming the court rules in your favor.

Unfortunately, in some jurisdictions, if you're granted the delay, the lender is then given the right to pursue a deficiency judgment against you if your house sells for less than the current amount you owe.

Consult an attorney in your area to find out whether you can file a demand to delay the sheriff's sale and what can happen as a result. An attorney can also assist you with preparing and filing the demand.

Relying on Court Delays

You won't find the wheels of justice at the Indy 500. They roll v-e-r-y s-l-o-w-l-y. When you're seeking justice, that's a bad thing. When you're facing a judicial foreclosure, however, court delays can work in your favor.

Unfortunately, you can't really count on long delays. A hearing may be held up by delays in mail delivery, someone getting sick, or one of the parties asking for a postponement, but these delays are typically only a few days at the most. In other words, don't count on court delays to gain a substantial amount of extra time.

One of the best ways to trigger a substantial delay is to demand a trial by jury, if this is an option in your jurisdiction. The court needs extra time to schedule a trial by jury, and you'll get additional time as the jury hears the case and deliberates. In addition, juries tend to favor poor, defenseless homeowners over big, bad banks.

Challenging the Process in Court

The foreclosure rules and regulations that your bank must follow are clearly laid out. If the bank or its attorney fails to follow those rules and regulations, you can point it out to the court to gain additional time. Here are some of the areas you may want to examine to determine whether you have a case against the bank:

- **Notification:** If you did not receive proper notification of the pending foreclosure, challenge the foreclosure. For example, if the rules in your jurisdiction state that the foreclosure notice must be posted for five weeks, and the bank posted it for only three weeks, the bank failed to honor your rights as a homeowner.

- **Redemption period:** The bank needs to inform you of any right you have to redeem your property. If the bank says you have three months to redeem your property after the sale, but your jurisdiction gives you six months, you can claim that the bank provided false information. In some cases, the court may grant you an entirely new redemption period starting on the date it issues its ruling.

- **Forfeiture:** If you purchased your home with a contract for deed or lease-option agreement, and the seller is abusing the terms of the agreement, bring your concerns before the court. In some cases, a seller may attempt to use a forfeiture clause to take immediate possession of a property in a jurisdiction where the seller is required to follow the foreclosure process to repossess the property. Know the rules and regulations that govern these contracts, and make sure the seller is not abusing her rights.

Challenging the foreclosure process in court is potentially costly, particularly if you hire an attorney. Calculate the cost/benefit ratio for yourself to determine if a legal challenge is worthwhile.

If you live in a state that requires judicial foreclosure, you already have a forum for raising defenses and objections to the foreclosure. If you're subject to a nonjudicial foreclosure, however, you must take the initiative to file suit to stop the foreclosure.

Filing for an Adjournment

Adjournment is a fancy legal term that means "delay." You can seek to adjourn either of the following:

- **Court date:** If you cannot attend a hearing that's scheduled on a specific date and time, let the court know that the date and time are inconvenient and state the reason why — but make sure it's a very good reason. A

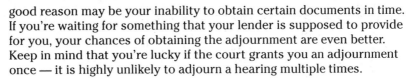

good reason may be your inability to obtain certain documents in time. If you're waiting for something that your lender is supposed to provide for you, your chances of obtaining the adjournment are even better. Keep in mind that you're lucky if the court grants you an adjournment once — it is highly unlikely to adjourn a hearing multiple times.

Judges are very perceptive and very good at sensing when someone is feeding them a bunch of baloney. Even when you're telling the truth, judges can be unwilling to accommodate your needs — they don't have the time or patience for shenanigans. If you're caught stretching the truth or making up stories, expect to receive even *less* compassion.

✔ **Sheriff's sale or nonjudicial foreclosure sale:** On rare occasions, you may be able to convince the lender to adjourn the sale, but you'd better have a darned good reason. Simply saying that you're trying to come up with the money to repay your debt isn't good enough. They've heard that song and dance before. If you can prove that you're making a good-faith effort to gather the money you need or to close the sale of your house, the bank may be willing to delay the sale. Contact the lender's attorney, let him in on the latest details, and be prepared to deliver the documented proof he asks for.

If your lender or the lender's attorney tells you over the phone that the sheriff's sale is going to be adjourned, make sure you record the details in your phone journal — who you talked to, when, and what the person told you. Ask if the person can mail or fax you a confirmation. We also recommend that you attend the sheriff's sale to confirm for yourself that your property is not sold. Bring a cellphone with you, so if you hear your property mentioned or see it on the list of properties to be auctioned, you can call the attorney for the lender immediately and ask what's going on. If you catch it early, they may pull it off the auction block, but the longer you wait, the less of a chance you have to stop the sale.

In some jurisdictions, sheriff's sale adjournments must be publicly posted. If this is the case in your area, make sure the adjournment has been properly posted. If it wasn't, you may have a case that the lender failed to follow proper procedures. It could be tough to prove, but it's worth a shot.

When appearing in court, dress professionally. You don't need to wear a suit and tie, but don't dress up like Farmer Brown, either. When addressing the judge, be respectful. Listen ten times more than you speak, and when you open your mouth, make sure you address the judge as "Sir," "Ma'am," or "Your Honor." You can get your point across and even be assertive when necessary, but being disrespectful is certain to harm your case. Be prepared. Write out some bullet points so that you can stay focused when you're given the opportunity to speak.

Filing for Bankruptcy

Filing for bankruptcy can be the mother of all delay tactics, but it also can be an attractive, affordable solution to foreclosure. In fact, you may be able to file for Chapter 13 bankruptcy for less than you'd have to pay a lender to obtain a temporary postponement of the sale.

As soon as you file for bankruptcy (see Chapter 10), you receive an automatic stay, which essentially surrounds you with a force field that keeps the bill collectors at bay. A three- to five-year Chapter 13 bankruptcy plan can give you the time you need to restructure your finances and pay off your loans. If the lender files to have the stay lifted and you don't qualify for bankruptcy relief, the court can reject your request and lift the stay, in which case you end up in the same situation you were in *before* filing for bankruptcy, except now you owe your attorney some money.

If you consult a bankruptcy attorney, steer clear of the mills. A *mill* is a bankruptcy office that churns out bankruptcy filings one after another and spends very little time with clients discussing their options. If you follow through with the bankruptcy, you must feel comfortable with the plan. Make sure that you can make the payments as scheduled, or you'll find yourself in a worse situation later.

If the automatic stay occurs just before your house is sold at auction, you may be able to have the sale *expunged* (erased). It's not easy and may not be possible in your situation, but if your house is sold soon after you file for bankruptcy, ask your attorney to look into having the sale expunged.

Another technique your bankruptcy attorney may attempt is the "cramdown," which is sort of like a short sale. For example, if you owe $400,000 on a $350,000 property, your attorney may be able to convince the court to reduce the amount owed to $350,000 — the value of the property.

Maximizing the Redemption Period

If you live in a jurisdiction that has a redemption period, you may be able to stretch out that redemption period to give yourself even more time in your rent-free pad. Here are some tactics that have been used in the past:

> ✔ **If you're going to challenge the foreclosure process (see "Challenging the Process in Court," earlier in this chapter), consider waiting until late in the redemption period before filing your challenge.** If the court rules in your favor, it may restart the clock on your redemption period. That's a big "if," however, so have a backup plan in place. Be careful: If you wait too long in a judicial foreclosure, the court may issue a default

judgment in favor of your bank, preventing you from challenging the foreclosure.

✔ **If you're going to file for bankruptcy, file late in the redemption period for the same reason mentioned in the preceding bullet.** This approach is a very dangerous one, however. Consult an attorney who really knows what she's doing as early as possible in the process, so she can recommend the most effective timing. In most cases, you're better off filing for Chapter 13 bankruptcy early rather than relying on redemption to pay the entire loan balance in full. Bankruptcy typically extends redemption rights for only about 60 days, whereas if you restructure under Chapter 13, you have three to five years to catch up on missed payments.

✔ **Request additional time to move, as explained in the following section.**

✔ **File bankruptcy separately from your spouse.** Your spouse can file for bankruptcy now and you can file later, or vice versa.

To find out more about filing for bankruptcy, check out *Personal Bankruptcy Laws For Dummies,* 2nd Edition, by James P. Caher and John M. Caher (Wiley).

Negotiating Additional Time to Move

When your redemption period expires or you don't have a redemption period, someone, usually the court officer, is going to ask you to vacate the premises. If you refuse, the officer and his crew can assist you by escorting you and your belongings out to the street.

Instead of taking the passive-resistance option, which usually leads to an ugly eviction, offer to move according to your schedule. Show up at the eviction hearing (technically called a *landlord/tenant trespassing action*) and ask the bank's attorney or the investor who purchased your property whether you can have two or three extra weeks to move. In most jurisdictions, ten days is the normal amount of time granted. Don't get your hopes up for much more, but if you really could use the extra time and have good reason for *needing* extra time, go for it.

Before you go in front of the judge, you usually have an opportunity to meet with the bank's attorney. You can talk to him about giving you more time. If he agrees, then you can both go in front of the judge to request a *consent judgment*.

Make a sincere promise not to trash the house and to leave it "broom clean" (remove all your belongings and sweep up after yourself) upon departure. By showing your willingness to cooperate and meet the needs of the person taking possession of the property, you have a much better chance of gaining the extra time you ask for.

If your redemption or ten-days-to-vacate period expires in December, your ability to gain extra time could be compromised or improved. If the period expires in early to mid-December, be prepared to move in a hurry. The eviction crews get paid based on the evictions they perform, so it's to their advantage to complete them quickly. If they can complete several close to the holidays, it puts a little extra Christmas money in their pockets. If the period expires near the end of December, you're likely to get more time for two reasons: First, the world shuts down from about December 23 to January 2, and second, nobody likes to kick families out of their homes around Christmas.

Chapter 17

Ten Scams and the Scumbags Who Perpetrate Them

In This Chapter

▶ Dodging deed-carrying con artists

▶ Steering clear of foreclosure rescue scams

▶ Avoiding agreements that set you up for failure

▶ Ducking the equity strippers

▶ Claiming your overbid money . . . without paying huge fees

As soon as word hits the streets that foreclosure is imminent, you become a prime mark for every con artist, shyster, and opportunistic real estate investor within 50 miles of your home (and, with the Internet, even distant "fraud trotters"). Dozens of people are going to be calling, phoning, and knocking on your door offering to "help," but only a select few are likely to be acting on the level.

Who can you trust?

In this chapter, we reveal ten all-too-common foreclosure scams and describe how they work, so you can tell the difference between a legitimate investor and a foreclosure con artist.

Hijacking Your Home with a Quit-Claim Deed

Signing a quit-claim deed (or any other type of deed for that matter) is the equivalent of waving the white flag of surrender. Essentially, it says, "I hand over any rights of ownership I have in this home to so-and-so." That so-and-so can then sell the property, use it as a collateral for a loan, or give the home to someone else, and then kick you out. Pretty scary, eh? That's why we warn you, in Chapter 9, to be extremely careful about any papers that you sign.

The most common methods that con artists employ to steal your home with a quit-claim deed or other types of deeds are the following:

- **Bait and switch:** The scammer convinces you to refinance your mortgage through him, and shows up with several stacks of documents you have to sign to take out the loan. Tucked in one stack is a single sheet of paper labeled *quit-claim deed* in tiny print. In the flurry of flipping through papers and signing on the dotted line, you don't even notice it. The scammer then files the deed at the register of deeds office, making himself the legal owner of your home. He can now borrow money against your home or even sell it, leaving you holding the bag.

- **Land contract (or contract for deed) scam:** This can start out as a legitimate way to save your home. You deed your property to the scammer, who is then supposed to use the deed to secure financing, pay off the sheriff's deed, and then sell your home back to you. Sure, it costs extra money, but you get to keep your home. Unfortunately, the deal doesn't go down as planned. The con artist may charge you rent for several months and fail to redeem the sheriff's deed; use the home as collateral to take out another fraudulent loan; or simply refuse to sell you the house back, claiming that you failed to honor the contract.

Don't sign anything unless you've read and clearly understand what you're signing and agree to it. If in doubt, ask questions. If still in doubt, consult a qualified real estate attorney, preferably someone who has experience in foreclosure.

Pulling Out the Rug with a Buy-Rent-Redeem Scam

If you live in an area that has a lengthy redemption period, you may feel fortunate, but this makes you a bigger target for the buy-rent-redeem scam. Here's how it works:

The scammer agrees to buy the home from you because you can't afford to make the payments on the mortgage. She agrees to purchase it for what you owe on the property and then rent the house back to you. The scammer is supposed to go down and redeem the property, no problem. This sounds good to you. You're currently paying 8 percent to 12 percent interest, so the "investor" can take out a 4.5 percent loan, pay off your high-interest mortgage, rent the home back to you for less than you're currently paying per month, and still earn a profit. Everybody wins.

The scammer may also offer to sell the property back to you after a certain amount of time under a lease-option agreement, as explained later in this chapter in the "Setting You Up for Failure with a Lease-Option

Agreement" section. Or, maybe you just want to rent until your son or daughter graduates high school in two or three years. As long as you make your monthly rent payments, everything is supposed to be okay.

Problems arise, however, when the scammer never redeems the house. What?! Why would the scammer pass up the golden opportunity to take out a loan at 4.5 percent and purchase this valuable piece of real estate? Because the scammer probably can't qualify for a mortgage. She's just out to collect some rent money from you.

You pay each month like clockwork, believing that everything is going along just fine. You may not own your home, but you're living there, and your life hasn't been disrupted, your family hasn't been uprooted. Months later, you receive a notice in the mail ordering you to appear at an eviction hearing. You think this must be a mistake, but it's not. The investor never redeemed the house, you paid four or five months' rent, and now you're going to be evicted. Unless the cops find the perpetrator, you're out of luck and out of your house.

Stealing Your Home with a Tax Deed

A complete stranger shows up at your home with a tax deed claiming that he is now the proud owner of your home. You knew you hadn't been able to pay your taxes for the past couple years, but could someone come along and buy your home just by paying the back taxes you owed? You bet!

In some states, an investor can buy a tax deed at auction and immediately, or in a very short time, become the official legal owner of the property. In other areas, the county sells tax liens, in which investors must go through the foreclosure process to get you booted out of your home.

In many cases, tax deed scams simply use the tax deed or lien as a vehicle to pull off some other type of scam. They scan the publicly accessible delinquent tax list to identify their marks and choose their targets. Then they pitch some quick-fix remedy to bail out the homeowners.

One such scam consists of offering the homeowners a high-interest loan for just enough money to cover the taxes. The scammer then slips a quit-claim deed into the loan papers, as discussed earlier in this chapter in the "Hijacking Your Home with a Quit-Claim Deed" section. With quit-claim deed in hand, the scammer can then take out a fraudulent mortgage on the property using a phony ID, leaving you and the new lender to sort out the mess.

When someone shows up at your door with a tax deed, claiming to be the new owner of your property, don't believe him. Contact a qualified real estate attorney right away. If you can't afford an attorney, head down to the register of deeds office and start asking questions. Don't take the "investor's" word for it. In most cases, you can redeem your property even if someone purchased the tax lien or deed at auction, as long as you haven't deeded the property to the person who purchased the tax lien or deed.

Cheating You Out of Your Redemption Period

When an investor purchases your mortgage at a foreclosure auction and you live in a jurisdiction that has a redemption period, you suddenly become one of the biggest obstacles sitting in the way of that investor making money. Until you move out and the investor can get in with a crew to rehabilitate the property, she can't fix and sell the property. Even worse, she may have the added expense of paying interest on any money she borrowed to make the purchase, along with property taxes and other costs.

Some investors in areas with lengthy redemption periods try to artificially shorten the redemption period by convincing you that you need to vacate the premises earlier than is legally necessary. The person may tell you that she just bought your house and you have to move out, failing to mention that you have six months to live in the home rent-free before you have to move. The investor may even try to bully or scare you out of the house by telling you that you really don't want to put your family through an ugly eviction.

As soon as you move out, you're at the mercy of the crooked investor. The investor can then record a fraudulent deed, redeem the house into her name, or have the house declared abandoned, shortening the redemption period. Without you around to challenge the claims, the investor can do whatever she wants. You probably won't even realize that you've been conned.

Stripping Your Equity with a Foreclosure Rescue Scam

Some of the lowest of the lowlifes pose as good guys in white hats coming to save the day. They have a special program that has helped hundreds of homeowners just like you avoid foreclosure and bankruptcy, and they can help you, too!

That's their story, anyway. The truth is that they're only going to help themselves . . . to *your* money — in the form of your house or the equity you have in it.

Foreclosure rescue scams take all shapes and forms. Here are a few of the more common scams:

- ✔ **Pyramid:** You pay $3,000 (or whatever the going rate) to assist someone in the group in paying off her mortgage. As more members join, you move higher up on the pyramid, until eventually it's your turn to have your mortgage paid off. For a one-time contribution of $3,000, you own your home free and clear! Sound too good to be true? It *is* too good to be true. Don't fall for it.

- ✔ **Legal technicalities:** The con artist explains (usually on the Internet) that you don't really owe the bank the money you borrowed. The government prints money and is involved in a scheme with the banks to defraud people out of their hard-earned cash. The con artist, posing as an attorney, promises to take your case to court and have your mortgage declared null and void. After that's accomplished, you can take out another mortgage, have that declared null and void, and walk away with the cash. Of course, the con artist wants a good chunk of the proceeds. Unfortunately, you end up with two unpaid mortgages and lose your house anyway.

  Savvy foreclosure attorneys do have legitimate ways to attack mortgages under Truth in Lending laws, but don't fall for a con artist who's simply setting you up for failure. If you think you have a case, hire a reputable attorney.

- ✔ **Refinance:** The foreclosure rescue specialist has a private lender who is willing to loan you the money. It's not cheap. You have to put $10,000 down and pay 10 points. Fortunately, the investor offers to roll all the fees back into the loan amount. You currently owe $100,000. After the refinance, you'll owe $125,000. "That's okay, though," the specialist explains, "because according to our appraiser, your house is worth $160,000, so you'll still have $35,000 in equity." The problem is that your house is really worth only $128,000. As soon as you refinance, all but about $3,000 of your equity is gone, and if you default on the loan, the lender can foreclose and take possession of your $128,000 home for the mere $100,000 the lender invested in paying off your previous mortgage.

Some foreclosure rescue services are legitimate. Just make sure you check them out carefully, work only with brick-and-mortar businesses that have real addresses and phone numbers, and verify everything they tell you with someone who knows foreclosure law.

Setting You Up for Failure with a Lease-Option Agreement

Remember the *Peanuts* cartoon in which Lucy always baits Charlie Brown into trying to kick the football? She convinces him that he can do it, and this time, she promises, she won't pull the football away at the last instant. Every time, poor Charlie Brown falls for it. He steps back, takes a running start, and just as he's about ready to boot the ball, Lucy pulls it away. Chuck whiffs the air, flies head over heels, and lands flat on his back, in desperate need of a chiropractor.

This is exactly what happens with investors who set up homeowners to fail with a lease-option agreement. The scammer approaches a couple who really want to save their home but can't, and he offers to buy the property for what the couple currently owes on it, lease the property back to them, and give them the option to purchase it for more money later. The scammer usually also requires a significant down payment.

The problem is, the couple really can't afford it, or the contract is laced with conditions that make it nearly impossible for the couple to honor. The contract usually includes a forfeiture clause as well, stating that if the homeowners fail to honor the contract, they lose their down payment, all of the rent they paid, and their home. In some cases, a payment that's one day late can trigger the forfeiture.

Don't get us wrong: Lease-option deals can be great. We actually use them to assist homeowners in staying in their home, and then buying back their property from us one to three years down the road when they're in a better financial position. But we don't recommend lease-option agreements to people who probably aren't going to be in a better financial position in the not-too-distant future. We don't believe in setting people up for failure, and you shouldn't allow anyone to do it to you.

Setting You Up for Failure with a Contract for Deed

The contract-for-deed (or land sale contract) scam is very similar to the lease-option scam. Both contracts usually contain a forfeiture clause that gives the seller the right to repossess the property in the event that the buyer fails to honor the contract. In the case of a contract for deed, the seller simply uses a contract instead of a mortgage to secure the debt when selling the property back to you.

In some jurisdictions, forfeiture clauses carry little weight. The seller/lender is still required by law to proceed with foreclosure to collect on the unpaid debt. However, some sellers may not know the law or may attempt to keep you in the dark about it. If the person you purchased the home from using a contract for deed or lease-option agreement attempts to kick you out of your home based on a forfeiture clause, be sure to check with a foreclosure attorney in your area to determine whether the person has the right to do that.

Stripping Your Equity with a Predatory Loan

Predatory lending can take many forms, but it boils down to unfair lending practices, such as the following:

- **Serial refinancing:** Convincing homeowners to keep refinancing to cash out equity. Every time you refinance, you pay financing fees, even though these fees may be rolled into the mortgage amount. This essentially strips the equity from your home.

- **Selling nonessential services:** Loan officers may try to sell costly mortgage insurance and other products or services to borrowers who don't need them, by saying that they're required in order for the loan to be approved.

- **Approving a risky loan:** Lenders may loan you money knowing that, in the near future, you're not going to be able to make the payments. The lender collects your payments for as long as you can afford to make them and then forecloses, takes your home, and sells it. This usually isn't in the best interest of the lender unless you have substantial equity in the property.

- **Selling high-interest loans to borrowers who qualify for low-interest loans:** Borrowers who have an excellent credit rating typically qualify for loans at lower interest rates. Some loan officers may try to sell these applicants higher-interest loans. This is why shopping around for a loan is so important.

Predatory lending often involves tempting borrowers with low introductory teaser rates that are scheduled to rise several months or years down the road. These loans also often come with stiff prepayment penalties to discourage borrowers from refinancing. The lenders are merely setting up borrowers to fail.

Selling Your Home at Way Below Market Value

Many homeowners have no idea what their homes' true market value is. Maybe you purchased your home 20 years ago for $75,000. If we told you that same house in today's market is worth $250,000, you'd never believe us, but in some popular neighborhoods, that can certainly be the case.

Con artists often rely on homeowner ignorance to scam them out of valuable real estate, especially when the pressure of foreclosure is added to the mix. The scammer may present you an appraisal showing that your home is worth far less than its true market value. Or the person may hire contractors to come over and provide an inflated estimate of the cost of repairs required to make the home marketable. We've seen cases where a con artist has convinced the homeowner to sell for $90,000 and then placed the property back on the market the next day for $155,000. This happened simply because the homeowner didn't realize what her home was really worth.

When someone comes along and tells you what your home is worth or how much it may cost to fix it up, get a second and third opinion. This is the only way to defend yourself against the purveyors of false information.

Cheating You Out of Your Overbid Money

The overbid scam is one of the most successful, because it's a "good" lie. The difference between a good lie and a bad lie is that a good lie contains some truth. The overbid scam is based on the fact that in some jurisdictions any funds collected at the sale in excess of what is owed to the mortgage holders belongs to the homeowners. That's the truth that the con artists use, but then they bend the truth by leading homeowners to believe that obtaining this money is terribly difficult — it's not.

Some of these overbid con artists charge as much as 50 percent of the proceeds to claim the overbid money. That's a little steep. If you really don't want to spend the time and effort driving down to the courthouse and signing a form, then hire someone to do it for 50 bucks or a small percentage of the take, but don't pay 50 percent. Just be sure the person you hire is trustworthy; otherwise, he may decide to walk off with 100 percent.

Chapter 18

Ten Ways to Rebuild Your Life after Foreclosure

"*L*ife goes on" may sound like a cliché, but no matter how devastating the experience, it's true: Life does goes on. How *well* it goes on for you hinges a great deal on how well you prepared for and controlled the foreclosure fallout, as well as on your financial resources and emotional frame of mind. In this chapter, we offer ten tips on how to recover from foreclosure and build a future that's far rosier than the painful past.

True failures in life occur only when people stop trying. As long as you're alive, you have opportunity. If you managed to keep your family together through these trying times, you have even more to start out with and keep you going. Some of the most successful people we know were baptized by fire.

Rebooting Your Life

As you run and then exit programs on a computer, those programs are not completely removed from your computer's memory. Over time, the computer's memory is overrun with errant instructions that slow it down and cause all sorts of mysterious problems. Rebooting the computer by shutting it down and restarting it often resolves the problem. The same is true in life. Sometimes a fresh start is all you really need to get back on track.

Whether you've been able to remain in your home or you're having to move out, you can now put the foreclosure behind you and get on with your life — assuming, of course, that the bank didn't hit you with a deficiency judgment that's going to follow you for several years. Leave all the bad stuff in the past, especially any mistakes that you or your partner may have made leading up to the foreclosure. You can't change the past. You can only make adjustments to ensure that history doesn't repeat itself.

Losing a home that's been dragging you down for so long can be liberating in a way. How long have you been living *for* your house instead of *in* your house? How many months or years have you been struggling to make those house payments? How long have you been living a charade in order to keep up appearances? As soon as you're free of the burden, you may have a clearer view of what matters most — health, happiness, friends, and family.

Use this opportunity to create a plan, commit your family to a disciplined financial strategy, and stick to it, and before you know it you'll be back up and running.

Swearing Off the Same Mistakes

If some human foible led to your foreclosure — overspending, not working hard enough, gambling, substance abuse, or some other weakness — own up to it and then make a commitment to change. The same applies to any errors of judgment you may have made, such as making your partner solely responsible for the finances or letting a loan officer convince you that you could "afford more house."

In some cases, you quickly learn from your mistakes and can easily avoid them in the future. When the mistake has something to do with your way of life, however, you may need to make some serious life changes to avoid repeating the mistake. Avoiding the mistake becomes more like trying to quit smoking or trying to lose that extra weight — you have to develop healthier habits.

Partner with someone who can hold you accountable. You can partner with your spouse, another relative, a close friend, or a colleague. Develop spending habits and budgets together. You may not see a positive change overnight and you may relapse into your old ways, but over time, you should see some real progress. Create a 12-month chart of where you are now and where you want to be by the end of the year. Track your progress over the course of the year. At the end of the year, draw up a new chart. Nothing is more motivating than seeing how far you've come and how close you are to your goal.

Leaning On Family and Friends

After foreclosure, whether you managed to keep your home or ended up losing it, friends and family can give you the support you need to get back on your feet:

✔ Encouragement and love to keep going

✔ Financial support in the form of loans or a job

✔ Watching your children, so you can take on an extra job

✔ Driving you to work and back if you have no reliable mode of transportation

✔ A temporary place to live

Foreclosure is nothing to be ashamed of. If your friend or relative were in the same situation and you were in a position to offer assistance, how would you feel if the person didn't ask you for help? You'd probably feel pretty bad, as though your friend or relative didn't trust you or feel close enough to you to ask. The same is true in your case. People need to be needed. When they're in a position to help, most people are more than willing to lend a hand.

Heading West . . . or East or North or South

Pulling up your tent stakes and migrating across the country may not be an option if you have a pretty good life where you are, your kids are in school, and you have plenty of support from family and friends. If you're living in an area that has been hard hit by an economic downturn, if everyone around you is highly critical of you for losing your home, or if you really have little reason to stay, consider heading out of town to a more promising destination.

The United States is a big country and jobs often move from one state to another. Consider moving to wherever the best-paying jobs are. Move to where the housing is cheapest. Move to where the schools are excellent and free. Whatever your most pressing needs are, research to find areas that are best suited to meet those needs. The loss of a job in Ohio may be just the opportunity you need to pick up and move to North Carolina. You lost or liquidated your house. You've sold as much of your belongings as possible. You don't have a job lined up. So, what's holding you back?

Slashing Expenses and Your Cost of Living

Chances are pretty good that when you first set out to seek your fortune, your standard of living was fairly low and you needed very little to survive. Perhaps you shared an apartment with a roommate, never went out to eat, purchased all your clothes at garage sales and discount stores, and hung out with friends instead of spending money on entertainment. You lived frugally, had plenty of time, and probably enjoyed life more than ever.

What's to stop you from doing that again? Do you really need a big house and all the trappings of "success"? Most people don't. Society has sold us a bill of goods, making most of us believe that happiness hinges on owning things.

You're essentially starting out from scratch, so learn a lesson from your youth — live frugally. Share living expenses. Cook your own meals from scratch. Ditch the car. Move closer to work. Rely on public transportation to get where you're going. You may find that you have less stuff but more time for the things in life that mean the most to you.

Downsizing to More Affordable Accommodations

Over the past 20 years or so, families have shrunk while houses have expanded. In the old days, a family of six managed just fine in a rinky-dink three-bedroom house. A second bathroom was considered a luxury. In modern homes, everyone has his or her own bedroom and each person shares a bathroom with, at the most, one other person.

You don't need much to live. Having a roof over your head, a place to sleep, a kitchen in which to cook meals, and a shared bathroom is sufficient for most families. It may feel a little cramped, but you can certainly get by until better days return.

As time goes on, the need to downsize generally increases. Your kids are going to move out someday, believe it or not. If your kids are one or two years from heading out to college, trying to hold onto that large house so your kids won't lose their rooms may not be practical.

Making a Lateral Move

People often feel like failures when they're not constantly ascending the ladder of success, but remember that you're in charge of defining what *success* means to you. You don't need to constantly strive for promotions. If you're good at what you do and you've simply lost your job, don't worry about finding something better. Look for something that can bring in about the same amount of income or even less, if you're able to make some lifestyle adjustments.

As more Americans become more highly educated, we find ourselves ruling out jobs that we would have jumped at in the past. Don't be afraid to slip into a secure job that's a lateral shift instead of a promotion. When security and peace of mind are the goals, any job that fills that role is a good job.

Pepping Up Your Pocketbook: Earning More

You downsized, slashed your budget, and are holding down a fairly steady job, but you still can't make ends meet. What do you do? Well, you have to find another source of income. You have to earn more. Here are some options:

- Pick up some overtime.
- Take on side jobs.
- Work shifts that offer premium or time bonuses.
- Moonlight by taking on a second job.
- Put other family members to work to cover some expenses.

Sometimes hard work has no substitute. If you have the extra time or can somehow free up some extra time, working more can be your lifeline.

Healing Your Bruised Credit

Although cutting up all your credit cards and paying for everything with cash is certainly a possibility, you need to think about rebuilding your credit for the long haul — especially if you're thinking about buying a house again someday. Take some positive steps to heal your bruised credit:

- ✔ **Get into the habit of paying all your bills on time every time.** Paying even one day late can harm your credit.

- ✔ **Apply for a credit card if you don't have one.** Use the credit card to pay for necessities only, and then pay off the balance in full when you receive your monthly statement.

- ✔ **Keep tabs on your credit report.** Check your credit report at least once a year (preferably more often), highlight any questionable items, and contact the credit reporting agency to clear up any discrepancies.

- ✔ **Start saving a little every month and socking the money away in a savings account.** Having money in the bank shows that you know how to manage your money.

For additional tips on how to heal bruised and battered credit, check out Chapter 15.

Getting Back into the Game of Life

When you suffer a series of minor setbacks or one big setback, you may feel as though life has just knocked the stuffing out of you. Perhaps you feel as though, no matter what you do, you can never get the break you need to make it.

However bad you feel, you need to wake up every day, get out there, and do it. Otherwise, you'll never get the big break you've been waiting for.

If you moved a significant distance from your old home as a result of the foreclosure, getting back into the game of life may be easier because you don't have to face your old peers. But even if you have to face your peers, what's most important is how you put your life back together, not what happened in the past. As people who've made it through foreclosure, you and your family are much stronger and much better prepared to handle future curves that life may throw your way. As long as you handle your comeback well, your foreclosure is a badge of courage, not of shame.

Glossary

· ·

acceleration clause: Language in the mortgage that allows the bank to call in the whole balance due on a loan in the event of missed payments. Without an acceleration clause, the bank must declare a separate default for each missed payment as the payment is missed. An acceleration clause allows a missed payment to be considered a default of the whole, and allows the bank to call the full balance due.

adjustable rate mortgage (ARM): A home loan whose interest rate can rise and fall. ARMs often contribute to triggering foreclosure when the interest rate jumps, making the monthly payments less affordable.

ARM: *See* adjustable rate mortgage (ARM).

automatic stay: A freeze imposed on lenders as soon as you file for bankruptcy. The stay prevents lenders from moving forward on debt collections. Bankruptcy automatically triggers the stay, but in some situations lenders can convince the bankruptcy court to lift the stay.

back-end ratio: Your debt ratio for your house and all other loans (such as a car loan). According to the Federal Housing Authority (FHA), your back-end debt ratio should not exceed 41 percent. *See also* debt ratio *and* front-end ratio.

bankruptcy: A legal process allowing the debtor to discharge certain debts or obligations without paying the full balance due or reorganize finances in order to repay all debts. The two most common forms of bankruptcy for homeowners are

- ✔ **Chapter 7:** Liquidation of all nonexempt assets to repay as much debt as possible and forgive all remaining debt
- ✔ **Chapter 13:** Reorganization of finances to pay off all or some debts over time

certificate of credit briefing: A document showing that you have received essential information about filing for bankruptcy from a certified credit counseling agency. At the time you file for bankruptcy, you must supply a certificate of credit briefing or a certificate of exigent circumstances. *See also* bankruptcy *and* certificate of exigent circumstances.

certificate of exigent circumstances: A written explanation of why you could not obtain credit briefing prior to filing for bankruptcy. *See also* bankruptcy *and* certificate of credit briefing.

Chapter 7: *See* bankruptcy.

Chapter 13: *See* bankruptcy.

clogging of the equity of redemption: A prohibited strategy used by some lenders to prevent you from taking advantage of your right to redeem. Instead of using a mortgage to secure the loan, the lender asks for a *deed absolute,* meaning that if you default on the loan, the lender takes immediate possession of the property. *See also* deed absolute.

contract for deed: A document that allows the seller of a home to finance the purchase and use the home as collateral to secure the loan. A contract for deed is very similar to a mortgage, but in this case, the seller rather than a bank or other lending institution is financing the purchase. Also known as a *land-sale contract.*

covenant to pay: Language in the mortgage that gives your personal promise to pay the debt in full. A covenant to pay may give the bank the right to a deficiency judgment in states in which deficiency judgments are allowed. *See also* deficiency judgment.

credit report: A statement that shows your credit history, including all of your accounts, balances, and late or missed payments. *See also* tri-merge credit report.

credit score: An indicator of how attractive you are as a borrower. Credit scores typically range from 300 to 900. Anything below about 680 starts to raise red flags.

debt ratio: The mathematical relationship between how much you pay out in monthly bills and your gross monthly income. Banks use your debt ratio to determine your ability to make monthly payments. Banks often examine both front-end ratio and back-end ratio. *See also* front-end ratio *and* back-end ratio.

deed: A legal document that identifies the official owner of a home. Deeds can come in several flavors. *See also* deed absolute, general-warranty deed, limited-warranty deed, quit-claim deed, sheriff's deed, *and* tax deed.

deed absolute: Transfers ownership of the property automatically and immediately to the lender in the event that the borrower defaults on the loan. *See also* deed *and* clogging the equity of redemption.

deed in lieu of foreclosure: An arrangement in which you hand over your home to the lender and, in exchange, the lender agrees not to foreclose. You have to be careful, though: A lender could still pursue you for any debt not covered by the proceeds from the sale of your home. If you offer a deed in lieu, make sure you also receive a document showing that the lender has accepted the deed as full payment of the loan.

default: The failure to honor an agreement. In foreclosure, default usually means failure to make monthly payments on the agreed-upon dates.

deficiency judgment: A court order that a borrower must pay the balance that remains on a loan after the foreclosure sale. In other words, if you owe $150,000 on your home and it sells for $125,000 at the foreclosure sale, in some states, the court could grant the lender a deficiency judgment, in which case, you would have to come up with the extra $25,000.

due on sale: A clause in a mortgage stating that you must pay the full balance of the mortgage loan in the event that you sell your home.

durable power of attorney: *See* power of attorney (POA).

encumbrance clause: Language in a mortgage designed to prevent homeowners from borrowing their way into a default situation. For example, a mortgage may have a stipulation that you cannot, without prior approval from the lender, take out another loan on your property.

equity: The amount of cash you have in your house. If you sold the house today and paid off all liens against it, equity is the money you could stuff in your pockets or purse.

eviction: The process of kicking someone out of the house in which he is residing and removing all his belongings from the house.

exempt assets: Stuff you own that cannot be taken and sold to repay debts to creditors. *See also* nonexempt assets *and* bankruptcy.

Federal Housing Authority (FHA): A division of the U.S. Department of Housing and Urban Development (HUD) that administers loan programs and issues loan guarantees to make housing more affordable and accessible. *See also* Housing and Urban Development (HUD).

FHA: *See* Federal Housing Authority (FHA).

forbearance: Curing the default to a mortgage by way of a payment plan. In most cases, you are required to make your normal monthly payment plus a portion of any past-due payments and penalties that have accrued as a result of the default.

force-placed insurance: Homeowner's insurance that is paid by the lender on behalf of the borrower to protect the bank's interest in the home. If you fail to insure your home, your lender may take out a policy on your home and then bill you for it.

foreclosure: The process by which a creditor can enforce repayment of a loan by selling the home at a public auction.

foreclosure auction: The public sale of a property to repay a debt for which the property was used as collateral. *See also* sheriff's sale.

foreclosure by advertisement: *See* nonjudicial foreclosure.

foreclosure rescue scam: A form of real estate fraud in which an individual or company promises to save you from foreclosure and ends up stealing your home or the equity you have in it.

forfeiture: A clause in a contract for deed or lease-option agreement stating that if the buyers of the property do not honor the agreement, they forfeit all their rights to the property. *See also* contract for deed *and* lease-option agreement.

front-end ratio: Your debt ratio for only your home. According to the Federal Housing Authority (FHA), it should not exceed 29 percent. *See also* debt ratio *and* back-end ratio.

general-warranty deed: Transfers ownership of the property from the seller to the buyer and guarantees that the seller is the rightful owner of the property, the title is free from any encumbrances, and the title will be good against any third parties seeking to establish title to the property. *See also* deed.

home equity line of credit: A mortgage loan that lets you borrow as much or as little money as you need against the equity in your home and pay interest on only the amount you borrow. *See also* equity *and* home equity loan.

home equity loan: A mortgage loan that enables you to cash out some or all of the equity in your home in a lump sum. *See also* equity and home equity line of credit.

Housing and Urban Development (HUD): The U.S. Department of Housing and Urban Development, which funds free or very low-cost housing counseling nationwide. Housing counselors can help you understand the law and your options, organize your finances, and represent you in negotiations with your lender if you need this assistance.

HUD: *See* Housing and Urban Development (HUD).

jointly: Together, as a group. Contracts may hold the people signing it jointly accountable, in which case all members can be named in a lawsuit as a group. *See also* severally.

judicial foreclosure: A foreclosure process that proceeds through the court system and is usually more costly and time-consuming for the lender who's trying to repossess a property. *See also* nonjudicial foreclosure.

junior lien: A legal claim to a home that is subordinate to the senior lien. A junior lien could be a second mortgage, a home equity loan or line of credit, or a loan taken out against the home for improvements, such as replacement windows. *See also* home equity line of credit, home equity loan, senior lien, *and* tax lien.

land-sale contract: *See* contract for deed.

lease-option agreement: A rent-to-own agreement between a seller and a buyer. The buyer typically agrees to make a down payment on the property and pay rent for a specified number of months, after which time, the buyer has the right, but not the obligation, to purchase the property.

limited power of attorney: *See* power of attorney (POA).

limited-warranty deed: Similar to a general-warranty deed, but guarantees the title only for the period of time that the seller owned the property. *See also* deed *and* general-warranty deed.

loan servicer: A company that works on behalf of your lender to collect and process your monthly mortgage payments.

loan-to-value (LTV) ratio: The mathematical relationship between how much you owe or will owe on your home and its appraised value. If you owe $80,000 on a home that appraises for $100,000, it has an LTV ratio of 80 percent.

loss mitigator: A person dedicated to assisting borrowers to avoid foreclosure and making sure the bank loses as little money as possible from bad loans.

LTV ratio: *See* loan-to-value (LTV) ratio.

means test: A provision in the bankruptcy code that determines whether you qualify for Chapter 7 bankruptcy or must file for Chapter 13 bankruptcy. If your income falls below a certain level, you may qualify for Chapter 7 bankruptcy. The means test is intended as a way to curb Chapter 7 bankruptcy abuse. *See also* bankruptcy.

mortgage: A document that pledges property as security for a loan. The note is your promise to pay. The mortgage pledges the property as collateral for the loan. *See also* mortgagee *and* mortgagor.

mortgage modification: An alteration of the mortgage agreement, typically to make the monthly payments more affordable. A lender can modify the mortgage in any number of ways, including adding time to the end of the mortgage or reducing the interest rate. *See also* mortgage.

mortgage satisfaction: A document filed with the register of deeds stating that the mortgage on a property has been paid in full.

mortgagee: The lender in a lender-borrower agreement. *See also* mortgage *and* mortgagor.

mortgagor: The borrower in a lender-borrower agreement. *See also* mortgage *and* mortgagee.

net worth: The amount of money that would remain if you were to sell all your stuff and pay all your debts. In other words, what you own minus what you owe.

no-asset case: A bankruptcy situation in which the value of nonexempt assets is not worth pursuing to repay debts. *See also* bankruptcy, exempt assets, *and* nonexempt assets.

nonexempt assets: Stuff you own that can be taken and sold to repay debts to creditors in bankruptcy. *See also* exempt assets *and* bankruptcy.

nonjudicial foreclosure: A foreclosure process that proceeds outside of the court system. With a nonjudicial foreclosure, the lender merely needs to publicly advertise its intent to foreclose for a set amount of time prior to the foreclosure auction. Also known as *foreclosure by advertisement. See also* judicial foreclosure.

non-monetary default: A condition that gives a party the right to take possession of your home for a reason other than nonpayment of a debt. Non-monetary defaults may include failing to properly maintain your property or violation of a restriction on the deed. *See also* default.

non-recourse debt: A loan in which the lender has the legal right to use only the value of the collateral the borrower put up as security for the loan to satisfy the debt. In other words, if you default on your mortgage, the bank can only take the property that was put up for security; it cannot come after your other assets.

note: A written promise to pay. Think of it as an IOU. When you take out a loan to finance the purchase of property, you usually sign a mortgage and a note. The note is your promise to pay. The mortgage pledges the property as collateral for the loan.

notice of default: A written announcement that a borrower has failed to honor the terms of payment stated in the mortgage. In most states, delivering the notice of default is the first step in the foreclosure process.

order of eviction: A directive of the court that allows the sheriff to evict the foreclosed-upon homeowners and turn the property over to whomever purchased the property at auction. Also known as a *writ of restitution.*

overbid: An amount of money bid at auction in excess of what is required to pay off all liens against the property. The homeowners who lost the property at auction are entitled to the overbid money and usually just have to show up at the sheriff's office and submit a form to claim it.

POA: *See* power of attorney (POA).

power of attorney (POA): A legal document that gives someone else the right to make decisions or act on your behalf. POAs come in two flavors:

- ✔ **Unlimited (or durable) power of attorney** assigns the grantee unlimited power to make decisions and take action on your behalf. The grantee can execute deeds, mortgages, bills of sale, and so on. The term *durable* means that the grantee holds this power and will continue to hold it even in the event that the grantor becomes incapacitated.

- ✔ **Limited (or specific) power of attorney** typically restricts the person's power to a specific transaction. This allows the grantee to handle the transaction as if the grantor were doing it herself, but it doesn't give the grantee the power to do anything else except what is specifically listed.

power of sale: A provision, typically in a mortgage document, stating that if you default on the mortgage, the lender has the right to foreclose on your home and sell it at auction to pay off the balance of the loan. This provision is often used in states that allow for nonjudicial foreclosure. *See also* nonjudicial foreclosure.

predatory lending: Any practices that are intended to cheat borrowers out of their money. Predatory lending includes placing homeowners who qualify for low-interest loans into high-interest loans, selling optional services as mandatory, charging hidden fees, and convincing homeowners to serially refinance their homes, stripping out the equity in refinancing charges.

pre-foreclosure: The time between when the bank first notifies homeowners of their missed or late payments and the foreclosure sale.

prepayment penalty: An amount or percentage of a loan that you must pay the lender if you pay off the loan earlier than the date specified in the mortgage. Lenders often use prepayment penalties to discourage borrowers from refinancing with another lender.

pro se: Acting as your own attorney.

property tax scam: A form of real estate fraud in which someone uses a tax deed or lien (either forged or legitimate) to falsely claim that she is the new owner of your home, and you are required by law to vacate the premises immediately.

quit-claim deed: A deed that makes no warranties or guaranties about title but conveys whatever ownership the grantor has (if any). *See also* deed.

real estate agent: A person licensed to negotiate and process a real estate transaction on behalf of the buyer or seller of a property. *See also* Realtor.

Realtor: A real estate agent who is also a member of the National Association of Realtors. Although the United States has over 2 million real estate agents, only about 1.2 million are Realtors. A Realtor has additional training and is held to a higher standard of ethics, which generally makes a Realtor a better choice for assisting people in buying or selling a home. *See also* real estate agent.

recourse debt: A loan in which the lender has the legal right to pursue any of your assets to collect on the balance of the loan. *See also* covenant to pay, deficiency judgment, *and* non-recourse debt.

redemption period: A specific amount of time after a foreclosure sale during which the foreclosed-upon homeowners can buy back their home. The homeowners must pay the person who purchased the property at auction the amount the person paid at auction, along with any qualified expenses the person incurred and filed an affidavit for having paid.

register of deeds: The county office in which legal documents related to the transfer of real property are recorded. Your county's register of deeds should be a great place to obtain foreclosure information and ideas for where to look for additional assistance.

reinstatement: Curing the default of a mortgage by catching up on past payments and paying any fees or penalties that resulted from the default.

secured loan: A loan that has some sort of collateral attached to it that the lender can take and sell if you don't repay the debt. Home mortgages and car loans are two examples of secured loans. *See also* unsecured loan.

senior lien: A legal claim to a home that takes precedence over all other liens, except a tax lien. *See also* junior lien *and* tax lien.

severally: Separately, as individuals. Contracts may hold the people signing it severally accountable, in which case each member can be named in a separate lawsuit. *See also* jointly.

sheriff's deed: Issued by the sheriff's office to the purchaser of a property at a foreclosure sale, indicating that the purchaser is the new owner of the property subject to certain conditions, such as a redemption period, where applicable. *See also* deed *and* redemption period.

sheriff's sale: A foreclosure auction typically conducted by the county sheriff. *See also* foreclosure auction.

short sale: An arrangement between lender and borrower in which the lender agrees to accept as full payment less than the total amount due. By negotiating a short sale, homeowners may be able to sell their home without having to take a loss on it. Rarely does a lender agree to a short sale if it means that the distressed homeowner profits from the sale.

specific power of attorney: *See* power of attorney (POA).

tax deed: Transfers the ownership of the property to the person who pays the delinquent or back property taxes due on the property at a specially held sale in states where tax deeds are used. *See also* deed *and* tax lien.

tax lien: A claim placed upon a property, typically by the county, to collect unpaid property taxes. The tax lien gives the person who purchases it the right to foreclose on the property to collect the unpaid taxes. In some states, tax deeds are used, in which case the buyer of the tax deed typically becomes the new owner of the property without having to foreclose or wait for a redemption period to expire. *See also* deed, tax deed, junior lien, *and* senior lien.

term: The duration of a loan. A 30-year mortgage, for example, has a term of 30 years.

tri-merge credit report: A document showing your credit history as reported by the three major credit reporting agencies. *See also* credit report.

unlimited power of attorney: *See* power of attorney (POA).

unsecured loan: A loan that is not backed up by collateral. Credit card debt and medical expenses are usually considered unsecured loans. *See also* secured loan.

writ of restitution: *See* order of eviction.

Index

BUSINESS, CAREERS & PERSONAL FINANCE

0-7645-9847-3

0-7645-2431-3

Also available:

- Business Plans Kit For Dummies
  0-7645-9794-9
- Economics For Dummies
  0-7645-5726-2
- Grant Writing For Dummies
  0-7645-8416-2
- Home Buying For Dummies
  0-7645-5331-3
- Managing For Dummies
  0-7645-1771-6
- Marketing For Dummies
  0-7645-5600-2

- Personal Finance For Dummies
  0-7645-2590-5*
- Resumes For Dummies
  0-7645-5471-9
- Selling For Dummies
  0-7645-5363-1
- Six Sigma For Dummies
  0-7645-6798-5
- Small Business Kit For Dummies
  0-7645-5984-2
- Starting an eBay Business For Dummies
  0-7645-6924-4
- Your Dream Career For Dummies
  0-7645-9795-7

HOME & BUSINESS COMPUTER BASICS

0-470-05432-8

0-471-75421-8

Also available:

- Cleaning Windows Vista For Dummies
  0-471-78293-9
- Excel 2007 For Dummies
  0-470-03737-7
- Mac OS X Tiger For Dummies
  0-7645-7675-5
- MacBook For Dummies
  0-470-04859-X
- Macs For Dummies
  0-470-04849-2
- Office 2007 For Dummies
  0-470-00923-3

- Outlook 2007 For Dummies
  0-470-03830-6
- PCs For Dummies
  0-7645-8958-X
- Salesforce.com For Dummies
  0-470-04893-X
- Upgrading & Fixing Laptops For Dummies
  0-7645-8959-8
- Word 2007 For Dummies
  0-470-03658-3
- Quicken 2007 For Dummies
  0-470-04600-7

FOOD, HOME, GARDEN, HOBBIES, MUSIC & PETS

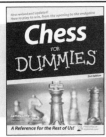

0-7645-8404-9

0-7645-9904-6

Also available:

- Candy Making For Dummies
  0-7645-9734-5
- Card Games For Dummies
  0-7645-9910-0
- Crocheting For Dummies
  0-7645-4151-X
- Dog Training For Dummies
  0-7645-8418-9
- Healthy Carb Cookbook For Dummies
  0-7645-8476-6
- Home Maintenance For Dummies
  0-7645-5215-5

- Horses For Dummies
  0-7645-9797-3
- Jewelry Making & Beading For Dummies
  0-7645-2571-9
- Orchids For Dummies
  0-7645-6759-4
- Puppies For Dummies
  0-7645-5255-4
- Rock Guitar For Dummies
  0-7645-5356-9
- Sewing For Dummies
  0-7645-6847-7
- Singing For Dummies
  0-7645-2475-5

INTERNET & DIGITAL MEDIA

0-470-04529-9

0-470-04894-8

Also available:

- Blogging For Dummies
  0-471-77084-1
- Digital Photography For Dummies
  0-7645-9802-3
- Digital Photography All-in-One Desk Reference For Dummies
  0-470-03743-1
- Digital SLR Cameras and Photography For Dummies
  0-7645-9803-1
- eBay Business All-in-One Desk Reference For Dummies
  0-7645-8438-3
- HDTV For Dummies
  0-470-09673-X

- Home Entertainment PCs For Dummies
  0-470-05523-5
- MySpace For Dummies
  0-470-09529-6
- Search Engine Optimization For Dummies
  0-471-97998-8
- Skype For Dummies
  0-470-04891-3
- The Internet For Dummies
  0-7645-8996-2
- Wiring Your Digital Home For Dummies
  0-471-91830-X

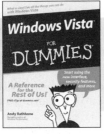

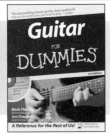

* Separate Canadian edition also available
† Separate U.K. edition also available

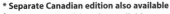

SPORTS, FITNESS, PARENTING, RELIGION & SPIRITUALITY

0-471-76871-5

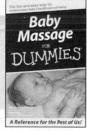

0-7645-7841-3

Also available:
- Catholicism For Dummies
  0-7645-5391-7
- Exercise Balls For Dummies
  0-7645-5623-1
- Fitness For Dummies
  0-7645-7851-0
- Football For Dummies
  0-7645-3936-1
- Judaism For Dummies
  0-7645-5299-6
- Potty Training For Dummies
  0-7645-5417-4
- Buddhism For Dummies
  0-7645-5359-3

- Pregnancy For Dummies
  0-7645-4483-7 †
- Ten Minute Tone-Ups For Dummies
  0-7645-7207-5
- NASCAR For Dummies
  0-7645-7681-X
- Religion For Dummies
  0-7645-5264-3
- Soccer For Dummies
  0-7645-5229-5
- Women in the Bible For Dummies
  0-7645-8475-8

TRAVEL

0-7645-7749-2

0-7645-6945-7

Also available:
- Alaska For Dummies
  0-7645-7746-8
- Cruise Vacations For Dummies
  0-7645-6941-4
- England For Dummies
  0-7645-4276-1
- Europe For Dummies
  0-7645-7529-5
- Germany For Dummies
  0-7645-7823-5
- Hawaii For Dummies
  0-7645-7402-7

- Italy For Dummies
  0-7645-7386-1
- Las Vegas For Dummies
  0-7645-7382-9
- London For Dummies
  0-7645-4277-X
- Paris For Dummies
  0-7645-7630-5
- RV Vacations For Dummies
  0-7645-4442-X
- Walt Disney World & Orlando
  For Dummies
  0-7645-9660-8

GRAPHICS, DESIGN & WEB DEVELOPMENT

0-7645-8815-X

0-7645-9571-7

Also available:
- 3D Game Animation For Dummies
  0-7645-8789-7
- AutoCAD 2006 For Dummies
  0-7645-8925-3
- Building a Web Site For Dummies
  0-7645-7144-3
- Creating Web Pages For Dummies
  0-470-08030-2
- Creating Web Pages All-in-One Desk
  Reference For Dummies
  0-7645-4345-8
- Dreamweaver 8 For Dummies
  0-7645-9649-7

- InDesign CS2 For Dummies
  0-7645-9572-5
- Macromedia Flash 8 For Dummies
  0-7645-9691-8
- Photoshop CS2 and Digital
  Photography For Dummies
  0-7645-9580-6
- Photoshop Elements 4 For Dummies
  0-471-77483-9
- Syndicating Web Sites with RSS Feeds
  For Dummies
  0-7645-8848-6
- Yahoo! SiteBuilder For Dummies
  0-7645-9800-7

NETWORKING, SECURITY, PROGRAMMING & DATABASES

0-7645-7728-X

0-471-74940-0

Also available:
- Access 2007 For Dummies
  0-470-04612-0
- ASP.NET 2 For Dummies
  0-7645-7907-X
- C# 2005 For Dummies
  0-7645-9704-3
- Hacking For Dummies
  0-470-05235-X
- Hacking Wireless Networks
  For Dummies
  0-7645-9730-2
- Java For Dummies
  0-470-08716-1

- Microsoft SQL Server 2005 For Dummies
  0-7645-7755-7
- Networking All-in-One Desk Reference
  For Dummies
  0-7645-9939-9
- Preventing Identity Theft For Dummies
  0-7645-7336-5
- Telecom For Dummies
  0-471-77085-X
- Visual Studio 2005 All-in-One Desk
  Reference For Dummies
  0-7645-9775-2
- XML For Dummies
  0-7645-8845-1

HEALTH & SELF-HELP

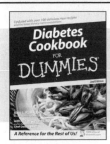

0-7645-8450-2

0-7645-4149-8

Also available:
- Bipolar Disorder For Dummies
  0-7645-8451-0
- Chemotherapy and Radiation
  For Dummies
  0-7645-7832-4
- Controlling Cholesterol For Dummies
  0-7645-5440-9
- Diabetes For Dummies
  0-7645-6820-5* †
- Divorce For Dummies
  0-7645-8417-0 †

- Fibromyalgia For Dummies
  0-7645-5441-7
- Low-Calorie Dieting For Dummies
  0-7645-9905-4
- Meditation For Dummies
  0-471-77774-9
- Osteoporosis For Dummies
  0-7645-7621-6
- Overcoming Anxiety For Dummies
  0-7645-5447-6
- Reiki For Dummies
  0-7645-9907-0
- Stress Management For Dummies
  0-7645-5144-2

EDUCATION, HISTORY, REFERENCE & TEST PREPARATION

0-7645-8381-6

0-7645-9554-7

Also available:
- The ACT For Dummies
  0-7645-9652-7
- Algebra For Dummies
  0-7645-5325-9
- Algebra Workbook For Dummies
  0-7645-8467-7
- Astronomy For Dummies
  0-7645-8465-0
- Calculus For Dummies
  0-7645-2498-4
- Chemistry For Dummies
  0-7645-5430-1
- Forensics For Dummies
  0-7645-5580-4

- Freemasons For Dummies
  0-7645-9796-5
- French For Dummies
  0-7645-5193-0
- Geometry For Dummies
  0-7645-5324-0
- Organic Chemistry I For Dummies
  0-7645-6902-3
- The SAT I For Dummies
  0-7645-7193-1
- Spanish For Dummies
  0-7645-5194-9
- Statistics For Dummies
  0-7645-5423-9

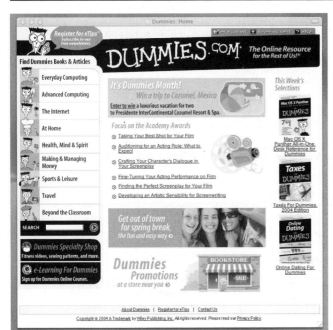

* Separate Canadian edition also available
† Separate U.K. edition also available